The Sempiternal Season

Seventeenth-Century Texts and Studies

Anthony Low, General Editor
Vol. 3

PETER LANG
New York • San Francisco • Bern
Frankfurt am Main • Berlin • Wien • Paris

P.G. Stanwood

The Sempiternal Season

Studies in Seventeenth-Century Devotional Writing

PETER LANG
New York • San Francisco • Bern
Frankfurt am Main • Berlin • Wien • Paris

Library of Congress Cataloging-in-Publication Data

Stanwood, P.G.
    The sempiternal season : studies in seventeenth-
century devotional writing / P.G. Stanwood.
        p. cm. — (Seventeenth-century texts and studies ;
vol. 3)
    Includes bibliographical references.
    1. English literature—Early modern, 1500-1700—
History and criticism.   2. Devotional literature, English—
History and criticism.   3. Herbert, George, 1593-1633—
Criticism and interpretation.   4. Donne, John, 1572-
1631—Criticism and interpretation. I. Title. II. Series.
PR438.D48S73 1992 820.9'382'09032—dc20   91-36045
ISBN 0-8204-1778-5   CIP
ISSN 0893-6900

Die Deutsche Bibliothek-CIP-Einheitsaufnahme

Stanwood, Paul Grant.:
The sempiternal season : studies in seventeenth-century
devotional writing.—New York; Berlin; Bern;
Frankfurt/M.; Paris; Wien: Lang, 1992
    (Seventeenth-century texts and studies ; Vol. 3)
    ISBN 0-8204-1778-5
NE: GT

The paper in this book meets the guidelines for permanence and durability
of the Committee on Production Guidelines for
Book Longevity of the Council on Library Resources.

To Christopher

and

To the Memory of Mary Louise

Acknowledgments

MOST OF THE ESSAYS in this collection appeared in earlier versions. I am therefore grateful to a number of journals, their editors, and various publishers for granting me permission to reprint them here.

"Time and Liturgy in Donne, Crashaw, and T. S. Eliot" originally appeared in *MOSAIC* 12 / 2 (Winter 1979): 91–105, in a special issue titled *Liturgy and Literature,* and is reprinted by permission of the editor. "Time and Liturgy in Herbert's Poetry" is reprinted from the *George Herbert Journal* 5 (Fall 1981 / Spring-Summer 1982): 19–30, by permission of the editor. "'Essentiall Joye' in Donne's *Anniversaries*" is reprinted from *Texas Studies in Literature and Language* 13:2 (Summer 1971): 227–38, by permission of the University of Texas Press. Chapter 5 first appeared as "Stobaeus and Classical Borrowing in the Renaissance, with Special Reference to Richard Hooker and Jeremy Taylor" in *Neophilologus* 59 (1975): 141–46, and is reprinted by permission of the editor. "Patristic and Contemporary Borrowing in the Caroline Divines" appeared in *Renaissance Quarterly* 23 (1970): 421–29 and is reprinted by permission of the Renaissance Society of America, the publisher of this journal. "John Donne's Sermon Notes" appeared in *The Review of English Studies* 29 (1978): 313–17, and it is reprinted by permission of Oxford University Press. "Milton's *Lycidas* and Earlier Seventeenth-Century Opera" is reprinted from *Milton in Italy: Contexts, Images, Contradictions,* edited by Mario A. Di Cesare, Medieval & Renaissance Texts & Studies, vol. 90 (Binghamton, N.Y., 1991), pp. 293–303, copyright, Center for Medieval and Early Renaissance Studies, SUNY Binghamton. "John Cosin and His *Devotions*" is a revised version of the introduction to *A Collection of Private Devotions* by John Cosin, edited by P. G. Stanwood with the assistance of Daniel O'Connor (Oxford: Clarendon Press, 1967), reprinted here by permission of Oxford University Press. "St. Teresa and Joseph Beaumont's *Psyche: or Loves Mysterie*" is reprinted from the *Journal of English and Germanic Philology* 62 (1963): 533–50, by permission of the editor and the publisher, the University of Illinois Press. "Christina Rossetti's Devotional Prose" is reprinted from *The Achievement of Christina Rossetti,* edited by David A.

Kent, copyright 1987 by Cornell University, and used by permission of the publisher, Cornell University Press.

A version of "A Portrait of Stuart Orthodoxy" appeared in the (now defunct) *Church Quarterly Review* 165 (1964): 27–39, whose late editor, J. W. C. Wand, onetime bishop of London, encouraged my work through his timely publication of my essay and through his own writing and knowledge, including *Anglicanism in History and Today* (London: Weidenfeld and Nicolson, 1961). "Henry More's *Democritus Platonissans* and the Infinity of Worlds" is a revised version of my introduction to *Democritus Platonissans* (1646) in the Augustan Reprint Society edition of that work, which appeared as publication number 130 (Los Angeles: William Andrews Clark Memorial Library, 1968). The essay on "Word and Sacrament in Donne's Sermons" began as a paper given at the John Donne Society Conference at Gulfport, Mississippi in February 1991, and it has received very helpful comments from students and faculty at the Vancouver School of Theology, especially Professor W. R. K. Crockett, who invited me to lecture to his denominational studies class on several occasions. The final, brief essay on "the Sonnet of Affliction" was given as a paper at the western meeting of the Conference on Christianity and Literature at Santa Clara University, in May 1989.

The frontispiece reproduces the engraved title-page of the first edition of *A Collection of Private Devotions* (1627) by John Cosin, and it appears by permission of the Bodleian Library, University of Oxford, shelfmark = Douce.c.79. The illustration on p. 74, opposite the beginning of chapter 7 on "John Donne's Sermon Notes," which shows Trinity College, Dublin, MS 419, f. 72^v, is given by permission of The Board of Trinity College Dublin. I wish also to thank Professor H. G. Edinger for his helpful assistance with a number of the translations, especially from classical texts.

Contents

Engraved title-page of the first edition of John Cosin's DEVOTIONS *(1627), in the Bodleian Library, Oxford (Douce.c.79).*

Preface

IN THE FOURTEEN ESSAYS that follow, I have brought together material on which I have worked for a number of years, revising much of it in order to take into account not only my own second thoughts but also the research of other scholars. For example, my early essays on "Time and Liturgy in Donne, Crashaw, and T. S. Eliot" and also on Herbert's poetry take note of the more recent criticism of Donne and Herbert by such scholars as Barbara Lewalski, Richard Strier, Debora Shuger, and others; but while I admire much of their work, I am not necessarily in accord with it, and so the fundamental direction of my own thought remains largely unchanged. I have not wished, however, to engage those with whom I disagree in argument, but rather to present my own ideas as clearly as possible. Thus my newest and previously unpublished essay on "Word and Sacrament in Donne's Sermons" examines an underlying implication of my thinking about "the liturgical mode"; for I believe now more firmly than ever that the essential belief of these Anglican writers depends upon an intense sacramentalism that the mystery of the Incarnation principally inspires.

Accordingly, most of the essays that form this book have changed little from their first presentation, usually as journal articles. But I believe that they are united by a common interest, style, and point of view. Although written over a long period of time and for a variety of occasions, they share a concern for discovering both the historical and the transcendent moment — a very elusive convergence of world and word; and they reveal in their sometimes historical, sometimes formalist, critical approach a persistent desire to understand literary texts that may, broadly speaking, be described as "devotional," or may be concerned in some way with the religious sensibility. Together these essays acquire more meaning than any one of them possessed independently, having the virtue now of "interfacing" with one another and looking toward a kind of *metacommentary;* yet the collection, composed of autonomous parts, is not fortuitous, but has a coherence which I hope the four-part division demonstrates.

The first part, called **TIME, LITURGY, AND GRACE,** includes four critical essays which take up a complementary and critical theme based upon what I describe as "incarnational time" and "the liturgical mode." In "Time and Liturgy in Donne, Crashaw, and T. S. Eliot," I explore the general terms of my discourse, pausing especially to consider Donne's "A Nocturnall upon S. *Lucies* day," and Crashaw's "The Weeper" and "The Flaming Heart"; and I write also of Eliot, who is particularly important to this discussion because he shows so eloquently the same tendencies as the earlier writers. *Four Quartets,* especially, is concerned with liturgical time, where "the point of intersection of the timeless with time" is apprehended — in "the sempiternal season." By *liturgy,* as I show further in the essay on Herbert's poetry, I mean to signify any religious rite or ceremony, not necessarily the eucharistic rite itself, which memorializes or consecrates a past action in order to give to it a present and continuing significance. Also, I assign to "liturgy" a literary function which expresses the ordered movement of time in space, conveying such movement in terms which often depend upon rhetorical invention. This concept leads to my reading of Donne's *Anniversaries* as a means of fulfilling the liturgical mode through the operation of "grace." The final essay in this group applies the suggestion implicit in them all, but only hinted, of sacramentality: for Donne's ability to celebrate the issues of life and death, particularly in his sermons, depends upon his incarnational theology and his eucharistic devotion, where "word and sacrament are one." In my discussion of Donne's religious work, I appeal also to Richard Hooker, on the one hand, and to Jeremy Taylor, on the other, writers who speak in the same tradition: *Of the Lawes of Ecclesiastical Polity,* for all of its magnitude and complexity, depends for its life on the incarnational theology inherent in the Anglican understanding of *participation* through a community of faith. *Holy Living* leads from admonition, precept, and prayer to an exuberant conclusion where all godly people (as if "Sprinkled and taught") may "approach, and taste / The churches mysticall repast."

The second part, **INFLUENCE AND COMPOSITION,** includes four historical studies which show some of the specific ways in which earlier seventeenth-century writers worked: mining for commonplaces in such anthologists as Stobaeus; borrowing of striking conceits from patristic writers and from one another — their own contemporaries; composing of sermons, illustrated through a set of notes taken down by one of Donne's auditors; responding to other arts, as Milton in his "monody." These essays lead to the third part of the book, where I look at **THREE CAMBRIDGE DIVINES** from a biographical and critical standpoint: John Cosin, whose contentious "cozening" *Devotions,* one of the most important devotional manuals of the period, helped lead to his expulsion from the mastership of Peterhouse at the outbreak of the civil war; Joseph Beaumont, protégé of Cosin, friend of Crashaw, author of the vast devotional epic *Psyche*; Henry More, the Cambridge Platonist and poet, a divine who refused preferment in favor of concentrated theological study. Each of these figures provides us with a glimpse of his culture and times, offering us also an insight into different kinds of devotional writing.

The book ends with two essays in a fourth part, or epilogue, of **VIC-TORIAN REFLECTIONS.** The first essay surveys the devotional prose of Christina Rossetti, who hoped, like many in the second generation of the Tractarian Movement, to find an Anglican "golden age" in the seventeenth century, and to practice patience, to wait for the knowledge of God's mysterious Incarnation. As a kind of reflective and brief peroration, the second essay studies closely one of G. M. Hopkins's sonnets in comparison with a sonnet by Donne, and another by Herbert. Thus this volume returns to its central focus on English devotional literature of the seventeenth century by suggesting once more the interrelationship of writers who set out "to redeem the time."

Vancouver, 1991

I

TIME, LITURGY, AND GRACE

1

Time and Liturgy in Donne, Crashaw, and T. S. Eliot

LITURGY APPLIES generally to all the public and written offices of the church and particularly to the eucharistic rite. But I use the term first of all broadly to describe any religious rite or ceremony which memorializes or consecrates a past action in order to give to it a present and continuing significance. Next and principally, I mean *liturgy* metaphorically and assign to it an aesthetic function which expresses ordered movement. In literature, I use liturgy to convey such movements which depend upon rhetorical and verbal invention, designed to make us feel both still and active, contracted and expansive, filled with the past and alive to the present. John Donne writes, for example, a liturgical poem in "A Nocturnall upon S. *Lucies* day" or in "The Sunne Rising" where the whole world, its motion, its size, its past, becomes centered upon the lovers around whom all else must reverentially turn. Time stops and space adjusts itself for these actors who are both transcendent and familiar. Their life is public but also private, and the poet's enactment of it is ceremonial and ritualistic. He celebrates a rite in verse which canonizes all things, and so he makes his own performance into a liturgical act. Liturgy in its ecclesiastical and metaphorical senses depends upon our doing or performing certain fixed actions in the same way, over and over again. Such patterns of action imply ceremony and the desire to perpetuate the past in the present; they advance faith in the future as if it were part of the present. And so time rests and takes its ease in literature which is liturgical. Time and liturgy meet together, like Mercy and Peace; they marry and lie down together with fit ceremony.

In my description, there lies an approach toward the fuller understanding and appreciation of much of the best seventeenth-century poetry, especially by the so-called metaphysicals, the Cavaliers, and Milton. The form, the structure, and the rhetoric of much of their poetry presupposes ritual, ceremony, and liturgical action. It is often, but not always, devotional poetry in the common and narrow sense, though seldom theological in any important way; but it is always marked by high and often exuberant ceremony which tries to defeat time, whether in "The Morning of Christ's Nativity," in "To His Coy Mistress," in Lovelace's "Grass-hopper," or in Richard

Crashaw's "Weeper" or "Flaming Heart." The inclusion of T. S. Eliot in this first essay, which focuses primarily upon Donne and Crashaw, is to indicate that at least one modern poet manifests the same tendencies occurring in the earlier writing. *Four Quartets* is especially concerned with the liturgical recording of time, where "the point of intersection of the timeless with time" is apprehended. Eliot celebrates the still point, from which life begins, by raising poetry to become "its own epitaph," and he helps us to understand Donne and Crashaw better because his work clarifies and summarizes their themes and meaning. In the next chapter, I shall further define these themes by studying them in Herbert's poetry.

One striking example of a liturgical poem is Donne's "A Nocturnall upon S. *Lucies* day, Being the shortest day" (written about 1617). It illustrates the fusion of the sphere as image and structural motif in a poetic process that is both forward and arrested, and it provides an ideal example of the style I want to describe, one that is profoundly sensitive to the values and implications of time and liturgy:

> 'Tis the yeares midnight, and it is the dayes,
> *Lucies,* who scarce seaven houres herself unmaskes,
>   The Sunne is spent, and now his flasks
>   Send forth light squibs, no constant rayes;
>   The world's whole sap is sunke:
> The generall balme th'hydroptique earth hath drunk,
> Whither, as to the beds-feet, life is shrunke,
> Dead and enterr'd; yet all these seeme to laugh,
> Compar'd with mee, who am their Epitaph.[1]
>   (1–9)

Donne draws upon the whole world of experience (the word *all* appears seven times within the forty-five lines of this poem). He modulates between the creation and his own present occasion, which he compacts into a microcosm. The midnight of the year is the end of the winter season and the beginning of the spring — the point yet neither from nor towards. The world reflects the season, for it has reached a zone of darkness and death which cannot be increased. The time is St. Lucy's Eve, the longest night or vigil, which precedes the shortest day of the year (according to the old reckoning); but Lucy, by her name, reminds us of light and the prospect of a new year.[2] Yet the occasion of the poem describes the desolation of the world, the winter season, the year, the day, the hour, and the poet's utter loss; someone has died (it makes no difference who), and the effect is shattering. But the poet implies that in this misery and awful melancholy, there is hope.

The poem begins and ends with the same line as if to suggest a circular movement and to recall that the end of the winter and the deepest night gives way to spring and the dawn of longer days. The poet calls himself the epitaph of the whole world, but new alchemy has transformed his deadness, even nothingness, and made him into another creature. Donne often frames his poems by devising an auditor within the poem to whom he teaches a moral or gives instruction. Here he addresses those

> who shall lovers bee
> At the next world, that is, at the next Spring.
>   (10–11)

He writes of his own experience in the past tense:

> For I am every dead thing,
> In whom love wrought new Alchimie.
>   For his art did expresse
> A quintessence even from nothingnesse,
> From dull privations, and leane emptinesse . . .
>   (12–16)

And he relates that

> . . . I am by her death . . .
> Of the first nothing, the Elixer grown.
>   (28–29)

The poet is the embodiment of a something which is the achievement of nothing. His existence is so paradoxical and so perfect that it cannot cast even a shadow; he is no "ordinary nothing," but the distillation of a body who has loved, and in loving has been a world. Donne's familiar theme of absence which makes two loves more nearly one and his conception that full love is a universe, a world or a sphere, finds its subtlest statement in this poem. For here the lovers are parted; yet the poet's love had re-begot him, and the death or loss of the beloved is meaningful only insofar as it has helped him to realize the elixir, the quintessence of love. Absence and darkness are indeed necessary to the possession of their opposites. Donne allows for hypothetical lovers in the next world, at the next spring; but he knows that his own love has been the world and that it will continue to be so into the summer season. This is a love so refined and purified that "the lesser Sunne" of the vulgar world must run to the Goat "to fetch new lust" for the ordinary lovers. In the poet's vigil is his eve, his Paradise and Eden, where there is time and time-lessness, where past and future meet in a momentaneous present, where the higher world of his love rests, and before which all other creatures must bow. "A Nocturnall" reveals the most advanced state of love of all Donne's poems. By contrast, the "soules language" in "The Extasie," to recall another poem with a comparable theme, has the sound of corporeality where "Loves mysteries in soules doe grow," but in the St. Lucy poem, Donne imagines an alchemical perfection of these mysteries that no longer relies upon the body for its book.

The movement of this poem is carefully modulated between process and fixity. Our knowledge grows as Donne reveals the sense of his love and the meaning of his vigil. Our feelings are perhaps like those of the lovers who are addressed and who are awakened to the meaning of unique love. Donne is describing a state perfect in its absence, as well as educating others in its significance; for this love possesses no possibility of alteration. Even the patterns of the poem reflect its principles. The five stanzas recall the fifth element around which the meaning of the poem turns. And the fifth line of each of the nine line stanzas is pivotal. This line is emphasized by its shortness (with six syllables) and its centrality. Moreover, it introduces a new rhyme to give us *abbacccdd*, with lines 1, 2, 6, 7, 8, and 9 containing ten syllables, lines 3 and 4, eight syllables. The whole poem, as well as its parts, suggest symmetry and balance, and the circles that draw themselves around the poem have at their center quintessential and unifying love, wherein one has become all. Time and space contract to a point, where we, like the lovers who shall be at the next world, may pause to worship with high ceremony and fit liturgy.

Donne's poetry commonly celebrates similar occasions. The *Anniversaries*, which together form his longest and most important poetic work, proclaim the liturgical mode.[3] The first lines of *The Second Anniversary* ("Of the Progres of the Soule") declare: "I ame / The Trumpet, at whose voice the people came" (527–28), a reference to Elizabeth Drury (the subject of the poem), to the poet himself and to Moses. In this way Donne merges the poet with the poem and its subject. Much earlier, at the end of *The First Anniversary* ("An Anatomy of the World"), Donne had identified himself with the voice of Moses and with God's voice which tuned his own, wittily observing that "incomprehensibleness" might not deter him (469). Now the two parts of the *Anniversaries* join together in a performance where the poet is both conductor and subject; this performance − a completed circle of experience − the poet offers to God as a gift consecrated to a higher end, where joy, harmony and heavenly wisdom embrace a complete and commemorative action in a single and everlasting time. In the *Anniversary* poems as in "A Nocturnall," Donne has declared the new life of power and the harmony that belongs to it; he has played his part both as poet in describing this life and as priest by consecrating it.

Yet Donne's literary and liturgical achievement should be measured by his sermons, many of which are poetic in style, especially in their compression and imagery. He is fascinated in the sermons by time and space, and by their liturgical interpretation. We see that he acts as a mediator for his congregation, as he did in the poetry for his readers. As readers of the sermons, we ourselves become members of Donne's congregation, for it continues, not being bound to an historical time and place. Donne celebrates the flow of time and its end which contains the beginning:

> [God's] eternity decayeth in no sense; and as long as his
> eternity lasts, as long as God is God, God shall never see

that soul, whom he hath accurst, delivered from that curse, or eased in it.

But we are now in the work of an houre, and no more. If there be a minute of sand left, (There is not) If there be a minute of patience left, heare me say, This minute that is left, is that eternitie which we speake of; upon this minute dependeth that eternity: And this minute, God is in this Congregation, and puts his eare to every one of your hearts, and hearkens what you will bid him say to your selves: whether he shall blesse you for your acceptation, or curse you for your refusall of him this minute: for this minute makes up your *Century,* your hundred yeares, your eternity, because it may be your last minute.[4]   (7:368–69)

The idea contained by this passage frequently occurs in his sermons:

This life is not a Parenthesis, a Parenthesis that belongs not to the sense, a Parenthesis that might be left out, as well as put in. More depends upon this life then so: upon every minute of this life, depend millions of yeares in the next, and I shall be glorified eternally, or eternally lost, for my good or ill use of Gods grace offered to me this houre.
(3:288)

With fascination, longing and tenderness, Donne regularly elaborates the contrast between eternity and finite time, and the everlastingness that must contain each of us. Consider his Christmas sermon, preached at St. Paul's in 1626, on Luke 2.29–30, "Lord now lettest thou thy servant depart in peace, according to thy Word: for mine eyes have seen thy salvation." It begins:

The whole life of Christ was a continuall Passion; others die Martyrs, but Christ was born a Martyr. He found a *Golgotha,* (where he was crucified) even in Bethlem, where he was born; For, to his tendernesse then, the strawes were almost as sharp as the thornes after; and the Manger as uneasie at first, as his Crosse at last. His birth and his death were but one continuall act, and his Christmas-day and his Good Friday, are but the evening and morning of one and the same day. And as even his birth, is his death, so every action and passage that manifests Christ to us, is his birth; for *Epiphany* is *manifestation. . . .*   (7:279)

Donne also preached at St. Paul's, on January 29, 1626, the second of his five prebend sermons, on Psalm 63.7, "Because Thou hast been my helpe, therefore in the shadow of Thy wings will I rejoyce." In this sermon, he characteristically links the literal, moral, and spiritual levels, managing to fuse

them with considerations of time past, time present, and time future until
meaning and time both reside in simultaneity. Donne thus treats in an explicit
way the currents within which many of his poems move; he sees a symbolic
occasion where meaning contracts but also expands in large and continuing
ringlets. In his prebendal office (for Chiswick), Donne was appointed to say
the five Psalms 62–66 daily at St. Paul's. The 150 Psalms together are "the
Manna of the Church," he says in the second of his sermons, and "as the
whole booke is Manna, so these five Psalmes are my Gomer [that is,
measure], which I am to fill and empty every day of this Manna" [cf. Exod.
16.33]. Donne continues, in his "Divisio" of the text, to show the particular
and historical situation assumed by it, and he interprets its significance both
for David, and by extension, for us:

> Now as the spirit and soule of the whole booke of Psalmes
> is contracted into this psalme, so is the spirit and soule of
> this whole psalme contracted into this verse. The key of the
> psalme [that is, its title] . . . tells us, that *David* uttered this
> psalme, *when he was in the wildernesse of Iudah;* There we
> see the present occasion that moved him; And we see what
> was passed between God and him before, in the first clause
> of our Text; (*Because thou hast been my helpe*) And then we
> see what was to come, by the rest, (*Therefore in the shadow
> of thy wings will I rejoyce.*) So that we have here the whole
> compasse of Time, Past, Present, and Future; and these
> three parts of Time, shall be at this time, the three parts of
> this Exercise; first, what *Davids* distresse put him upon for
> the present; and that lyes in the Context; secondly, how
> *David* built his assurance upon that which was past;
> (*Because thou hast been my help*) And thirdly, what he
> established to himselfe for the future, (*Therefore in the
> shadow of thy wings will I rejoyce.*) First, His distresse in the
> Wildernesse, his present estate carried him upon the
> memory of that which God had done for him before, And
> the Remembrance of that carried him upon that, of which
> he assured himselfe after.   (7:52)

There is no pause after this last statement which points still to David's condition, now in its metaphorical sense, and before the following address to all
people:

> Fixe upon God any where, and you shall finde him a Circle;
> He is with you now, when you fix upon him; He was with
> you before, for he brought you to this fixation; and he will
> be with you hereafter, for *He is yesterday, and to day, and
> the same for ever.*   (7:52)

The application epitomizes the movement of the sermon; it draws out the higher sense of the text by declaring its universal nature while yet depending upon and emerging out of a specific occurrence. This example of fixity and of globular perfection, with its blending of different times into universal time, recalls a similar process in the St. Lucy's Day poem. In the poem, we identify with the lovers at the next spring although we are made aware of, but unable to share wholly in love's quintessence. In the sermon, David's circumstances give a glimpse of the possible and the obtainable, and the preacher helps us to make use of a past which ought to be present for us. There is a richness and a maturity about the sermon that even so remarkable a poem as "A Nocturnall" does not quite capture; and its greater possibilities lie, not in the difference of theme or idea, but in the nearness "of afflictions in generall, and the inevitableness thereof."

Donne begins the exposition of his text by discussing first of all David's present condition; such a beginning is important for opening up the analogues of the currency of grief, for this time is like that earlier one. "But then," says Donne, "there is *Pondus Gloriæ, An exceeding waight of eternall glory,* and that turnes the scale" (7:55). The dangers of temporal afflictions are nothing compared with spiritual miseries. David's banishment was like an excommunication, "an excluding of him from the service of God" (7:59). Yet God had given him help before; there is a past at work in the present, a tradition and a pattern of expectation. "The surest way, and the nearest way to lay hold upon God, is the consideration of that which he had done already" (7:63). So with David, and so with us. In these promises and assurances of past mercies there is support for the present, and there is also confidence for the future. As David will rejoice, so "we must ascend to a holy joy, as if all were done and accomplished" (7:65). The future gathers up the past and the present: they are all one. Our conclusion rests upon mercy, joy, and hope:

> I would always raise your hearts, and dilate your hearts, to a holy Joy, to a joy in the Holy Ghost. . . . There may bee a just jealousie, and suspition too, that [men] may fall into inordinate griefe, and diffidence of Gods mercy. . . . And therefore I returne often to this endeavor of raising your hearts, dilating your hearts with a holy Joy, Joy in the holy Ghost, for *Vnder the shadow of his wings,* you may, you should, *rejoyce.* . . . The everlastingnesse of the joy is the blessednesse of the next life, but the entring, the inchoation is afforded here.   (7:68–69)

Misery gives way to glory, in fact is the occasion of glory, as death provides for the Resurrection.

As Donne moves into the conclusion of his sermon, he joins himself with his auditors and with all who hear him. David's situation is ours, and his past overlaps with and contains our own time. When we are told at the con-

clusion of the sermon to delight in everlasting joy, we remember the advice at
the beginning, "Fixe upon God any where, and you shall finde him a Circle":

> In the face of Death, when he layes hold upon me, and in
> the face of the Devill, when he attempts me, I shall see the
> face of God, (for, every thing shall be a glasse, to reflect
> God upon me) so in the agonies of Death, in the anguish of
> that dissolution, in the sorrowes of that valediction, in the
> irreversiblenesse of that transmigration, I shall have a joy,
> which shall no more evaporate, then my soule shall
> evaporate, A joy, that shall passe up, and put on a more
> glorious garment above, and be joy super-invested in glory.
>   (7:71)

Donne's achievement in this sermon, as with "A Nocturnall" or with the
Anniversaries, is to transform the circumstances of the moment, of the present occasion, of the text before us, through "joy super-invested in glory";
thus the literal confinements of grief or of mortal time are transcended and
dissolved in the shimmering deliquescence of eternity. In this mysterious
force, there lies the ultimate measure of time and liturgy: we are persuaded
into the unbroken realm of the unending circle, without beginning or
terminus, where evocative moments, such as the desolations of the poet in "A
Nocturnall," or of the "Anatomy of the World" (where "all coherence is
gone"), or of David in the prebend sermon, become types pointing to a state
of achieved spirituality. Donne expresses a sentiment like this in another
sermon by means of holy and paradoxical mathematics: "If my span of life
become a mile of life, my penny a pound, my pint a gallon, my acre a sheere;
yet if there be nothing of the next world at the end, so much peace of con-
science, so much joy, so much glory, still all is but *nothing* multiplied, and that
is still nothing at all. 'Tis the *end* that qualifies all" (4:171). This end returns
us to our beginning; there we may rest in well-made ceremony and in
celebration that raises time to the land of spices, where everything is nothing
understood.

2

Between Richard Crashaw and his older contemporary Donne, it is difficult
to see any real affinity, as Douglas Bush observes when he suggests that the
motto of Crashaw's poetry might be "Over-ripeness is all."[5] While Crashaw's
themes and interests are less wide ranging than Donne's, the two poets
nevertheless share a similar intensity and excitement, and as with Donne, so
Crashaw's sense of time is compacted and concentrated on a single point.
Their poetry employs different figures, but both poets move toward the same
end into which and out of which everything spins and radiates in the oneness
of worshiper and the object of worship. Consecration, ceremony, unity of
experience, and publicly formalized yet personal feeling — all features of the

liturgical mode — belong as much to Crashaw as to Donne.

The common view of Crashaw is expressed not only by Bush, but by one of Crashaw's recent editors, who says: "Richard Crashaw may be considered the most un-English of all the English poets. As his native poetic genius developed, it absorbed continental influences, both sacred and secular, to such a degree that Crashaw eventually removed from Puritanism and England to Roman Catholicism and Rome."[6] While Crashaw certainly moved easily in Tridentine devotion, he wrote in ways common to many other Englishmen of his time, but in a richer and better informed manner. Crashaw should not be read in isolation (though he often is) from Giles and Phineas Fletcher, Henry Hawkins, Joseph Beaumont, Edward Benlowes, William Chamberlayne, Abraham Cowley, and from such prose writers as Robert Shelford for whose *Five Pious and Learned Discourses* (1635) he wrote a commendatory poem, and Anthony Stafford, author of *The Femall Glory: or, the Life, and Death of our Blessed Lady, the Holy Virgin Mary, God's owne immaculate Mother* (1635). Puritanism and England spawned much that was exotic, unlike our expectations. Crashaw's ceremonial, adorational mode of expression, his passion, and his alleged Catholic flamboyance are familiar in other and non-Roman writers contemporary with him, as well as in Donne and in earlier English poets such as Sidney and Spenser.

Above all, Crashaw is concerned with the experience of faith and only secondarily with doctrine. Like Donne, he seeks to describe complete moments in a continuously moving world in terms where the end of time is its beginning with "æternity shutt in a span." The urgency of Crashaw's devotion is single-minded and heated, as much public as it is private. He is as if present at the altar of God, offering his poetry and our aspirations to be a fit and sufficient thanksgiving and sacrifice. Crashaw is a poet of the liturgical mode, where the Incarnation informs his every gesture and speech: word and world, preacher and sermon, offering and receiving, going and returning, history and eternity meet in the point around which all else turns. Here ceremony is performed not for its own sake, but for the sake of liturgical rightness.

Crashaw illustrates best — or most prominently — the features of these paradoxes and the qualities of this worship in the "Hymn of the Holy Nativity." He writes from the standpoint of a rapt observer in the period of a literal time past, but one which is currently and continuously present:

> We saw thee in thy baulmy Nest,
>   Young dawn of our æternal DAY!
> We saw thine eyes break from their EASTE
>   And chase the trembling shades away.
> We saw thee; & we blest the sight
> We saw thee by thine own sweet light.
> . . . .
> Wellcome, all WONDERS in one sight!
>   Æternity shutt in a span.
> Sommer in Winter. Day in Night.

> Heauen in earth, & GOD in MAN.
> Great little one! whose all-embracing birth
> Lifts earth to heauen, stoopes heau'n to earth.
>
> WELLCOME. Though nor to gold nor silk.
>   To more than Cæsar's birthright is;
> Two sister-seas of Virgin-Milk,
>   With many a rarely-temper'd kisse
> That breathes at once both MAID & MOTHER,
> Warmes in the one, cooles in the other.[7]
>   (31–36, 79–90)

Crashaw's carefully controlled and restrained breathlessness, his use of antithesis, of oxymoron, of homoioteleuton, and of other rhetorical figures, urge us to abandon ordinary time in preference to another higher and paradoxical time. This new time describes the world correctly, being of an infinite dispensation, and it provides for and clothes the earthly order in a liturgical setting, where the poet portrays himself in the role of worshiper at an eternal scene demanding total attention.

"The Weeper" is often felt to be Crashaw at his worst; but even the most celebrated stanzas have power and integrity. Crashaw stretches the resources of poetic language as far as he can; his subject is, indeed, nothing less than the exaltation of penitential tears into an independent and autonomous world.[8] We may not like to think of tears in this way, but that is the way Crashaw intends us to see them and this was a convention of his time. We may wonder over the details of their metamorphosis:

> Hail, sister springs!
> Parents of syluer-footed rills!
> Euer bubling things!
> Thawing crystall! snowy hills,
> Still spending, neuer spent! I mean
> Thy fair eyes, sweet MAGDALENE!
> . . . .
> Vpwards thou dost weep.
> Heaun's bosome drinks the gentle stream.
> Where th'milky rivers creep,
> Thine floates aboue; & is the cream.
> Waters above th'Heauns, what they be
> We'are taught best by thy TEARES & thee.
>
> Euery morn from hence
> A brisk Cherub somthing sippes
> Whose sacred influence
> Addes sweetnes to his sweetest Lippes.

Then to his musick. And his song
Tasts of this Breakfast all day long.

Not in the euening's eyes
When they Red with weeping are
For the Sun that dyes,
Sitts sorrow with a face so fair,
No where but here did euer meet
Sweetnesse so sad, sadnesse so sweet.
. . . .
But can these fair Flouds be
Freinds with the bosom fires that fill thee
Can so great flames agree
Æternal Teares should thus distill thee!
O flouds, o fires! o suns ô showres!
Mixt & made freinds by loue's sweet powres.

Twas his well-pointed dart
That digg'd these wells, & drest this Vine;
And taught the wounded HEART
The way into these weeping Eyn.
Vain loues auant! bold hands forbear!
The lamb hath dipp't his white foot here.

And now where're he strayes,
Among the Galilean mountaines,
Or more vnwellcome wayes,
He's follow'd by two faithfull fountaines;
Two walking baths; two weeping motions;
Portable, & compendious oceans.
                    (1–6, 19–36, 97–114)

The tears of the penitent Magdalen take on a life of their own, and
later in the poem begin to speak. But they are not merely the result of devotion; they are themselves objects of devotion, and they offer themselves for a
devotional end, which is to wash *our Lord's feet.* Here is a new world made of
tears which worship and ask for worship. I see nothing inherently different
about Crashaw's ambition in this poem and Donne's in "A Nocturnall," since
both poems make preposterous statements and claim to be complete and
encompassing experiences. Finally, both are liturgical poems, and both
demand wholehearted assent.

Some commentators have dismissed "The Weeper," and especially
these stanzas of it, as a collection of mere *bonbons* and not even delectable
ones. But Crashaw nearly always knew what he was doing; he was a constant
reviser of his work and this version of "The Weeper," for example, contains
thirty-one stanzas as opposed to an earlier version of twenty-three. Crashaw

is right in expanding his effects, in urging us in ceremonial yet familiar terms to wonder at the singleness of devotion. His exotic fantasies turn out to be no different in kind, let us say, from Donne's invitation at the end of "Death's Duell" — his last sermon — where he urges us to climb the Cross and suck at the bloody wounds of Christ, a conceit which seems not to have troubled anyone as either outrageous, tasteless, or atypically English. T. S. Eliot was right in saying that Crashaw was a poet with intelligence: "Crashaw's images ... give a kind of intellectual pleasure — it is deliberate conscious perversity of language, a perversity like that of the amazing and amazingly impressive interior of St. Peter's. There is brain work in it."[9]

Crashaw writes of extremes and carries them as far as metamorphosis and consuming passion will permit. His intensity is both a credit and a shortcoming — helpful in producing highly colorful performances but limiting since it narrows the range of possible subjects. Incarnation, penitence, martyrdom, mystical death — these are Crashaw's principal topics, and these he offers in a variety of ritualized forms. The Magdalen is one saint who engaged his imagination, while Teresa of Avila is a second. The last lines of "The Flaming Heart" are well known, but they should be recalled in view of the theme of time and liturgy. Here Crashaw joins himself to St. Teresa and hopes he may become one with her in order to defeat the corruption of common time and space. As well, he celebrates her ecstasy both for her sake and for his own and suggests that in her life and death we may see the true and sufficient pattern of all life. The poem may be witty, baroque, and metaphysical, but it is indeed liturgical:

> O thou vndanted daughter of desires!
> By all thy dowr of LIGHTS & FIRES;
> By all the eagle in thee, all the doue;
> By all thy liues & deaths of loue;
> By thy larg draughts of intellectuall day,
> And by thy thirsts of loue more large then they;
> By all thy brim-fill'd Bowles of feirce desire
> By thy last Morning's draught of liquid fire;
> By the full kingdome of that finall kisse
> That seiz'd thy parting Soul, & seal'd thee his;
> By all the heau'ns thou hast in him
> Fair sister of the SERAPHIM!
> By all of HIM we haue in THEE;
> Leaue nothing of my SELF in me.
> Let me so read thy life, that I
> Vnto all life of mine may dy.
>
> (93–108)

Crashaw intends this conclusion as a litany, where there is a perfect meeting of public ritual and personal desire. His language reminds us of Cranmer's Litany in the Book of Common Prayer, which of course Crashaw knew: "By the mystery of thy holy Incarnation; by thy holy Nativity and Circumcision; by thy Baptism, Fasting, and Temptation, *Good Lord, deliver us.* By thine Agony and Bloody Sweat; by thy Cross and Passion; by thy precious Death and Burial; by thy glorious Resurrection and Ascension; and by the Coming of the Holy Ghost, *Good Lord, deliver us.* . . . " In such forms are particular desires offered in one common prayer. Crashaw recalls one ritual in performing another, and in his triumph he writes liturgically. "It is the world of man's inner life at its mystical intensity," writes Austin Warren, "the world of devotion expressing itself through the sacraments and ceremonial and liturgy; it is a world which knows vision and rapture, tears and fire; it is a world of the supernatural, wherein the miraculous becomes the probable; and this world manifests itself to the senses in a rhetoric brilliant, expressive, and appropriate."[10] It is also a world comparable in many ways to Donne's: the flames of passion sometimes rise higher in Crashaw, but the desire is similar in both writers; for in both, the literary creation contains the world and is one world, and we are bound to this world by admiration and prayer.

3

While T. S. Eliot is far from the earlier seventeenth century in time, he is close to it in spirit. Eliot knew the period well, wrote often about it, and distilled in his own poetry much of the liturgical mode I have been discussing. As a poet he is conscious of a living and continuing tradition in literature and history, and he desires to preserve and to make use of these traditions. Eliot is preoccupied with time and liturgy, and so it is fitting to look at his work for insight and advice.

I am primarily interested in *Four Quartets,* Eliot's most sustained and successful poem. The *Quartets* may be treated as one poem, but each of the four parts has a completeness; each becomes a portion of a fuller, and finally a spherical pattern.[11] The climax of *Four Quartets* occurs late in the final poem, in parts IV and V of "Little Gidding." These final sections, which grow from the preceding poems, operate by a system of progressive revelation. We make a pilgrimage in reading *Four Quartets,* as Eliot does in writing them, and this movement may be likened to the progress of the lovers in Donne's St. Lucy's Day poem, or to that hoped for "joy super-invested in glory" of the second prebend sermon, or to Crashaw's joining of himself to the mystical death of St. Teresa.

Eliot wrote *Murder in the Cathedral* in the same year as "Burnt Norton" (1935), the first of the *Quartets,* and the two works have much in common. There is the same interest in time and the same desire for its redemption. Thomas says before his execution:

> It is not in time that my death shall be known;
> It is out of time that my decision is taken
> If you call that decision
> To which my whole being gives entire consent.[12]

Throughout *Four Quartets,* we notice a special forward movement, whose end is also the beginning and surrender of time. The reaching out to "a condition of complete simplicity" in "Little Gidding" follows the excitement of our finding it located in historical place and time: "Quick now, here, now, always" points to the redemption of time. This same line occurs in an earlier variation at the end of "Burnt Norton":

> Quick now, here, now, always —
> Ridiculous the waste sad time
> Stretching before and after.[13]

Here time is as yet uninformed by a coherent vision. Much of "East Coker," the second of the *Quartets,* describes this fallen world: "O dark dark dark. They all go into the dark . . . " (p. 199). The soul struggles with aridity in its dark night, with "dull privations, and leane emptinesse," and the poet addresses his soul; he still suffers from the sadness of a world that God seems to have left:

> I said to my soul, be still, and let the dark come upon you
> Which shall be the darkness of God.
> ("East Coker" III, p. 200)

"Dry Salvages" — the next of the *Quartets* — represents a stage further along the way of discovery. Water and voyaging are central symbols in this poem, as well as the effort of "prayer, observance, discipline, thought and action" (V, p. 213). What one still does not entirely understand is Incarnation, where "the impossible union / Of spheres of existence is actual." But "Little Gidding" does reveal this "incomprehensibleness," draws together earlier hints and guesses, and leads the soul to the end of its journey, to the point it started from. So life ought to be the recapturing of Eden, the opening of the door into the rose-garden, where all is purified by a "new Alchimie."

The most historically centered of *Four Quartets* is "Little Gidding." It is the most concrete, but with a theme nevertheless as abstract as that of the elusive "Burnt Norton." Perhaps Eliot's purpose here is more obvious; the indefinite "you" is now invited to come "this way" in midwinter spring, the "sempiternal" season. You would come "from the place you would be likely to come from," and you would come like King Charles who once sought refuge here, and like the modern pilgrim who still comes to Little Gidding

> not . . . to verify,
> Instruct yourself, or inform curiosity
> Or carry report.
> (p. 215)

Here in this present you may meet the past, and in prayer grasp the timeless moment; for prayer carries us across history and "beyond the language of the living" (p. 215). This informed moment is Incarnation, "all Wonders in one sight," in Crashaw's words; it is the center where we start from and the place where we return. It is the timeless moment, the perfect pattern, the liturgical circle of time and space. "At the still point of the turning world" locates the place in and out of time where there is

> . . . neither arrest nor movement. And do not call it fixity,
> Where past and future are gathered.
> ("Burnt Norton" II, p. 191)

This image, to which Eliot returns, would have been a congenial one to Donne or to Crashaw; for, like Eliot, they had recourse to paradoxical geometry. Truth, to complete the metaphor, is contained by circles which turn about their first pitch, the point of starting, and they imply both arrest and movement, continuing yet finished.

Eliot begins "Burnt Norton" with a vision of "our first world," a time past which it is his aim to recover "at the still point"; he looks forward with Donne into "the dayes deep midnight," or with Crashaw to "the full kingdome of that finall kisse." While there is yet life to be lived in this world, all three poets take heart in the adumbrations of the promised end of ceaseless love and joy. Eliot concludes "with the drawing of this Love and the voice of this Calling" (p. 222), where Love is like Donne's joy in the prebend sermon, or Crashaw's "intellectual day," all of these being terms or phrases attempting to express the pattern of eternal and endless time. The dialogue the poet has with "the first-met stranger" (in "Little Gidding" II) ends when the "dead master"

> In the disfigured street
> . . . left me, with a kind of valediction,
> And faded on the blowing of the horn.
> (p. 219)

Since Eliot locates this scene during a raid on London in wartime, the sound is literally the "all clear." It is also a metaphorical horn which accentuates the advice of the master, that his pupil must be "'restored by that refining fire / Where you must move in measure, like a dancer'" (p. 219). The fires of London are purgatorial ones, imbued with salvation as well as destruction; the message of this Dantesque verse recalls also the dance as pattern and form, and it reminds us of the image, first introduced in "Burnt Norton," of the still point where the dance is; of Donne's "quintessence even from nothingnesse," his "joy super-invested in glory"; of Crashaw's "æternity shutt in a span" or "æternal Teares," and his desire for mystical death.

The Pentecostal flames which enter this world refine and redeem it. The poet's simple question is difficult, the answer profound and paradoxical: "Who then devised the torment? Love" (p. 221). "Little Gidding" ends with a vision of perfection, in which having survived fire by fire, we learn that "the fire and the rose are one" (p. 223). Fire and rose, emblems of God's love, are possible through Incarnation, the center of illumination for Donne, Crashaw, and Eliot. Donne teaches the intense need people have for salvation beyond themselves; Crashaw, the destruction of self in the harmony of devotion; Eliot, much influenced by mystical theology, emphasizes the contemplative value of charity and love. His use of Julian of Norwich is important to the theme of "Little Gidding" and to *Four Quartets* as a whole because it underlines his understanding of redemption:

> Sin is Behovely, but
> All shall be well, and
> All manner of thing shall be well.
>
> (p. 219)

The dissolution of time in timelessness is an overarching theme in all the works I have mentioned. This is a literature of momentaneousness, where each work becomes a world complete in itself, seemingly unable to exist simultaneously with another. It is a literature which exalts and celebrates, not necessarily but often in religious terms, the wholeness of a faith or idea, and demands our single-hearted assent. Such literature seems to stand in isolation, with each work on its own, always asking and inviting us to join in it with full participation, as if we should become grafted to it and share in a solipsism. The poetry remains static in spite of its inner movements and patterns; but our every repetition makes possible a fresh and unaltered performance of its ritual and its liturgy, for

> Every phrase and every sentence is an end and a beginning,
> Every poem an epitaph.
>
> ("Little Gidding" V, p. 221)

Notes

1. Quotations are from John Donne, *The Elegies and The Songs and Sonnets,* ed. Helen Gardner (Oxford: Clarendon Press, 1965), 84–85.
2. The poem probably recalls the canonical office of nocturn, a division of the traditional night office or "lauds," the first office of the day. This point has been noted by Clarence H. Miller, "Donne's 'A Nocturnall upon S. Lucies Day' and the Nocturns of Matins," *Studies in English Literature* 6 (1966): 77–86.
3. See John Donne, *The Epithalamions, Anniversaries, and Epicedes,* ed. W. Milgate (Oxford: Clarendon Press, 1978), from which I quote.
4. See John Donne, *The Sermons of John Donne,* ed. George R. Potter and Evelyn M. Simpson, 10 vols. (Berkeley: University of California Press, 1953–62). Volume and page number are cited in the text.

5. See Bush, *English Literature in the Earlier Seventeenth Century 1600–1660,* 2nd ed. (Oxford: Clarendon Press, 1962), 147.

6. The statement is by George Walton Williams in his edition of *The Complete Poetry of Richard Crashaw* (Garden City, N.Y.: Doubleday Anchor, 1970), xv. But see *New Perspectives on the Life and Art of Richard Crashaw,* ed. John R. Roberts (Columbia, Mo.: University of Missouri Press, 1990), especially the introductory essay on "Crashavian Criticism: A Brief Interpretive History" by Lorraine M. Roberts and John R. Roberts, 1–29.

7. Richard Crashaw's poetry is quoted from *The Poems English Latin and Greek,* ed. L. C. Martin, 2nd ed. (Oxford: Clarendon Press, 1957), 248–51, 308–14, 324–27.

8. See Anthony Low's sensitive analysis of Crashaw's "The Weeper," in *Love's Architecture: Devotional Modes in Seventeenth-Century English Poetry* (New York: New York University Press, 1978), 133–45: "The poem moves by the logic of affection and the dream-logic of association rather than intellectual analysis" (138). See also Paul A. Parrish, "'O Sweet Contest': Gender and Value in 'The Weeper,'" in *New Perspectives on the Life and Art of Richard Crashaw,* cited in n. 6.

9. See "A Note on Richard Crashaw," in *For Lancelot Andrewes* (1928; repr. London: Faber and Faber, 1970), 96.

10. See Warren, *Richard Crashaw: A Study in Baroque Sensibility* (1939; repr. Ann Arbor: University of Michigan Press, 1957), 206.

11. My indebtedness to Helen Gardner may be generally evident. See especially her *Art of T. S. Eliot* (1950; repr. New York: E. P. Dutton, 1959), and also *The Composition of* Four Quartets (London: Faber and Faber, 1978), esp. chap. 3, "The Sources of *Four Quartets*": "In writing [*Little Gidding*] Eliot deliberately gathered up themes and images from his earlier meditation on Time's losses and Time's gains, to make the poem not only complete and beautiful in itself but the crown and completion of the exploration of man in Time he had begun in *Burnt Norton*" (71).

12. See Eliot, *Murder in the Cathedral,* in *Collected Plays* (London: Faber and Faber, 1962), 46.

13. Quotations from *Four Quartets* are taken from *Collected Poems 1909–1962* (London: Faber and Faber, 1963), 189–223.

2

Time and Liturgy
in Herbert's Poetry

AT THE BEGINNING of my discussion of Donne and Crashaw, I noted that liturgy in its narrow or ordinary sense has an ecclesiastical significance, with reference principally to the eucharistic rite, especially of the Eastern churches. Originally, in Greek, the term was applied to a public duty of any sort, not exclusively religious, then later it came to be applied to the services of the Temple. In English, the term is used to describe all the services of the church, not necessarily (though frequently) the eucharist or Holy Communion. But I apply liturgy in a further, metaphorical sense to describe a way of seeing and ordering experience.

Liturgy, of course, makes use of time; for it is within time that all of our actions take place. Yet the end of liturgy is to fix time in an everlasting present, to rescue time from mutability, to redeem the present moment by conquering the threat of loss and triumphing over decay — even the dissolution of mortality itself. Liturgy always implies patterns of action which recall us to a time that is past, but continuing and also instantaneous. These external forms of worship consecrate and perpetuate our desire not merely to remember or memorialize the past, but really to transcend the physical confinements of time and space; thus, in the eucharist there is the living presence of Christ's Incarnation.

Now it may be possible to understand the wider significance of liturgy in literature, notably of poetry which consciously attempts to organize past actions and movements into a framework that celebrates an unending present and looks forward implicitly to the future. Poetry in the liturgical mode depends upon an atmosphere where time and space mingle ceremoniously, and where the literary creation asks to be taken as self-sufficient and complete. This kind of poetry is distinctive because the liturgical text is or aims to be a ritual that, in playing with time and redefining space, directly asks for independence. We are able to enter a new and perfect world — "a little world made cunningly" — and find in it the timelessness of compacted space. The desire to make poems out of particular moments made imaginatively present rather than merely remembered is a quality of the liturgical mode; there is spatial and temporal collapse, where everything pivots on one point, past and future become single in the present, infinity is finite, and the sphere and circle provide natural figures of description.

I have tried to demonstrate the usefulness of this description in better understanding many of Donne's poems, particularly "A Nocturnall upon S. *Lucies* day, Being the shortest day," "The Ecstasie," and the *Anniversaries*. In these and in other poems, Donne offers a performance through recourse to a completed circle of experience; he offers up an object dedicated to a higher end, and by this action lifts up the past into a single and everlasting time. Where there is an effort to reduce all to one time, to one point of con- vergence which has a transcendent or spiritual end, we find a liturgical work. The ideal liturgical text describes action that really occurs in an instant, in that "Bright effluence of bright essence increate" (*Paradise Lost*, 3.6), or where "the fire and the rose are one" ("Little Gidding" V).

Now my purpose is to describe George Herbert's use of time and liturgy in *The Temple;* my hope is thus to show another way of understanding and responding to this remarkable book. Herbert was careful to plan his whole work in order to unfold the theme of worship, or, in the words intended for Nicholas Ferrar (as reported by Walton), to present "a picture of the many spiritual Conflicts that have passed betwixt God and my Soul." Such conflicts are a part of worship; they always imply the two sides of effort and the resistance or discouragement that effort often provokes, as if an outer design impinges on an inner desire. The implicit connection between these two movements makes worship itself effective; and while the "conflicts" of hope and action face each other, they also contain the fundamental pattern of liturgy. Spiritual conflict, indeed, presumes the need for worship, and wor- ship demands a liturgy, whether willingly offered or not. F. H. Brabant many years ago wrote of the relationship between liturgy and worship: "all liturgi- cal acts . . . have a double function: one directed Godwards, expressing in outward form the thoughts and feelings of the worshipers, the other directed manwards, teaching the worshipers how they ought to think and feel . . . ."[1] By an easy analogy, *liturgy* describes the "structure" and the design of *The Temple* itself − the outward form − while *worship* encloses the spirit that domiciles it everywhere, teaching us how to think and feel.

This dual nature of liturgy (rule and order) and worship (feeling and desire) points to the divided way in which most of us see Herbert. Beguiled by the insecure assumption that a knowledge of his technique reveals his art, on the one hand, or else bemused by the dazzling beauty and strength of the poetry (an older view, perhaps), on the other hand, we ought better to look for a resolution of our double vision in the power of liturgy. Like the speaker in "The Collar" who always is calling, or like the key to Doubting Castle that Bunyan's Pilgrim finds in his heart, conflicts contain their own peaceful antidotes; expectations call for responses, and the answers mysteriously appear, not in distant but in near places. In movement that goes ahead in order to look back, Herbert's book gathers up ringlets of ever increasing sig- nificance; the final result is an elaborate design that rises above time while still existing within it, a liturgical work that exalts action while reducing it to the common and all embracing experience of single and perpetual time.

In individual poems and in the entire work, Herbert celebrates circularity; at the end, we have found the beginning, for "The Altar" is where "Love (III)" occurs; yet in each poem is a completeness quite independent of the other. It is often suggested that *The Temple* is not an anthology or a random collection of poems, but a work where each poem is integral to the purpose of the whole book and has a specific position within this whole. Thus Herbert carefully contrived to make a large design within which there are independent but associated parts, inextricably bound together to form one circle. We may say that each poem is a microcosm; these little spheres together form the larger circle which must contain the meaning of the whole.[2]

Circles and spheres and patterns of the whole lead us to the contemplation of paradoxical geometry, and to the sound in the universe of "mystical mathematics," where music particularly offers a supporting theme. Ideas about music and the spheres must naturally occur in *The Temple,* and such imagery frequently reminds us that a true consort (like *The Temple* itself) is made up of parts harmoniously playing together (like the poems that make up *The Temple*); or that the tuning of the lute, like the longing heart, must be done time and again "To make the musick better" ("The Temper [1]," 24).[3] *The Temple* is a universe of spheres that together turn, from which music emanates and within which all music plays. It is a place of worship in which everything and every creature is worshiping; it is an object but also an activity, an outer circle comprising inner ones that simultaneously move and are still, mutually attracted to one another. In this liturgical kind of celebration is the inevitable joining of the particular and the universal into a timeless and orderly universe, into a "temper" of true harmony in which "Thy power and love, my love and trust / Make one place ev'ry where" ("The Temper [I]," 27–28).

Herbert's plan is cumulative and reverberative; no one poem can be fully known without our reading all the others. Yet each poem speaks separately as well as contextually. While *The Temple* is no more than the sum of its parts, it is also but one of these parts alone, for the part is the whole. No way of describing *The Temple* may be entirely satisfactory, so complex is Herbert's achievement; but I think the great sweep of his work may be considered on a liturgical point, where worship is the worshiper, the center the circumference, the universe a globe. The hand of God describes nature in circles, as Sir Thomas Browne was also quick to understand: "In eternity there is no distinction of Tenses," nor beginning, middle, or end.[4] Many poems in *The Temple,* indeed, depend explicitly upon circles or on a "circular" kind of interconnectedness – and many more imply circularity – as if to illustrate the design of the whole while likewise contributing to it.

One such poem is "Clasping of hands." With its two stanzas, each of ten lines, its interlocking rhyme scheme, and its verbal play on "mine" and "thine," this poem well reveals Herbert's particular skill and wide intentions.

The title, which is not subsequently defined except by implication, points to the theme of mutual trust and love between God and man. The point of view in the first stanza is of the tentative desire of man for God, of his dependence, and of his preoccupation with his own restoration. The emphasis changes in the second stanza, from "Lord, thou art mine, and I am thine" (1) to "Lord, I am thine, and thou art mine" (11); the difference is subtle, but it calls attention to a different direction in the relationship. (One may compare "The Quip," where "I am thine" refers both to God and to the speaker of the poem.) The closing couplets of each stanza speak of this alteration, and they point finally to that higher ambition in which differences are obliterated:

> If I without thee would be mine,
> I neither should be mine nor thine.
>
> (9–10)

This is the first couplet, and it expresses a conditional and an impossible situation; for without thee, I might be independent and yet I could be nothing:

> O be mine still! still make me thine!
> Or rather make no Thine and Mine!
>
> (19–20)

Herbert's prayer contains the insight of deep belief, with "still" at its heart — remaining forever, always at the quiet center, where God and man meet separately and together with hands clasped, while the language of the poem plays over the terms of conjunction.

"Sinnes round" describes the persistence of desire within the conviction of sin. Its three stanzas imitate the regular motion of offences that "course it in a ring" by repeating linked lines and also the first line of the first stanza and the final line of the last. Thus the poem is itself in a round, or a musical circle, yet the poet cries "Sorrie I am" in the midst of this round which is self-perpetuating, repetitious, and indulgent. The theme is frequent in Herbert: beginnings meet endings in the exclamation of sorrow or hope, of love or praise. Similarly, "A Wreath" is a poetic imitation of the subject itself, where the repetition becomes a form of liturgy:

> A Wreathed garland of deserved praise,
> Of praise deserved, unto thee I give,
> I give to thee, who knowest all my wayes,
> My crooked winding wayes, wherein I live,
> Wherein I die, not live: for life is straight,
> Straight as a line, and ever tends to thee,
> To thee, who art more farre above deceit,
> Then deceit seems above simplicitie.
> Give me simplicitie, that I may live,

> So live and like, that I may know, thy wayes,
> Know them and practise them: then shall I give
> For this poore wreath, give thee a crown of praise.
>   (1–14)

The poet would give to God "A wreathed garland of deserved praise," a poor wreath which may be exchanged for "a crown of praise" providing he gives up his own winding ways for the simplicity that may direct him to God's ways. The rhyme pattern suggests a wreath, with its woven and matched pieces and its repetition of key words: praise, give, ways, live (die), straight, thee, deceit, simplicitie, and especially *give*, which occurs crucially at first and last: "unto thee I give," "then shall I give . . . give thee. . . ." This word echoes Herbert's customary desire to offer his thanksgiving and his suffering to God as a true worshiper in his church.

The priesthood is one of Herbert's regular themes — the priesthood of all believers which includes those who are specially ordained as priests in the church. Of the many poems that deal explicitly with this theme, "Aaron" perhaps speaks most forcefully, and with geometrical clarity. The poem encloses the action which it illustrates, making us see spherically in a linear world. The name with its five letters anticipates the five stanzas of five lines in each; in their short and long lengths (six, eight, ten, eight, six syllables) the stanzas suggest the shape of bells, or circles, or a combination of lines within circles, which make a *theta (Ø)*, or, in solid geometry, an inverted *chi (X)* (a conceit that appealed to Browne in *The Garden of Cyrus*[5]). Indeed, the central line of the poem (13), as well as the middle line of each stanza, might be said to be the center point of the *chi* (the first letter of Christ), for significantly they are all about music (or doctrine) for dealing with the dead:

> Onely another head
> I have, another heart and breast,
> Another musick, making live not dead,
> Without whom I could have no rest:
> In him I am well drest.
>   (11–15)

The music of the bells on the fringe of Aaron's garment sounds as he dresses for his priestly office; but the bells need tuning and the vestments need refitting to suit the man who stands in place of Aaron, the new man whose vocation is to celebrate "My doctrine tun'd by Christ":

> So holy in my head,
> Perfect and light in my deare breast,
> My doctrine tun'd by Christ, (who is not dead,
> But lives in me while I do rest)
> Come people; Aaron's drest.
>   (21–25)

In "Aaron," old and new, type and fulfillment, passion and order, death and life all meet and demonstrate the calling of the true priest. The poem is splendidly liturgical, for it exalts a moment into an eternity and it links earth with heaven. The meaning of this poem is like a sphere, or else a completed circle which continues to move and turn in space and time. In "Aaron," Herbert lets us hear the truest voice of *The Temple,* for there is no other sound but this one.

     The voice of this calling is God's speech to us, and Herbert hears it also in "The Collar," whose title itself may conceal the right sound. He would be free and unbound, able to make life as he wishes to form it. The anguish, frustration, and raging of the early part of the poem is set out primarily in terms of questions that in fact contain their answers. "Shall I ever sigh and pine?" "Is the yeare onely lost to me?" The reply must be "no," as if to a child who petulantly asks why he must routinely follow another's directions. Yet independence must be lonely and selfish; and the freedom that lies in perfect service and obedience really comes from one's heart's desire. "But there is fruit" expressed through the natural drawing of love and the grace of affection:

> But as I rav'd and grew more fierce and wilde
>   At every word,
> Me thoughts I heard one calling, *Child!*
>   And I reply'd, *My Lord.*
>   (33–36)

The poet's sudden discovery is well anticipated; in his recollection he reaffirms the link of nature that has always been present, persistently appealing to the inevitable connection of *mine* and *thine.* This theme "prevents" or reviews (depending upon the direction of our reading) the "Clasping of hands," and so we may see in a brief sequence of poems a circle of meaning. "The Collar" is followed by "The Glimpse," with its longing for renewed illumination: "Whither away delight?" The heart still hopes for a breaking forth of light, so that "Assurance," the next poem, looks forward to the realization of God's promises. It ends, as so many of Herbert's poems do, on a tentative and witty point that remembers the conflicts taken up in the previous lines while declaring a new paradox:

> What for it self love once began,
> Now love and truth will end in man.
>   (41–42)

The final lines of "Assurance" lead us to "The Call," next in this sequence begun by "The Collar." With "The Glimpse" and "Assurance" forming a bridge of expanded meaning, the sound of "The Call" is especially clear. The "call" is from God, and it is also from the heart of man: "Come, my Way, my Truth, My Life" (1), Herbert writes, taking the words of Christ in Matthew

11.28, and making them describe two directions at once: "Come unto me, all ye that travail and are heavy laden, and I will refresh you." The call of the poem is really for God, but it is God's call to which we respond. The inevitable connection and interrelationship of calling and called, of choosing and chosen, of going out and returning join here, and they meet still again in the "Clasping of hands," the poem which follows "The Call." All of these poems, from "The Collar" through the "Clasping of hands," closely related by theme and language, form a circle of meaning, though each poem lives also by itself. Herbert here conspires to remind us of worship in his "temple," where all patterns of action are one and the same, associated in a place of benediction and liturgical fullness. And where do sequences truly begin or end?

The Temple is filled with many sequences such as this one, of poems whose order is important for displaying or working out a theme in a circlet of "invention." The truth is that wherever we touch Herbert's work, we discover a beginning and an ending, and we may find ourselves at home anywhere. Each poem sets up its own special relationship between an inner desire and an outer attraction, between the little and the large, between man and God. While each poem is independent, with its own truth and value, and moves within its own time, it forms as well a part of the whole and exists within the wider time of *The Temple*. Few thoughtful readers of Herbert should have missed this point, nor failed to recognize the elaborate wordplay and the linking of multiple meanings in so many of his poems. "The Bunch of Grapes," with its extraordinary final lines, provides another and notable example of an action, complete in itself and emblematic of the whole:

> But can he want the grape, who hath the wine?
> I have their fruit and more.
> Blessed be God, who prosper'd *Noahs* vine,
> And made it bring forth grapes good store.
> But much more him I must adore,
> Who of the Laws sowre juice sweet wine did make,
> Ev'n God himself being pressed for my sake.
> (22–28)

God himself is crushed to make the new wine; he is the fruit of our salvation, but we need to "drink" and adore him. The idea involves wise dedication and a mature calling; it depends upon reciprocity and mutuality (that is, Atonement); the conceit should arouse in us the desire to understand better the meaning of worship within a liturgical sphere, where the fruit is the wine, and the wine the fruit.

Further instances seem unnecessary for urging my essential point: the backward and forward movement of the poems in *The Temple* reflects the simultaneous Godward and manward movement of all worship; and the structural motif of *The Temple* is the circle or the sphere — the true liturgical design — where time is everywhere and nowhere. Thus "The Altar" is appropriately the first poem of "The Church" (once we are ready to enter *The Temple* itself). The sacrifice of the stony heart takes place there, and in fact the heart constitutes the altar. Herbert prays, "O let thy blessed SACRIFICE be mine, / And sanctifie this ALTAR to be thine" (15–16). This prayer turns us in toward the poem in order to know its theme and "shape," but it lets us look beyond the poem itself to "mine and thine," the transcendent figure of the whole book. The poem that closes "The Church" could also have opened it, for "Love (III)" and "The Altar" are but aspects of the same liturgical movement, but arcs in common around the same circle:

> Love bade me welcome: yet my soul drew back,
> > Guiltie of dust and sinne.
> But quick-ey'd Love, observing me grow slack
> > From my first entrance in,
> Drew nearer to me, sweetly questioning,
> > If I lack'd any thing.
>
> A guest, I answer'd, worthy to be here:
> > Love said, You shall be he.
> I the unkinde, ungratefull? Ah my deare,
> > I cannot look on thee.
> Love took my hand, and smiling did reply,
> > Who made the eyes but I?
>
> Truth Lord, but I have marr'd them: let my shame
> > Go where it doth deserve.
> And know you not, sayes Love, who bore the blame?
> > My deare, then I will serve.
> You must sit down, sayes Love, and taste my meat:
> > So I did sit and eat.

Herbert echoes the Prayer of Humble Access (traditionally placed after the consecration in the Anglican rite of Holy Communion):

> We do not presume to come to this thy Table (O merciful Lord) trusting in our own righteousness, but in thy manifold and great mercies: we be not worthy so much as to gather up the crumbs under thy table: but thou art the same Lord, whose property is always to have mercy: grant us therefore (gracious Lord) so to eat the flesh of thy dear Son Jesus Christ, and to drink his blood, that our sinful bodies may be made clean by his body, and our souls washed through his most precious blood; and that we may evermore dwell in him, and he in us.[6]
>
> > (Book of Common Prayer, 1559)

The graceful and courtly phrasing closely touches Herbert's purpose; familiar terms follow us through *The Temple:* mercy and trust, worthy and unworthy, sinful and clean, we in him and he in us. All of these ideas occur in "Love (III)": guilty and worthy, diffident and desiring; the admonition at last to sit "and taste my meat," and above all the sense of reverence and mystery, of restful, domestic joy in the midst of God's majesty – a peculiarly Anglican kind of spirituality. The principle around which *The Temple* turns and in which it is exalted lies within the force of liturgy. This poem, like the others that precede it, speaks of a living moment, harmoniously tuned by unending liturgical life, of the same moment that *The Temple* as a whole consecrates.

Notes

1. See "Worship in General," in *Liturgy and Worship,* ed. W. K. Lowther Clark (1932; repr. London: SPCK, 1959), 12.1.
2. I am generally indebted to a number of works, among which are Leigh DeNeef, *"This Poetick Liturgy": Robert Herrick's Ceremonial Mode* (Durham, N.C.: Duke University Press, 1974); Lowry Nelson, Jr., *Baroque Lyric Poetry* (New Haven: Yale University Press, 1961); and Joseph H. Summers, *George Herbert: His Religion and Art* (Cambridge: Harvard University Press, 1954). Much of the recent criticism of Herbert focuses on his supposed "protestantism," to which mode notably belongs Barbara K. Lewalski's impressive book, *Protestant Poetics and the Seventeenth-Century Religious Lyric* (Princeton, N.J.: Princeton University Press, 1979), esp. chap. 9, and Richard Strier's *Love Known: Theology and Experience in George Herbert's Poetry* (Chicago: University of Chicago Press, 1983). Other writers see a poet whose religious attitudes are less important than the method of his book, which they assume lacks coherence and lies in fragments and broken pieces. Thus, Stanley Fish discovers Herbert "in dissolution" in *Self-Consuming Artifacts: The Experience of Seventeenth-Century Literature* (Berkeley: University of California Press, 1970) and seeks oddly to rehabilitate him in *The Living Temple: George Herbert and Catechizing* (Berkeley: University of California Press, 1978), while Barbara Leah Harman continues the process of exploring Herbert's "collapsing poems" and his general failure to write connectedly in *Costly Monuments: Representations of the Self in George Herbert's Poetry* (Cambridge, Mass.: Harvard University Press, 1982). But I believe that Herbert is an Anglican poet whose Arminian views place him in the company of William Laud, John Cosin, and Nicholas Ferrar. I see also *The Temple* as a carefully conceived whole. See Stanley Stewart, *George Herbert* (Boston: Twayne, 1986), with whose views I am largely in agreement. His book is cogently reviewed by Claude Summers in the *George Herbert Journal* 12 (1989): 60–66. A valuable historical description of the ecclesiastical situation during Herbert's lifetime is Nicholas Tyacke's "revisionist" *Anti-Calvinists:*

The Rise of English Arminianism c. 1590–1640 (1987; repr. Oxford: Clarendon Press, 1990).

3. The quotations from Herbert's poetry are from the edition of his *Works,* ed. F. E. Hutchinson (1941; repr. Oxford: Clarendon Press, 1959).

4. See *Religio Medici,* 1.11, ed. L. C. Martin (Oxford: Clarendon Press, 1964), 11.

5. "Of this Figure *Plato* made choice to illustrate the motion of the soul, both of the world and man; while he delivereth that God divided the whole conjunction length-wise, according to the figure of a Greek *X,* and then turning it about reflected it into a circle; By the circle implying the uniform notion of the first Orb, and by the right lines, the planetical and various motions within it. And this also with application unto the soul of man, which hath a double aspect, one right, whereby it beholdeth the body, and objects without; another circular and reciprocal, whereby it beholdeth it self" (chap. 4). Quoted from *Religio Medici and Other Works,* ed. Martin, 168.

6. See Chana Bloch, *Spelling the Word: George Herbert and the Bible* (Berkeley: University of California Press, 1985), whose "Reading of 'Love, III'" also points to the liturgical significance of the Prayer of Humble Access. Michael C. Schoenfeldt writes, less tactfully, of this poem and of Herbert's achievement, mostly in sexual terms which I think inappropriate to the context and finally unconvincing: "'That Ancient Heat': Sexuality and Spirituality in *The Temple*" in *Soliciting Interpretation: Literary Theory and Seventeenth-Century English Poetry,* ed. Elizabeth D. Harvey and Katherine Eisamen Maus (Chicago: University of Chicago Press, 1990), 273–306. Cf. his extended discussion of Herbert in *Prayer and Power: George Herbert and Renaissance Courtship* (Chicago: University of Chicago Press, 1991).

3

"Essentiall Joye" in Donne's

ANNIVERSARIES

THE ANNIVERSARY POEMS of John Donne are at once the longest and the most complex and elusive of his poetic works. A judge usually so perceptive as Ben Jonson thought that they might properly be about the Blessed Virgin Mary but instead unfortunately described Elizabeth Drury, who could hardly be worthy of such effusive compliment. Jonson is reported to have said "that Dones Anniversarie was profane and full of Blasphemies."[1] The *Anniversaries,* indeed, still trouble readers who search too far for historical, allegorical, structural, or secular meaning without understanding enough of their devotional significance. Of course, these are poems with various concerns and numerous confusions, but above all else they give triumphant expression to God's glory and to the art of verse.[2] Here is a single ambition with a "divine" end − to celebrate God's grace and his glory by means of the verse which itself is the offspring of the very grace being celebrated.

My wish is to explore the essentially religious and Christian quality of the *Anniversaries,* and especially their teaching about grace, a term which I use in a theological sense, particularly to indicate "sanctifying," rather than "actual" grace. The latter is a passing help for the production of some good act, but sanctifying grace is a permanent quality inhering in the soul. It is "the reality produced in man by God's creative love . . . [and] the result of the gracious love of God . . . received by man as a favor or free gift."[3] Man's redemption and salvation depend upon the sacramental life made possible by the Incarnation; for God through Christ restores man to his original state by his Passion and Resurrection, and God thus makes the free offering of grace. The *Anniversaries* likewise reveal the same bounteous gift of grace by their redeeming of time. By this I mean that they mediate for God on behalf of Christ, with the poet himself acting a priestly office by turning his poetry and himself into a holy sacrifice, into which and out of which grace may flow. Donne's language is often oblique, for it tries to express the ineffable; but we must, at the last, know the faith which the poet has declared is possible for us to have by means of grace. Like Elizabeth Drury, we, too, must let our bodies think.

Although Donne's *Anniversaries* are poems of meditation in the way that Louis L. Martz has shown, they are also poems of vision, possessing a special kinship with the work of such later poets as Yeats and Eliot. The traditional patterns of prayer, however, of the sort that evidently inspired the structure of the *Anniversaries,* appear only tentatively in such modern poets. Poetry of meditation becomes something freer in them, though no less rigorous an exercise in introspection. Yet even poetry like the *Anniversaries,* while remaining "Ignatian," certainly cannot be defined by its formal structure, for its external plan both encloses and releases its inner movement, that "interior drama of the mind" that produces an action leading to the consciousness of a moment of illumination.[4] Such inner and progressive movement leads to and overtakes the climax and so lets our appreciation of extrinsic form disappear into a higher wisdom. And it is this illumination itself, rather than the formal means for disclosing it, that underlies my theme.

1

The narrative voice of the *Anniversaries* searches for colorful, strident, and dramatic tones. Above all, the *Anniversaries* are allegedly about someone, the person of Elizabeth Drury being always plainly before us (although she is never actually named). Yet few readers have been content to take Donne at his literal word. Surely Elizabeth Drury, a young girl whom Donne never knew, cannot be herself but rather an emblem for Queen Elizabeth, or for the Blessed Virgin, or for Justice and Truth and Divine Wisdom. O. B. Hardison, Jr., is close to the best sense when he says that "she is a virtuous young woman concerning whom Donne had received 'good report' and whom he undertook to celebrate in two elegies based on traditional topics and images."[5] While Hardison is right in appreciating the relationship of Elizabeth Drury to Renaissance epideictic theory, and consequently in recognizing that Donne meant us to take her historically and not as a *figura* of the *logos* or of anything else, he inadequately characterizes Elizabeth's full role in the poems.

Elizabeth Drury remains herself — she is not allegorical. But Donne does use her in order to describe the life of grace in its fullness and in its withdrawal. The world is a carcass for the anatomist to dissect and Donne's autopsy has shown foul disease in the old world that Elizabeth had inhabited; that world which only Elizabeth could keep alive is dead with her own death. She had provided sweetness and joy when in the world, though she herself was not altogether free of its corruption (for it was, after all, fatal): "Shee, shee embrac'd a sicknesse, gave it meat, / The purest Blood, and Breath, that ere it eat" gives testimony of the disease (*The Second Anniversary. Of The Progres of the Soule,* 147–48).[6] Donne thus gives report of the world uninformed by grace. Having once been so lavishly embodied in Elizabeth Drury, grace retired with her; now that it is deprived of its richest expression, the world can exist only as a dead thing, "a dry cinder." This is what Donne meant by the Idea of a Woman: Elizabeth Drury stands for herself, who is

the idealized, the saintly embodiment of God's free gift of sanctifying grace.
Once this is gone, or seems to have disappeared, life cannot wholly function
again.

Donne's *First Anniversary,* or *An Anatomy of the World,* therefore,
recalls the Old Dispensation, the Law uninformed by grace. Although
Elizabeth Drury belonged to the old world, she provided it with a glimpse of
the new one to come by leaving the old with her instructive model. Donne
expresses such a view in these lines from *The First Anniversary:*

> And though she have shut in all day,
> The twi-light of her memory doth stay;
> Which, from the carcasse of the old world, free,
> Creates a new world; and new creatures be
> Produc'd: The matter and the stuffe of this,
> Her vertue, and the forme our practise is.
> And though to be thus Elemented, arme
> These Creatures, from home-borne intrinsique harme,
> (For all assum'd unto this Dignitee,
> So many weedlesse Paradises bee,
> Which of themselves produce no venemous sinne,
> Except some forraine Serpent bring it in)
> Yet, because outward stormes the strongest breake,
> And strength it selfe by confidence growes weake,
> This new world may be safer, being told
> The dangers and diseases of the old.
>
>   (73–88)

The old world is dead; the new one is not in fact the world of Donne's poems,
but one, discovered through grace, within ourselves. Donne again has in mind
the old world in the concluding lines of *An Anatomy of the World* where he
sees himself, with Moses, as the instrument of God's song. He thus recalls
the Old Covenant, which the *Anatomy* has analyzed, and Moses' commandments and "last, and lastingst peece, a song":

> [God] spake
> To *Moses,* to deliver unto all,
> That song: because he knew they would let fall,
> The Law, the Prophets, and the History,
> But keepe the song still in their memory.
> Such as opinion (in due measure) made
> Me this great Office boldly to invade.
> Nor could incomprehensiblenesse deterre
> Me, from thus trying to emprison her.
>
>   (462–70)

In the *Essayes in Divinity,* Donne refers again to Deuteronomy 32.4, the scriptural passage alluded to in these lines, and comments on its further implications: "One benefit of the Law was, that it did in some measure restore them [Abraham and his children] towards the first light of Nature: For, if man had kept that, he had needed no outward law; for then he was to himself a law, having all law in his heart."[7] *The First Anniversary* concludes with the poet looking back to a dark and graceless world. But with the pun on "fall," he can also look forward to being celebrant once more, both as poet and priest, of a joyful world where grace has returned to revitalize all and make of man's heart a paradise within, happier far. Such an office can hardly comprehend or encircle all God's fullness. But "of his fulness have all we received, and grace for grace. For the law was given by Moses, but grace and truth came by Jesus Christ" (John 1.16,17).

2

I have mainly referred to *The First Anniversary,* an almost unrelieved rehearsal of the calamitous state of the world. Donne has performed an anatomy by stripping away, layer by layer, the skin and tissue of its body, and shown at last, as Vesalius did his man, only the skeleton to be left.[8] That is, Donne would perform so complete an anatomy if the world's carcass would outlast its own putrefaction (435–40). What remains afterwards is our sense of corporal and spiritual darkness. Our physical senses remind us of the present rottenness of the inmost parts, a world of stinking flesh, a world deprived of grace: the smell is unpleasant to hear, Donne wittily observes; the outward expression of the interior ruin tells us of the abundance of corruption. This is the fallen world in need of the grace which Elizabeth embodied. *The Second Anniversary* builds upon this frail base; the progress is upward, starting from the "fall" – the fall of the world from grace (partly because Elizabeth Drury left the world, but mostly because of man's intrinsic sinfulness) and the death-fall of the poet as well as Elizabeth. We must "trust th'immaculate blood to wash [the] score" (106), a wretched one, indeed. *The Progres of the Soule* is not only about such a movement; it is the movement itself. Donne does not commonly refer in his poetry to the poet in the process of writing: he does not look over his shoulder to see what it is that the creative process is in the very act of creating.[9] In being forced to go beyond Elizabeth Drury herself – or better to say, to accompany her on her progress – one recognizes that the poetic act embodies her, as she embodied all virtue. *The Second Anniversary* is a poem about Elizabeth Drury, but it is also, and more important, about the creative power of the soul itself, above all about the power of the poet who interprets and prophesies and gives form to the highest truth. This truth is the life of grace made possible by God, through the Incarnate Christ, in the Holy Spirit – and it infuses everything.

Donne ended *The First Anniversary* by referring to the Old Law, to life in the Old Dispensation. "Fall" appears at several points in *The Second Anniversary,* and first of all at its beginning where the term acts as a bridge for bringing us from the previous poem into this next one:

> Nothing could make mee sooner to confesse
> That this world had an everlastingnesse,
> Then to consider, that a yeare is runne,
> Since both this lower worlds, and the Sunnes Sunne,
> The Lustre, and vigor of this All,
> Did set; 'twere Blasphemy, to say, did fall.
>   (1–6)

The pun on "fall" is multiple — the fall of man, the fall of Elizabeth, the fall of the Sun-Son, the fall of the world.[10] These fallings prepare us for the bold simile that follows, of the beheaded man whose head drops from his body and leaves a double jet of blood, "One from the Trunke, another from the Head" (11). Still his eyes "twinckle" and his tongue "will roll, / As though he beckned, and cal'd backe his Soul" (13–14). The truncated body still seems to grasp and try to reach its departing soul. This, with the other similes that immediately follow, is proof that there is "motion in corruption," that the "fall" is not final.

Later, when Donne is enjoining his soul to go up, and from its position in the watch-tower to "see all things despoyld of fallacies" (295), he aims to go

> Up to those Patriarckes, which did longer sit
> Expecting Christ, then they'have enjoy'd him yet.
> Up to those Prophets, which now gladly see
> Their Prophecies growne to be Historee.
>   (345–48)

The direction is the forward one for which the lines about Moses and the prophets in *The First Anniversary* have prepared us. *The First Anniversary* had looked to the past and present world, but *The Second Anniversary* to the present and to the future one. Donne is embracing all time in these poems. His subject is grace, made possible by Incarnation, or, in T. S. Eliot's expression, by the "intersection of the timeless moment" ("Little Gidding" I). Donne is revealing the new life of love in the progress of a soul that makes an ending which is also a beginning, and he is fascinated by just proportion and the fitting together of the embracing circle. He complains in *An Anatomy of the World* (especially ll. 249–324) that the world's beauty is gone and disproportion has become true form:

>   nor can the Sunne
> Perfit a Circle, or maintaine his way
> One inche direct . . .
>   (268–70)

But *The Second Anniversary* answers by revealing the vision of the saint:

> Shee, who by making full perfection grow,
> Peeces a Circle, and still keepes it so.
>   (507–509)

Elizabeth Drury, whose soul has emigrated to Heaven, possesses enduring joy. Donne, who speaks for his own and the world's soul, sees the lesson to be learned: she who has shown us the way must inspire us to work even harder, for the knowledge that grace increases in Heaven should move us toward realizing the grace here within us all the more. The spiritual and intellectual effort required recalls Satyre III, where Truth, the object of all our search stands

>   on a huge hill,
> Cragged, and steep . . . and hee that will
> Reach her, about must, and about must goe.
>   (79–81)[11]

From *The Progres of the Soule:*

>   whither who doth not strive
> The more, because shee'is there, he doth not know
> That accidentall joyes in Heaven doe grow.
> But pause, my soule, and study ere thou fall
> On accidentall joyes, th'essentiall.
>   (380–84)

Manley's reading of these lines is incomplete: "The essential joy of heaven is the everlasting possession of the Beatific Vision; all others are its accidents."[12] The Beatific Vision, which forms the end of all our striving and the end of these poems, is *essential* because it is complete and continuing, and we can never be deprived of it. Donne had said at the beginning of *The Progres of the Soule,* "Thou seest mee strive for life" (31). Surely this is the life of grace, "the seed of glory," the "positive share or participation in the life of God Himself."[13] Grace, too, is traditionally understood, as Donne would have known, to be *accidental.* It is, in orthodox theology, a given reality or entity, an "accident," something added to a person who is already a completely constituted being and inhering in him. Grace adds a divine quality, a supernatural and additional abundance. In our earthly life, we may live in the life of grace intermittently; but in our heavenly existence, we live fully within it. Accidental joys grow, or increase, in Heaven because they flourish uninterruptedly, and there our sight of God's love and grace cannot be darkened by mortal sin and the corruption of a primitive and fallen world. One may "fall" on accidental joys — Donne is characteristically punning — in the sense that having made a beginning in the life of grace, having started his study, one may not see how to complete it. The answer comes in the sight of the essential joy of heavenly grace. Donne is thus saying that we should study the vision, the essence, the object of grace, even before we start, and perhaps fail or fall along the way. There is essential joy on earth, of course, as well as in Heaven, but here it is transitory, and Donne is eager in the next fifty lines to demonstrate this fact:

> whil'st you thinke you bee
> Constant, you'are howrely in inconstancee.
> (399–400)

Thus "accidentall" means "but a casuall happinesse" (412) while it also defines in a technical way the meaning of grace as taught by the Fathers and the Schoolmen.

The climactic lines of *The Second Anniversary,* indeed of both poems, for they are one long poem united by a single purpose and direction, begin at line 435:

> Then, soule, to thy first pitch worke up againe;
> Know that all lines which circles doe containe,
> For once that they the center touch, do touch
> Twice the circumference; and be thou such.
> Double on Heaven, thy thoughts on Earth emploid;
> All will not serve; Onely who have enjoyd
> The sight of God, in fulnesse, can thinke it;
> For it is both the object, and the wit.
> This is essentiall joye, where neither hee
> Can suffer Diminution, nor wee;
> 'Tis such a full, and such a filling good;
> Had th'Angels once look'd on him, they had stood.
> To fill the place of one of them, or more,
> Shee whom we celebrate, is gone before.
> Shee, who had Here so much essentiall joye,
> As no chance could distract, much lesse destroy.
> . . . .
> Whose twilights were more cleare, then our mid day,
> Who dreamt devoutlier, then most use to pray;
> Who being heare fild with grace, yet strove to bee,
> Both where more grace, and more capacitee
> At once is given: . . .
> (435–50, 463–67)

The passage is a brilliant one: the first pitch to which the soul is enjoined to work up again recalls its Edenic state, its highest elevation before the Fall. Pitch is a musical image, too, and appropriate here for the fact that it recalls other musical references, central to the purpose of both poems. In *An*

Anatomy of the World, Elizabeth Drury was seen as "a part both of the Quire, and Song," one who sings and is sung about; in *The Progres of the Soule,* Donne indicates that he will propagate a child each year by writing a hymn in Elizabeth's honor. Punning on *hymns,* Donne says that he shall continue to let his verses be Elizabeth's children: she, as much as the poet, makes this issue possible, and so her posterity will be enriched until "Gods great Venite change the song" (44), until the Resurrection of the body and the end of time. Elizabeth Drury thus teaches us the first pitch, the best harmony. Pitch also leads into the next metaphor by carrying a geometrical meaning, for one pitches a circle — *pitch* in this sense (see *OED,* sb., III.10) is the point from which one describes the circle — here the point or center is Donne's soul itself.

Again, we may recall the numerous images in these poems that have relied upon and called for the harmony of the circle. Elizabeth has pieced the circle together, or shown how it is complete (508), for the circle, indeed, represents the Beatific Vision for which we all long. Donne, who speaks for us, lives on earth, not always with the sight of God, and his life is the line which transects the center, the soul on earth, longing to touch Heaven (the circumference) twice. "Double" is an imperative, associated with thoughts; in touching the circumference with them, our time crosses earth, where the soul presently stays, and links it with Heaven. "All" is opposed to "Onely," in line 440. But "all" suggests that to have one's thoughts on Heaven in double the number of one's thoughts on earth is insufficient; only the whole circle, the whole vision of God is enough, and only those who have had it can "thinke it." Here *think* is related to Elizabeth Drury, whose body thought (246) — she did have "the sight of God, in fulnesse." This sight is both *object,* the known thing, seen in itself, and the *wit,* the very mode of perceiving. Object is realization complemented by wit, or the means of realizing. And such is essential joy, or grace unending, where one has a reciprocative share in the supernatural life. Indeed, had all the angels looked on God, none of them would have fallen. "No chance" could distract Elizabeth, who lived in grace, no accident. Her twilights were clearer than our brightest hours (the same image occurs in the passage of *The First Anniversary,* 73–74, quoted earlier), but still she labored for more grace.

The Progres of the Soule ends by recalling its beginning: *An Anatomy of the World* showed the disease of earthly life under the Old Dispensation; *The Progres of the Soule,* of life in grace, which the poet will continue to celebrate until God's last Venite. The image of "great Grand-children of [her] praises," the role of the verse itself described at the beginning of *The Progres of the Soule,* Donne recalls at the ending of the poem. By being Elizabeth's child, this poem is also Donne's, for he asks her to be the father of his chaste muse (33–36). Elizabeth, having pieced the circle of harmony in which we may see and discover the embodiment of grace, would be worthy of an invocation. But Donne does not invoke her name; he remembers his purpose has been to commemorate Elizabeth by declaring that God has given her power to be well remembered and him the poetic ability to write well of her:

> Since his will is, that to posteritee,
> Thou shouldst for life, and death, a patterne bee,
> And that the world should notice have of this,
> The purpose, and th'Authority is his;
> Thou art the Proclamation; and I ame
> The Trumpet, at whose voice the people came.
> (523–28)

The poet merges with the poem and its subject; the voice of Moses with which Donne identified at the end of *An Anatomy of the World* is now God's song of the New Dispensation of grace whose pattern Elizabeth was able to proclaim. Both of the *Anniversaries* have been tied together by the motif of song, at first struggling to be heard (Moses knew the people would not hear) and at the last triumphantly sounding − the people come to hear the sound of the last trumpet which announces the general resurrection (1 Cor. 15.52,55). The poems are a performance in which the poet has been both conductor and subject. Yet he still waits for God's last calling of the faithful together, his last *Venite* when all voices shall join in a hymn of praise: "O come, let us sing unto the Lord: let us heartily rejoice in the strength of our salvation."[14]

The trumpet commonly signifies the inspired prophet. Donne again calls all men to a general resurrection at the conclusion of one sermon where he compares his own "lower and infirmer voice" to the last trumpet: "as at the last resurection, all that heare the sound of the Trumpet, shall rise in one instant, though they have passed thousands of years between their burialls, so doe all ye, who are now called, by a lower and infirmer voice, rise together in this resurrection of grace." Moreover, in the second prebend sermon, Donne points to Christ's joyous *Venite*: "The everlastingnesse of the joy is the blessednesse of the next life, but the entring, the inchoation is afforded here. For that which Christ shall say then to us, *Venite benedicti, Come ye blessed,* are words intended to persons that are coming, that are upon the way, though not at home; Here in this world he bids us *Come,* there in the next, he shall bid us *Welcome.*" Beginning, entering, coming, welcoming − *Venite* has many voices.[15]

But there is a further point, and that is to see the poet as priest, who, through God's grace, has offered up his performance to God. As priest, Donne has taken the ordinary world and consecrated it so that *The Progres of the Soule* can end with joy, harmony, and heavenly wisdom. When opposing accidental to essential joy, and yet mingling them, Donne intends a eucharistic meaning. Joy is grace, and grace, as we have seen, is an accident, an objective *quality*; the dull and common world is also an accident, but of *quantity,* in need of priestly blessing. Donne, who himself accompanies Elizabeth on a progress, and identifies himself with her, transforms, by means of the grace available through Christ and embodied in Elizabeth Drury, the vulgar world; for he has made possible its transubstantiation. While appearances remain the same, the substance of life is totally altered. In *The First Anniversary,* Donne had dwelt primarily upon insubstantial, accidental forms; in *The Second Anniversary,* he declares the new life of power in grace, the essential and substantial life of the spirit, the real presence of Christ. If the Beatific Vision, and the harmony that accrues and belongs to it, is the end of this poem, then we may say that the poet has consciously played his part both as poet in describing this new life and as priest, by God's power, in consecrating it and making it holy. Although Donne does not use the term, he is fully conscious of it: Incarnation makes possible, through Christ, a sacramental way for the stream of grace to flow to us all.[16]

In embracing all experience, from decay and disorder through joy and grace, from old covenant to new order, these extraordinary poems speak on different levels, but in one harmony. While Elizabeth Drury always remains herself and the world goes on being corrupt, both can be informing and informed through the creative acts of poetry and of grace. Donne has shown the turning of sorrow into joy and offered up himself and his poetry to the God of grace as a fit sacrifice of praise and thanksgiving; having cried out from the depths of his experience, he heard at first his own voice in this calling, but at last only Love's, drawing him with promises of plenteous redemption, and revealing what he had always known, in speech which never began and has no ending. Donne takes us where we may know "the souls bloud, / The land of spices; something understood."

Notes

1. "Ben Jonson's Conversations with William Drummond of Hawthornden," quoted in Ben Jonson, *Works,* ed. C. H. Herford and Percy Simpson (Oxford: Clarendon Press, 1925), 1:133. Donne commented in his letter "To Sir G. F.," written about 1612, that "it became me to say, not what I was sure was just truth, but the best that I could conceive" (quoted in *The Life and Letters of John Donne,* ed. Edmund Gosse [London, 1899], 1:306). Cf. T. S. Eliot's passing remark that the *Anniversaries* are "the finest of Donne's long poems," in "The Devotional Poets of the Seventeenth Century," *The Listener* 3 (March 26, 1930): 552.

2. See Rosalie L. Colie, *Paradoxia Epidemica: The Renaissance Tradition of Paradox* (Princeton, N.J.: Princeton University Press, 1966), 428–29. I am indebted to Colie's discussion of Donne's *Anniversaries,* and also to Antony F. Bellette, "Art and Imitation in Donne's *Anniversaries,*" *Studies in English Literature* 15 (1975): 83–96. See as well Dennis Quinn, "Donne's *Anniversaries* as Celebration," *Studies in English Literature* 9 (1969): 97–105, and Carol M. Sicherman, "Donne's Timeless *Anniversaries,*" *University of Toronto Quarterly* 39 (1970): 127–43. Marjorie Hope Nicolson's important

study, *The Breaking of the Circle: Studies in the Effect of the "New Science" upon Seventeenth-Century Poetry,* rev. ed. (New York: Columbia University Press, 1960), chap. 3, "The Death of a World," is nevertheless misleading. Richard E. Hughes relies on slight historical and textual evidence for an archetypal or mythic explanation of the poem in *The Progress of the Soul: The Interior Career of John Donne* (New York: Morrow, 1968). Barbara K. Lewalski's magisterial work, *Donne's* Anniversaries *and the Poetry of Praise: The Creation of a Symbolic Mode* (Princeton, N.J.: Princeton University Press, 1973), seeks to understand the *genre* of these poems by examining their literary and theological contexts. I am less inclined than she to represent Donne as strongly "protestant," the reformist elements of his thought seeming to me very much overstated. For another, recent view see Edward W. Tayler, *Donne's Idea of a Woman: Structure and Meaning in* The Anniversaries (New York: Columbia University Press, 1991).

    3. See P. Gregory Stevens, *The Life of Grace,* The Foundations of Catholic Theology (Englewood Cliffs, N.J., 1963), 108. Cf. E. Towers, "Sanctifying Grace," in *The Teaching of the Catholic Church,* 2nd ed. (London: Burns & Oates, 1952), chap. 16. Cf. also *OED,* II.6, esp. b., for its definition of "grace."

    4. See *The Poetry of Meditation,* rev. ed. (New Haven: Yale University Press, 1962), 330 and app. 2, "The Dating and Significance of Donne's *Anniversaries,*" a reply to Nicolson and some others who have organized Donne into too careful a shape. Martz himself, whose description of the *Anniversaries* seems at times too rigid, recognizes that "the central point of both poems lies in the assertion that religious virtue is the greatest of all human values . . . [that Donne] is celebrating the values of 'interior peace'" (356).

    5. O. B. Hardison, Jr., *The Enduring Monument: A Study of the Idea of Praise in Renaissance Literary Theory and Practice* (Chapel Hill, N.C.: University of North Carolina Press, 1962), 186.

    6. See Harold Love, "The Argument of Donne's *First Anniversary,*" *Modern Philology* 64 (1966): 125–131. He argues that Elizabeth Drury's death is cause as well as consequence of the innate corruption of the natural world, "that the death of Elizabeth has been caused by the death of the world" (127). Quotations from Donne's *Anniversaries* are from the edition by W. Milgate, *The Epithalamions, Anniversaries, and Epicedes* (Oxford: Clarendon Press, 1978). Cf. the edition, with commentary, by Frank Manley, *John Donne: The Anniversaries* (Baltimore: Johns Hopkins University Press, 1963), and especially *The Donne Variorum,* vol. 6, ed. Gary Stringer and others (Columbia, Mo.: University of Missouri Press, 1992).

    7. *Essayes in Divinity,* ed. Evelyn M. Simpson (Oxford: Clarendon Press, 1952), 92.

    8. See Devon L. Hodges, *Renaissance Fictions of Anatomy* (Amherst, Mass.: University of Massachusetts Press, 1985), esp. chap. 1, "Of Anatomy." Hodges reproduces a number of the illustrations in Vesalius's *De Corporis*

Fabrica (1543), and discusses the "anatomy" as a cultural, scientific, and literary phenomenon of the later sixteenth and earlier seventeenth centuries.

9. "Hymne to God my God, in my sicknesse" is one exception. Donne thinks of himself and the poem he is writing as simultaneous offerings.

10. Ben Jonson's ode "To the immortall memorie, and friendship of that noble paire, Sir Lucius Cary, and Sir H. Morison" (from *Under-Wood,* 1640) also plays on *fall* and attempts to disclose a model life which has the perfection of the sphere:

> Alas, but Morison fell young!
> He never fell: thou fall'st, my tongue.
> He stood, a soldier to the last right end,
> A perfect patriot, and a noble friend;
> But most, a virtuous son.
> All offices were done
> By him so ample, full, and round,
> In weight, in measure, number, sound,
> As, though his age imperfect might appear,
> His life was of humanity the sphere.
>
>   (43–52)

Ben Jonson, ed. Ian Donaldson (Oxford: Oxford University Press, 1985), 396.

11. *The Satires, Epigrams and Verse Letters,* ed. W. Milgate (Oxford: Clarendon Press, 1967), 13.

12. See the commentary to his edition of *The Anniversaries,* 194.

13. See Robert W. Gleason, S.J., *Grace* (London, 1962), 3; of particular interest is app. 4, "Grace and Philosophy."

14. Psalm 95, "Venite, exultemus Domino," stands traditionally at the beginning of the office of matins (or morning prayer in the Book of Common Prayer).

15. See Manley's commentary, p. 200, which cites Ezek. 33.1–7, and passages from Donne's sermons. The first of these, which is quoted above, occurs at the conclusion of a Lincoln's Inn sermon (preached about 1621), in *Sermons of John Donne,* ed. George R. Potter and Evelyn M. Simpson (Berkeley: University of California Press, 1957), 3:133. Donne preached the second of his prebend sermons at St. Paul's on January 29, 1626, and Simpson and Potter call attention in their introduction (*Sermons,* 7:3–4) to close connections between this sermon and a number of lines of *The Second Anniversary.* The passage quoted appears near the end of the sermon (p. 69). *Venite benedicti* are the first words of Matt. 25.34. Cf. chap. 1, pp. 8–10.

16. Donne may indirectly be referring to the sacrament of the eucharist in *The Progres of the Soule,* 45–47. He has just looked forward to "Gods great Venite," but his "insatiate soule" must meanwhile serve its thirst "with Gods safe-sealing Bowle." See Manley, p. 177, who recognizes the commonplace equation of sacraments to seals. But he does not suggest which sacrament; the reference to Apoc. 7.3–4 is not helpful when Donne seems to have the eucharist in mind.

4

Word and Sacrament in Donne's Sermons

IN THEIR introductory remarks on "The Literary Value of Donne's Sermons," Potter and Simpson say that "in prose Donne belongs to the school of Hooker and Jeremy Taylor, of Milton and Sir Thomas Browne."[1] By this judgment, Donne's editors mean that all of these writers learned first to write Latin prose and then modeled English syntax on classical forms. This general view may be commonly held though imperfectly understood and troublesome to demonstrate. For the present, however, let us imagine Donne at school with only two of these persons, whose shared interest is not so stylistic as theological, that is, with the older Hooker, on the one hand, and the younger Taylor, on the other. Here is a text, as Donne might say, in which our division shall be short, and our whole exercise but a larger paraphrase upon the words of the Prophet Jeremy, *Surge et descende, Arise and go down* (Jer. 18.2). "Our grave is upward," according to Donne, "and our heart is upon *Iacobs* Ladder" (4:51).

My wish is to focus primarily on eucharistic celebration, or the sacramental sense in Donne, especially in the sermons, and to suggest that Donne's interest in the issues of life — and death — is representative of that most compelling feature of Anglican spirituality — its incarnational theology.[2] I shall notice also Hooker's *Lawes* and Taylor's *Holy Living* as further examples of the tradition which Donne, as the central figure in this discussion, inherited and sustained. He would certainly have agreed with Hooker, that "there are but fower thinges which concurre to make compleate the whole state of our Lord Jesus Christ, his deitie, his manhood, the conjunction of both, and the distinction of the one from the other beinge joyned in one"; and Taylor would have given assent to them both in his guides to a sanctified life and to a blessed death.[3]

Donne's 160 extant sermons, preached over about fifteen years, are, as we should expect, quite varied in occasion, subject, and style. Some readers see in them, for example, a change in language, an enriching of metaphor, and a deepening seriousness. This may be true, but I have not noticed a substantial shift in tone from early to late, though perhaps Donne has become more skillful in organizing and embellishing his material. Still if no dates could be attached to any of the sermons, we would have difficulty in deciding their order; for their likenesses are greater than any dissimilarities. Their common features are most impressive, and they lie at the heart of my analysis.

Donne always preaches on a text by exploring its significance at several levels, by extending its literal sense to a wider, spiritual one, and by finally relating the text with all its accumulated meanings to the special circumstances of himself and his audience. Occasionally in a sermon Donne is specifically preparing his congregation for receiving the Holy Communion, but usually his sermons formed part of what used to be generally known as "ante-communion," or else morning prayer (or matins). The particular liturgical occasion did not so importantly affect his sermons (except in a few obvious cases, such as the one preached at the funeral of Sir William Cokayne); but Donne usually kindles them with a universal concern for unfolding and exalting the mystery of faith and for allowing all persons to rest in some comfortable understanding of it. Seen in this way, most of Donne's sermons, ending so often at a moment of supreme exaltation and desire, lead to a celebration of the eucharistic feast.

This idea can be illustrated through reference to the second prebend sermon, preached at St. Paul's, January 29, 1626, on the text from Psalm 63.7, "Because thou hast been my helpe, therefore in the shadow of thy wings will I rejoyce" (*Sermons,* 7, no. 1)[4]. The text, Donne says, comprises "the whole compasse of Time, Past, Present, and Future": David's present situation, what passed between him and God, and what was to come *"in the shadow of thy wings"* (7:52). After carefully studying the text from the point of view of two time planes, Donne eagerly moves to the third, where he sustains his argument on the metaphor of wings:

> Though God doe not actually deliver us, nor actually destroy our enemies, yet if hee refresh us in the shadow of his Wings, if he maintaine our subsistence (which is a religious Constancy) in him, this should not onely establish our patience, (for that is but halfe the worke) but it should also produce a joy, and rise to an exultation.   (7:68)

Carried on wings and permeated by the transforming presence of sacramental joy, Donne is moving his congregation (in which he surely must include himself) to an exalted state of consciousness:

> The Holy Ghost, who is a Dove, shadowed the whole world under his wings; *Incubabat aquis,* He hovered over the waters, he sate upon the waters, and he hatched all that was produced, and all that was produced so, was good. Be thou a Mother where the Holy Ghost would be a Father; Conceive by him; and be content that he produce joy in thy heart here.   (7:70)

Thus one may possess Heaven uninterruptedly in the face of Death or of the Devil "in the irreversiblenesse of that transmigration" where joy is "super-invested in glory." Donne has typically achieved two ends in this sermon: he has given the ordinary circumstances of his text and of his auditory transcendent value, and he has turned what is low or what is dying into triumphal life. Here is surely a foretaste of that mystical banquet where love is both known and understood.

The theme is further elaborated in the Easter Day sermon preached at St. Paul's in 1628, on 1 Corinthians 13.12, "For now we see through a glass darkly, but then face to face; now I know in part, but then I shall know, even as also I am knowne" *(Videmus nunc per speculum in ænigmate: tunc autem facie ad faciem. Nunc cognosco ex parte: tunc autem cognoscam sicut et cognitus sum).* Although the text makes no reference to "light," it obviously depends upon light, Simpson and Potter counting the word *light* or its derivatives *enlighten* and *enlightened* seventy-one times, remarking that the idea of the Beatific Vision is implicit in the text and in Donne's theme (8:20). The knowledge of God is what we long for, the sight of him now, partially, in this world, but then, entirely, in the world to come. In a remarkable though characteristically ingenious transition from *nunc* to *tunc*, from this *now* to that *then*, in which he recalls the points of his division, Donne turns from facing earth to imagining Heaven:

> Now, as for the sight of God here, our Theatre was the world, our *Medium* and glasse was the creature, and our light was reason, And then for our knowledge of God here, our Academy was the Church, our *Medium* the Ordinances of the Church, and our Light the light of faith, so we consider the same Termes, first, for the sight of God, and then for the knowledge of God in the next life.   (8:231)

Since Donne is preaching on a text from St. Paul's famous discourse on charity, he naturally sees the link between human and divine love, the one acting as a mirror of the other. He also was evidently anticipating the Lord's Supper or Holy Communion that would follow his sermon — Easter being one of the days on which the eucharist was invariably celebrated, when all should be "in love and charity." He ends his sermon with a summary of its arguments and with an exhortation:

> Only that man that loves God, hath the art to love himself; doe but love your selves; for if he love God, he would live eternally with him, and, if he desire that, and indeavour it earnestly, he does truly love himself, and not otherwise. And he loves himself, who by seeing God in the Theatre of the world, and in the glasse of the creature, by the light of reason, and knowing God in the Academy of the Church, by the Ordinances thereof, through the light of faith,

> indeavours to see God in heaven, by the manifestation of
> himselfe, through the light of Glory, and to know God him-
> self, in himself, and by himself, as he is all in all; Con-
> templatively, by knowing as he is known, and Practically, by
> loving, as he is loved.   (8:236)

Yet once more, Donne raises us from darkness, from the obscurity of
mortality, to the light of glory.

In turning to Donne's sermon at Whitehall, preached on the first
Friday of Lent 1628, on Acts 7.60, the last words of St. Stephen, "And when
he had said this, he fell a sleep," we may touch especially the imagery of
mortality, which, because of its frequency in the sermons (and elsewhere),
has seemed to many readers indication of an unhealthy preoccupation with
death. But Donne is usually as much concerned with life as death, his emphasis being on the result of dying, not just the details of dissolution and
putrefaction, but the triumph of new life. In this sermon, he begins with the
representative figure: "He that will dy with Christ upon Good-Friday, must
hear his own bell toll all Lent; he that will be partaker of his passion at last,
must conform himself to his discipline of prayer and fasting before" (8:174).
The idea is essential to Taylor's frequent admonitions in *Holy Living* that one
must spend a lifetime making ready to die. The tolling of the bell invoked in
this sermon is a well known figure in Donne's writing, the sound of death but
the call also to repentance and a better life to come. "Preparatives" are
necessary, of course; and Lent with Good Friday leads to Easter; the Passion
anticipates the Resurrection. So in this place, Donne sees his text as a means
of calling together his congregation to die in order to live, a process
reenacted in the sermon which itself helps us to receive the Blessed Sacrament. "You would not go into a Medicinal Bath without some preparatives,"
he says; "presume not upon that Bath, the blood of Christ Jesus, in the Sacrament then, without preparatives neither" (8:174). In a striking image, on
which we see many variations, Donne remarks that "no Martyr ever lack'd a
grave in the wounds of his Saviour" (8:186); but in the death-bed, which one
may embrace, is "a sleep" that "delivers us to a present Rest; . . . a future
waking in a glorious Resurrection" (8:191). Thus Stephen's sleep and our
own sleep are but promises and emblems of the simultaneous death and life
of the Cross. The sermon ends with another vision of beatitude, where there
are "no ends nor beginnings, but one equall eternity" (8:191).

Christmas is the Feast of the Incarnation, the Nativity of Christ, and
Donne, as so many preachers of his day – Lancelot Andrewes perhaps
preëminent among them – treats the occasion with special solemnity and
particular joy. In his sermons for this occasion, Donne naturally gives promi-
nence to the doctrine that underlies so much of his work, and he is able to
manifest well that sacramental sense inherent in it. In one sermon, preached
perhaps in 1629, on John 10.10, "I am come that they might have life, and
that they might have it more abundantly," Donne wittily plays on the directions of the text (in a way reminiscent of Andrewes's well known Christmas

sermon of 1622, where the Magi had "a cold comming"). His aim is to gather up all directions of all persons in all times in order to lead them into the celebration of this time. In "the beating of the pulse of this text" is our panting after the joys of the abundance of the spiritual life of grace. While Donne is reaching for such a "coruscation," such an "incomprehensibleness," he meditates the direction of the Shepherd and the Sheep, Him and Them, God and Men:

> What eye can fixe it self upon East and West at once? And
> he must see more then East and West, that sees God, for
> God spreads infinitely beyond both: God alone is all; not
> onely all that is, but all that is not, all that might be, if he
> would have it be. God is too large, too immense, and then
> man is too narrow, too little to be considered; for, who can
> fixe his eye upon an Atome? and he must see a lesse thing
> then an Atome, that sees man, for man is nothing.   (9:134)

Crashaw would later write of the Nativity as "Æternity shutt in a span"; and we remember Donne's readiness to collapse different time planes into one, as in the second prebend sermon, or as in another and earlier Lincoln's Inn sermon for Trinity Sunday, preached perhaps in 1621:

> When I see . . . *Iesus,* accomplishing my salvation, by an
> actuall death, I see those hands stretched out, that stretched
> out the heavens, and those feet racked, to which they that
> racked them are foot-stooles; I heare him, from whom his
> nearest friends fled, pray for his enemies, and him, whom
> his Father forsooke, not forsake his brethren; I see him that
> cloathes this body with his creatures, or else it would wither,
> and cloathes this soule with his Righteousnesse, or else it
> would perish, hang naked upon the Crosse. . . .   (3:308)

The impulse in all of these selections, and the direction of so much of Donne's work is toward temporal collapse, the finite in the infinite; or, in sacramental terms, the Word made flesh, and Christ's death, Resurrection, Ascension, and coming again in glory.

"Deaths Duell," with its striking conclusion, demonstrates the process and movement we have been seeing. Donne's text for this presumably last sermon is from Psalm 68.20, "And unto God the Lord belong the issues of death, i.e. from death." In this sermon, he returns to the motifs and the imagery we have often seen: the point is that death belongs to the Resurrection: "Fixe thy self firmly upon that beliefe of the generall resurrection, and thou wilt never doubt of either of the particular resurrections, either from sin, by Gods grace, or from worldly calamities, by Gods power. For that last resurrection is the ground of all" (4:61). These are lines near the end of a sermon preached some ten years before Deaths Duell, on 1 Corinthians

15.26, "The last enemie that shall be destroyed, is death." So in the last sermon: we come into the world seeking a grave, as the Incarnation reveals; and we may leave "with a *dangerous damp* and *stupefaction,* and *insensibility*"; but Christ "suffered *colluctations* with *death,* . . . and an *agony* even to a *bloody sweate* in his *body,* and *expostulations* with *God,* and *exclamations* upon the crosse" (10:240). Our own time is well spent if we take this present day and celebrate Christ's life in it, and in the sacrament itself discover the whole history of faith. Donne leaves this sermon by leaving us in contemplation of that blessed dependency, that meeting of world and word, of death and life, of emptied graves and incorruption:

> There wee leave you in that *blessed dependancy,* to *hang* upon *him* that *hangs* upon the *Crosse,* there *bath* in his *teares,* there *suck* at his *woundes,* and *lye downe in peace* in his *grave,* till hee vouchsafe you a *resurrection,* and an *ascension* into that *Kingdome,* which hee *hath purchas'd for you,* with the *inestimable price* of his *incorruptible blood.*
> (10:248)

Word and sacrament meet in this vivid image, at the intellectual and spiritual climax of the sermon, and perhaps of Donne's life.

To call upon Richard Hooker at this point might seem to bring at most a distant echo; yet his *Lawes of Ecclesiastical Polity* unfold just this sense, so stirringly felt and portrayed in Donne, of the unity of all persons in the eucharist. Indeed, the *Lawes* is such a vast work that one may easily miss certain of its fundamental principles in the details of argument. Having spent his first four books on "generalities," on the natural law and its universal operation, Hooker turns to the particular application of those laws to the practice of religion in a "politic society."

In the preface to his whole work, Hooker sets out his great design by which he intended to answer the objections of those reformers who attacked the Church of England. His plan is to display the universal reasonableness of the church against the unreasonable assertions of these unenlightened opponents. Hooker develops his argument into a noble description of the pattern of laws established and defined by God, the authority of which is unchanging and absolute; and he depicts those who would not be conformed to these laws as mischievous and blind.

Hooker is careful to distinguish the different, yet interlaced, kinds of law; for all persons are subject to many laws, which ask for a variety of responses. There are thus eight kinds of law: "[1] The lawe which God with himselfe hath eternally set downe to follow in his owne workes; [2] the law which he hath made for his creatures to keepe, [that is,] the law of naturall and necessarie agents; [3] the law which Angels in heaven obey; [4] the lawe whereunto by the light of reason men finde themselves bound in that they are men; [5] the lawe which they make by composition for multitudes and politique societies of men to be guided by; [6] the lawe which belongeth unto each nation; [7] the lawe that concerneth the fellowship of all; [8] and lastly the lawe which God himselfe hath supernaturally revealed."[5] Each law is distinct yet the *law* altogether rests in the "bosome of God; her voyce [is] the harmony of the world, all thinges in heaven and earth doe her homage, the very least as feeling her care, and the greatest as not exempted from her power, but Angels and men and creatures of what condition so ever, though ech in different sort and maner, yet all with uniforme consent, admiring her as the mother of ther peace and joy."[6]

Everything in Hooker's work follows from this initial discussion of the law both "natural" − emanating from God, and thus immutable − and "positive" − deriving from human interpretation and authority, which may change. Hooker's genius is to distinguish between divine and human law and yet to draw them together. The long fifth book thus turns from the description and general presence of universal law in order to deal with "the power of Ecclesisticall order," by taking up the principles and detailed contents of the Book of Common Prayer, that is, the formularies of the established church. In the middle of his whole work on the *Lawes*, Hooker now turns unmistakably from one to another view that shows ideal conjunction, *The union or mutuall participation which is betweene Christ and the Church of Christ in this present worlde* (chap. 56). On the interconnectedness of God and man in hypostatic union, he writes:

> He therefore which is in the father by eternall derivation of beinge and life from him must needes be in him through an eternall affection of love. His incarnation causeth him also as man to be now in the father and the father to be in him. For in that he is man he receiveth life from the father as from the fountaine of that everlivinge deitie which in the person of the worde hath combined it selfe with manhood and doth thereunto imparte such life as to no other creature besides him is communicated.[7]

Hooker's central doctrine is *participation,* the steady belief that "we may evermore dwell in him, and he in us":

> God hath his influence into the verie essence of all thinges, without which influence of deitie supportinge them theire utter annihilation could not choose but followe. Of him all thinges have both receaved theire first beinge and theire continuance to be that which they are. All thinges are therefore pertakers of God, they are his ofspringe, his influence is in them, and the personall wisdome of God is for that verie cause said to excell in nimblenes or agilitie, to pearce into all intellectuall pure and subtile spirites, to goe through all, and to reach unto everie thinge which is.[8]

Hooker's concern with the sacramental life of the church is at the heart of his vast treatise, for it touches and harmonizes all experience. The eucharist itself, Hooker knows, provides the consummation of our eternal yet mortal life in Christ. Indeed, one of the most vivid and stirring passages of the *Lawes* occurs in chapter 67, *Of the sacrament of the body and blood of Christ,* where Hooker approvingly recalls Cyprian:

> These mysteries doe as nailes fasten us to his verie crosse,
> that by them wee draw out, as touchinge efficacie force and
> vertue, even the blood of his goared side, in the woundes of
> our redemer wee there dip our tongues, wee are died redd
> both within and without, our hunger is satisfied and our
> thirst for ever quenched, they are thinges wonderfull which
> hee feeleth, greate which hee seeth and unheard of which he
> uttereth whose soule is possest of this pascall lamb and
> made joyfull in the strength of this new wine, this bread
> hath in it more then the substance which our eyes behold,
> this cup hallowed with sollemne benediction availeth to the
> endles life and wellfare both of soule and bodie, in that it
> serveth as well for a medicine to heale our infirmities and
> purge our sinnes as for a sacrifice of thanksgiving, with
> touching it sanctifieth, it enlightneth with beliefe, it trulie
> conformeth us unto the image of Jesus Christ; what these
> elementes are in them selves it skilleth not, it is enough that
> to me which take them they are the bodie and blood of
> Christ, his promise in witnes hereof sufficeth, his word he
> knoweth which way to accomplish, why should any cogita-
> tion possesse the minde of a faithfull communicant but this,
> *O my God thou art true, O my soule thou art happie*?[9]

Most great and long works have their simplicities as well as complications; for Hooker these words express an essential point that guides his grand design, even as they anticipate and embrace Donne's last sermon −   where we are left hanging in "that *blessed dependancy.*"[10]

With Hooker, as with Donne, so also with Taylor and many other Anglican divines − Andrewes and Herbert come at once to mind − we are in a teacher's presence. It is easy to think of any of these writers as instructors and guides, beckoning us toward what we should know. But of these figures, only Jeremy Taylor is primarily interested in writing a guidebook for the direction of souls, for he was specifically responding to the particular events of his time in a way that he believed most useful. In 1649, the year in which Taylor probably wrote *Holy Living,* the Church of England was in the midst of the most difficult period of its history. The King had been executed that year, four years after Archbishop Laud. Episcopacy had by then been abolished, the Book of Common Prayer banned, and the Church dis-established. Many of the Anglican clergy, having been turned out of their livings, like Taylor himself, were in want and penury. In the aftermath of the civil war, though the Rump of the Long Parliament still existed, the army and Cromwell in fact exercised all real power. This was the state of affairs, as Taylor says in his dedication, that prompted him to write *Holy Living*. At a time when he has seen "Religion painted upon Banners, and thrust out of Churches," when men "prefer a prosperous errour before an afflicted truth," and the "Ministers of Religion are so scattered that they cannot unite to stop the inundation" of truth by error, he offers the book as a means to help keep the impoverished Church alive.[11] The book presents in "one body those advices which the severall necessities of many men must use at some time or other, and many of them, daily." It is a "collection of holy precepts," or "rules for conduct of soules," that supplies a need in "the want of personall and attending Guides" (pp. 5–6). This description of *Holy Living* explains its comprehensive form. Since it is meant to supply a need in the absence of appropriately organized religious teaching (as Taylor believed), the scope of the book extends to all areas in which guidance is necessary, including in its province every concern of the Christian life.

In *Holy Living* Taylor wishes to show that the attainment of salvation is vitally dependent on living a holy and religious life. He makes clear at the very beginning of the book that religion is not confined merely to acts of ritual worship: "as every man is wholly Gods own portion by title of creation: so all our labours and care, all our powers and faculties must be wholly imployed in the service of God, even all the dayes of our life, that this life being ended, we may live with him for ever" (p. 17). Religion, in this sense, is the same as a holy life, and each action of a man is a religious duty:

> ... it becomes us to remember and to adore Gods good-
> nesse for it, that God hath not onely permitted us to serve
> the necessities of our nature, but hath made them to
> become parts of our duty; that if we by directing these
> actions to the glory of God intend them as instruments to
> continue our persons in his service, he by adopting them
> into religion may turn our nature into grace, and accept our
> natural actions, as actions of religion.   (p. 18)

The structure of *Holy Living* is determined by this understanding of religion.

The opening paragraph of chapter 2 quotes St. Paul in the Epistle to Titus (2.12): *"For the grace of God bringing salvation hath appeared to all men; teaching us that denying ungodlinesse and worldly lusts, we should live 1. Soberly, 2. Righteously, and 3. Godly in this present world, looking for that blessed hope and glorious appearing of the great God and our Saviour Jesus Christ"* (p. 60). On the basis of this passage, Taylor divides Christian religious practice into the three parts of sobriety, justice, and religion. Taylor defines these three qualities thus: "The first contains all our deportment in our personal and private capacities, the fair treating of our bodies, and our spirits. The second enlarges our duty in all relations to our Neighbour. The third contains the offices of direct Religion, and entercourse with God" (p. 60). Religion accordingly has its private, public, and spiritual aspects and consists of man's duties towards himself, towards others, and towards God. This threefold division forms the basis of the structure of *Holy Living*. Of its four chapters, the first introduces the reader to the fundamental requirements of the life of religion and piety, and the subsequent chapters each present one of the three aspects of Christian life.

The several parts or divisions of *Holy Living* are not, however, equal. The chapters move progressively so that the fourth and longest in the book, "Of Christian Religion," is the climax to the previous three. Taylor uses the word "religion" in a special sense, defining it through the Pauline "godly." Religion is "that part of duty which particularly relates to God in our worshippings and adoration of him, in confessing his excellencies, loving his person, admiring his goodnesse, believing his Word, and doing all that which may in a proper and direct manner do him honour" (p. 174). Having defined religion as worship of God, Taylor divides religious action into two kinds: internal and external. The internal actions of religion are those "in which the soul onely is imployed" (p. 174), and comprise the virtues of faith, hope, and charity. The external actions of religion are those in which the body as well as the soul is involved (p. 195), and include reading or hearing scripture, fasting, prayer, the giving of alms, repentance, and, above all, receiving the Holy Communion.

We may properly conclude that the end of *Holy Living*, as of Donne's sermons and of Hooker's *Lawes*, is to prepare us to see "the Altar of the Crosse." "The celebration of the holy Sacrament," Taylor writes in the final, long section of *Holy Living*, "is the great mysteriousnesse of the Christian religion," and also the end of our striving (p. 254):

> This is the sum of the greatest mystery of our Religion: it is the copy of the passion, and the ministration of the great mystery of our Redemption; and therefore whatsoever intitles us to the general priviledges of Christs passion, all that is necessary by way of disposition to the celebration of the Sacrament of his passion: because this celebration is our manner of applying or using it.   (pp. 255–56)

Now Taylor offers a number of precepts for assuring the reverent ministration and reception of this sacrament, urging all persons worthily to come to the eucharistic feast.

Taylor reaches for an exaltation at the conclusion of *Holy Living*, when describing "the effects and benefits of worthy communicating." God is known to us in this life through his Incarnation, and in the life to come through his Resurrection. Our affections are instructed through discourse with God by means of the sacramental life he has made possible to us. Taylor's direction, like Hooker's or Donne's, reflects such an "essentiall joye." In his conclusion Taylor remembers St. François de Sâles: "'that as those Creatures that live amongst the snowes of the Mountains turne white with their food and conversation with such perpetual whitenesses': so our souls may be transformed into the similitude and union with Christ by our perpetual feeding on him, and conversation, not onely in his Courts, but in his very heart, and most secret affections, and incomparable purities" (p. 262). Mortality leads upwards where word and sacrament, time and eternity, are one.

Notes

1. See *Sermons of John Donne,* ed. George R. Potter and Evelyn M. Simpson (Berkeley: University of California Press, 1953–62), 1:83, afterwards cited in the text and in the notes below.

2. The most fundamental of Christian doctrines is that of the Incarnation, affirmed at Nicea in A.D. 325 (in the familiar Nicene Creed), and reaffirmed as the Definition of Chalcedon (A.D. 451): that Jesus Christ exists as One Person in Two Natures, united "unconfusedly, unchangeably, indivisibly, inseparably." Donne refers once to the Council of Chalcedon, in a sermon of 1629, on Gen. 1.26, "And God said, let us make man, in our image, after our likenesse," where he is demonstrating the significance of words, even small words, about which the whole church has busied herself. At Chalcedon, the concern was "but for a syllable, whether *Ex,* or *In.* The Heretiques condemned then, confessed Christ, to be *Ex duabus naturis,* to be composed of two natures, at first; but not to be *in duabus naturis,* not to consist of two natures after: and for that *In,* they were thrust out" (9:71). Donne sustained this incarnational teaching – he was not to be one of the heretical monophysites – and his deep sympathy for the greatest of Christian paradoxes inspires his life and work.

In a wider sense, the Incarnation, thus traditionally defined, informs the idea of time and eternity, of finitude and infinity. That Donne should so commonly use imagery expressing linear progress (lines) or spherical motion (circles) is not surprising. For example, Donne writes in a sermon: "If you carry a Line from the Circumference, to the Circumference againe, as a Diameter, it passes the Center, it flowes from the Center, it looks to the Center both wayes. God is the Center; The Lines above, and the Lines below, still respect and regard the Center; Whether I doe any action honest in the sight of men, or any action acceptable to God, whether I doe things belonging to this life, or to the next, still I must passe all through the Center, and direct all to the glory of God, and keepe my heart right, without variation towards him" (9:406–7).

3. See *Of the Lawes of Ecclesiastical Polity,* 5.54.10 in *Works of Richard Hooker,* ed. W. Speed Hill (Cambridge, Mass.: Harvard University Press, 1977), 2:226. John Donne is hardly a "creative" theologian in the sense we understand when we describe the thought of Hooker or William Perkins or even William Laud; but Donne reflected theological attitudes,

commonly interpreting and expounding them, often in memorable ways. In a sermon of 1622, he warns his auditors against too much or unnecessary learning, particularly advising them to avoid the infirmities of pre-Reformation religion, but rather "to live according to that Religion which you have, then to enquire into that from which God hath delivered you":

> To end all, embrace Fundamental, Dogmatical, evident Divinity; That is express'd *in Credendis,* in the things which we are to believe in the Creed. And it begins with *Credo in Deum,* Belief in God, and not in man, nor traditions of men. And it is expressed *in petendis,* in the things which we are to pray for in the Lords Prayer; and that begins with *Sanctificetur nomen tuum, Hallowed be thy Name,* not the name of any.   (4:143–44)

Such a faith may be profound, but it does avoid theological controversy. Sir Thomas Browne captures well this *ethos* of the church within which both he and Donne define themselves: "In Divinity I love to keepe the road, and though not in an implicite, yet an humble faith, follow the great wheele of the Church, by which I move. . . . By this meanes I leave no gap for Heresies, Schismes, or Errors. . . " (*Religio Medici,* I:6, ed. L. C. Martin [Oxford: Clarendon Press, 1964], 7).

    4. Cf. my discussion of this sermon in chap. 1, pp. 7–10, above.

    5. See *Of the Lawes of Ecclesiastical Polity,* 1.16.1 in *Works of Richard Hooker,* ed. Georges Edelen (Cambridge, Mass.: Harvard University Press, 1977), 1:134.

    6. Ibid., 1:142.

    7. See *Lawes,* 5.56.4 in *Works,* ed. Hill, 2:236.

    8. Ibid.

    9. See *Lawes,* 5.67.13, in *Works,* 2:343.

    10. I am generally indebted to the work of John E. Booty, and, for the present discussion, especially to his survey of "Richard Hooker," in *The Spirit of Anglicanism: Hooker, Maurice, Temple,* ed. William J. Woolf (Wilton, Conn.: Morehouse-Barlow, 1979), 1–45. Cf. the recent "neo-historicist" study of Hooker and his age by Debora Kuller Shuger, *Habits of Thought in the English Renaissance: Religion, Politics, and the Dominant Culture* (Berkeley: University of California Press, 1990), esp. chap. 1. Shuger's thoughtful work nevertheless seems to me to miss the context, the religious sensibility, and the literary significance of Hooker, as well as of Andrewes, Donne, and Herbert, the other figures she principally considers. But see William O. Gregg, who argues that Hooker regarded the sacraments to be of the *esse* of the church, in "Sacramental Theology in Hooker's *Laws:* A Structural Perspective," *Anglican Theological Review* 73 (1991): 155–76.

    11. See my edition of Taylor's *Holy Living* (Oxford: Clarendon Press, 1989), 5. Subsequent references to this work appear in the text. I have quoted from my general introduction to this edition, esp. pp. xxxviii–xlii, adapting it to the present discussion.

II

INFLUENCE AND COMPOSITION

5

Stobaeus and Classical Borrowing
in the Renaissance

ALTHOUGH Joannes Stobaeus is vaguely remembered by classical scholars as a transmitter of texts, he is almost totally unknown by everyone else. Yet he affected the composition of late Renaissance English writers to an enormous extent, and his influence should be compared with the more familiar names of Valla, Erasmus, Vivès, and even Natalis Comes. Because Stobaeus, like these well-known figures, provided a ready-made work of reference, his importance should also be widely acknowledged and his name often invoked.[1]

The only anthology to have come down to us from classical literature in anything approaching a complete state is by Stobaeus (that is, of Stobi in Macedonia),[2] who flourished in the middle of the fifth century, not much later than Hierocles (c. 450), the latest author whom he cites. Stobaeus is supposed to have intended his anthology in the first instance for the instruction of his son Septimius, but little else is known of him. Originally, his work consisted of four books which came to be grouped later under the separate titles Ἐκλογαὶ and Ἀνθολόγιον, but there is no real distinction of subject matter. His plans provided for an elaborate division into 206 sections, each denoted by a short motto, dealing at first with metaphysics and politics, and later with ethical questions, these forming by far the greater part of the whole. The extracts follow the motto; they are first in verse, then in prose, with at least 500 writers in all being represented. Stobaeus gives only Greek authors, ranging from Homer to Themistius; he includes many neo-Platonists and neo-Pythagoreans, but no Christian writers. He is known mainly for his citations from earlier literature or from authors who have otherwise perished; many of the fragments of the dramatists, with a generous number by Menander, are preserved in him. Photius (fl. 858–86), who describes Stobaeus's compilation in his *Bibliotheca* (cod. 167), had commended the work for its usefulness to writers and speakers; in England its appeal waited for the Renaissance.

Such an anthology was bound to be attractive at a time when students cultivated the classics, often at one or more removes, and produced numberless books of *sententiae*. The earliest printed text of Stobaeus, a selection of his work, appeared in Latin as *Apophthegmata ex variis autoribus,* in the edition by Camertus, at Rome, in 1517. There were other selections, especially the 'Εκλογαὶ ἀποφθεγμάτων: *Collectiones sententiarum,* ed. V. Trincavelli (Venice, 1536); Γνωμολογία ἑλληνικολατίνη: *Gnomologia Graecolatina,* ed. M. Neander (Basel, 1557); *Sententiarum . . .* (Paris, 1557); and *Eclogarum libri duo, graece,* ed. G. Canter (Antwerp, 1575). But the most important edition, being both the fullest and the most reprinted, was that by C. Gesner, who provided a Greek-Latin text, published in Zürich, 1543; its successors include Basel, 1549, 1551 (a German translation); Paris, 1552, 1557; Zürich, 1559; Frankfurt, 1581; Lyons, 1608, 1609.[3] During his imprisonment at The Hague, Hugo Grotius completed the *Dicta Poetarum* (Paris, 1623); he extracts the verse only and translates it into Latin, but he preserves the headings of Stobaeus before each major division or section. Grotius is said to have reached the 49th section, "On the Criticism of Tyranny" (Περὶ ψόγου τῆς τυραννίδος), when the pen was snatched from his hand.[4] In referring to the various parts as "Florilegia," Grotius describes these *Sententiae* by their most usual name.

Writers have always borrowed ideas from each other and from whatever sources lay at hand, quite usually without acknowledgment; and Renaissance authors, too, keenly dipped into handy stores, especially of classical knowledge where their learning was frequently at second hand. Stobaeus offered still another and very common supply. But his pervasiveness is hard to measure because he must have served much as a dictionary or general encyclopaedia does today, where one seldom sees need to give credit for "discoveries" made through the help of reference books in a well-stocked library. Consequently, while I have found only a few writers who mention Stobaeus explicitly, I think there can be no doubt that many others knew and probably made use of him. There is thus no surprise, on the one hand, in finding Richard Hooker making acknowledged and extensive use of Stobaeus in his *Lawes of Ecclesiastical Polity* or Jeremy Taylor in his various treatises; but one need not be puzzled, on the other hand, to find no specific mention of him in Sir Thomas Browne or John Milton, to take a different and equally learned pair. Without drawing up cumbersome lists of allusions or searching indefinitely for possible references, my point is plain enough: Stobaeus is a regular and palpable presence to Renaissance writers, and we are better informed about their writing for being aware of him. For showing how Stobaeus was used in a particular context, examples from Hooker and Taylor should be sufficient.

In Book 8.2 of the *Lawes,* Hooker described the role of the king as both an ecclesiastical and a secular head. He writes:

> Sometime it pleaseth God himself by speciall appointment
> to choose out and nominate such as to whom *Dominion*
> shalbe given, which thing he did often in the *Commonwealth*
> of *Israel:* They who in this sort receive power have it
> immediatelie from God by meer divine right, they by

humane on whom the same is bestowed according unto mens discretion when they are left free by God to make choise of their owne governoure. By which of these meanes soever it happen, that *Kings* or governours be advanced unto their seates, we must acknowledg both their lawfull choise to be approoved of God, and themselfs for *Godes Livetenantes* and confesse their power his.[5]

To give breadth to his discussion, Hooker, relying upon a large section contained in Sermo 46 of Stobaeus, "Admonitions for the King" (Ὑποθῆκαι περὶ βασιλείας), cites Ecphantus, along with several others:

Τὸ μὲν σκᾶνος τοῖς λοιποῖς ὅμοιος, οἷα γεγονὼς ἐκ τᾶς αὐτᾶς ὕλας, ὑπὸ τεχνίτα δ᾽ εἰργασμένος λῷστω, ὃς ἐτεχνίτευσεν αὐτὸν ἀρχετύπῳ χρώμενος ἑαυτῷ.
(A King in regard of the tabernacle of his body is like to other men; as made of the same matter, but fashioned by the best workman, who artificially framed him: using himself for the pattern.)[6]

Hooker writes more about the power which kings claimed to have in former times and refers to Ecphantus again, whose view of the monarch puts the king in the role of a mediator between God and man.

In contrast with this religious conception of kingship, Hooker sets the teaching of Archytas, whom Stobaeus cites in Sermo 41, "On the Republic" (Περὶ πολιτείας):

We can not properlie terme him a king, of whom it may not be sayd, at the least wise, as touching certaine the very chiefest affayres of state αὐτῷ μὲν ἄρχειν, ἄρχεσθαι δὲ ὑπ᾽ οὐδενός, his right in them is to have rule, not subject to any other predominant.[7]   (3:341)

. . . .

Most divinely therefore *Archytas* maketh unto publique felicitie these four steppes, every later whereof doth spring from the former as from a mother cause, Ὁ μὲν βασιλεὺς νόμιμος, ὁ δὲ ἄρχων ἀκόλουθος, ὁ δὲ ἀρχόμενος ἐλεύθερος, ἁ δ᾽ ὅλα κοινωνία εὐδαίμων *(The king ruling by Lawe the magistrate following, the subject free and the whole society happie)*, adding on the contrary side, that where this order is not it commeth by transgression thereof to passe that the *King* growes a *Tyrant,* he that ruleth under him abhorreth to be guided and commanded by him, the people subject unto both have freedome under neither and the whole communitie is wretched.[8]   (3:342)

Still further along in Book 8, Hooker refers again to Archytas in a marginal note where he is discussing the role of the church in making laws:

> It is undoubtedly a thing even naturall that all free and independent societies should them selves make their own lawes, and that this power should belong to the whole not to any certaine part of a politique body though happilie some one part may have greater sway in that action then the rest. Which thing being generally fitt and expedient in the making of all lawes we see no cause why to think otherwise in lawes concerning the service of God, which in all well ordered States and Commonwealths is the first thing that law hath care to provide for: Δεῖ τὸν νόμον τὰ περὶ θεοὺς καὶ δαίμονας καὶ γονέας, καὶ ὅλως τὰ καλὰ καὶ τίμια πρῶτα τίθεσθαι, δεύτερον δὲ τὰ συμφέροντα· τὰ γὰρ μήονα τοῖς μείξοσιν ἀκολουθεῖν καθήκει. *Archyt[as]. de leg[ibus]. et just[itibus]*. That is, *it behooveth the Law first to establish, or settle those things which belong to the Gods, and divine powers, and to our parents, and universally those things which be vertuous and honourable. And in the second place those things that be convenient or profitable: for it is fit that matters of the lesse weight should come after the greater.*[9] (3:390–91)

Hooker turns to Stobaeus for extended extracts on government in order to develop his own arguments, using Ecphantus and Archytas by claiming the fullest support he can of them.

But Jeremy Taylor gathers a wide variety of material from Stobaeus, generously filling out and embellishing his own discussions on ethical or moral themes. We need to look in his *Great Exemplar* (1649, often called *The Life of Christ*), in *Holy Living* and *Holy Dying* (1650, 1651), in the sermons, and especially in his great casuistical work, *Ductor Dubitantium* (1660), to find Stobaeus. Taylor searched such sections as these: "That life is brief and mean and full of care" (Περὶ βίον, ὅτι βραχὺς καὶ εὐτελὴς, καὶ φροντίδων ἀνάμεστος, §96); "Marriage precepts" (Γαμικὰ παραγγέλματα, §72); "On sickness, and the easing of vexation" (Περὶ νόσου, καὶ τῆς τῶν κατ᾽ αὐτὴν ἀνιαρῶν λύσεως, §98); "That parents should always be obeyed"(῞Οτι χρὴ τοὺς γονεῖς τῆς καθηκούσης τιμῆς καταξιοῦσθαι παρὰ τῶν τέκνων, καὶ εἰ ἐν ἅπασιν αὐτοῖς πειστέον, §77). *Ductor Dubitantium*, 3.5, "Of laws domestic; or the power which fathers of families have to bind the consciences of their relatives," corresponds with this last section in subject.[10] Taylor enriches his discussion from the beginning, on Rule I, with a line from Menander, one of the most commonly quoted authors in his works, generally by means of Stobaeus. Taylor likes to develop a theme by welding together the words of apt authorities. "He that reviles and speaks evil of his father [with a reference to Plato, *Republic,* 4.8], does blaspheme God; for Θεοὶ μέγιστοι τοῖς φρονοῦσιν οἱ γονεῖς, God is the great Father of the world, and therefore He hath by the greatest religion immersed the fathers' honour" (10:452).[11] In continuing his argument on the relationships of fathers to their families, Taylor recalls the story of Leontius the Bishop of Tripolis in Lydia whose only son was of an ill nature; he "prayed to God that his son might die young, lest he should fall into impiety: and God heard the father's prayer" (10:453). Here Taylor uses the line of Orpheus given in this same section of Stobaeus (that is, §77), "Δειναὶ γὰρ κατὰ γαῖαν ἐριννύες εἰσὶ τοκήων, 'The curses of parents are grievous upon the earth.'"[12]

On the reverence which is the duty of children, Taylor takes from Stobaeus the line from Philemon, "Βούλου γονεῖς πρώτιστον ἐν τιμαῖς ἔχειν, 'above all things have your parents in honour'" (10:455).[13] At the opening of Rule II, on the limitations of paternal power, Taylor quotes from Timocles in Stobaeus, giving the Latin translation exactly as it appears in Gesner's edition,[14] "Quicunque patrem timet ac reveretur, / Hic in bonum civem evadet procul dubio," which Taylor renders as "he that fears and obeys his father, without peradventure as he is a good man so he will make a good citizen" (10:457). There is further borrowing from this section of Stobaeus, on the honor due to parents, in an earlier part of *Ductor Dubitantium,* 2.2, on the law of nature as it is contained by Christian law. In this place, Taylor is distinguishing between moral precepts and precepts not moral: "it must necessarily and naturally follow that children must pay to their parents the duties of love and obedience,

> Ὅστις δὲ τοὺς τεκόντας ἐν βίῳ σέβει,
> ὅδ᾽ ἐστὶ καὶ ζῶν καὶ θανὼν θεοῖς φίλος."

These lines from Euripides, Taylor observes, represent "the voice of nature" (9:469).[15]

On a similar theme, Taylor writes about the duty of superiors in *Holy Living,* and in chapter 3, section 2, "Rules for married persons," he refers to Menander, making use of Stobaeus's Sermo 65, "Praise of nuptials" (Ὅτι κάλλιστον γάμος). Taylor begins, "Husbands must give to their wives, love, maintenance, duty, and the sweetnesses of conversation . . . wives must pay to them all they have, or can," with the note,

> Ἔνεστ᾽ ἀληθὲς φίλτρον εὐγνώμων τρόπος·
> Τούτῳ κατακρατεῖν ἀνδρός εἴωθεν γυνή.
> (There is one genuine love-philtre —
> considerate dealing. By this the woman is
> apt to sway her man.)[16]

Taylor writes more about the relationship of husbands and wives in his sermon "The Marriage Ring" (4:228), borrowing from Stobaeus's section of "Marriage precepts" (72). Along with many other classical references, he refers to Juvenal (6.134), "A ruling woman is intolerable . . . faciunt graviora coactae / Imperio sexus . . . " (their behavior is worse when it is the imperiousness natural to their sex which drives them on), and to Menander: she also is miserable, for

τὰ δεύτερ' ἀεὶ τὴν γυναῖκα δεῖ λέγειν,
τὴν δ' ἡγεμονίαν τῶν ὅλων τὸν ἄνδρ' ἔχειν.
(In speaking, wives should have the second call,
In guiding, husbands should be all in all.)[17]

Taylor is on such easy terms with Stobaeus, and his use of him is so frequent that these examples are only selected from many. As with Hooker, quotation and paraphrase form part of the texture of his composition, although Taylor ranges more widely in the pages of Stobaeus, not so much to improve his argument as to color the atmosphere. Perhaps Taylor prepared to write as Erasmus had long before advised, by setting down extracts from classical literature under systematically chosen headings. Of course, Erasmus supposed his writer would consult first-hand the original sources, not extracts in someone else's commonplace book; he could not have anticipated the helpfulness of Stobaeus, who came to be a friend indeed to Jeremy Taylor. But Stobaeus, I am sure, was never far from any literate man's mind as he began to strain for seemly words situated in a column of traditional ideas.

Notes

1. Stobaeus receives no mention in DeWitt T. Starnes, *Renaissance Dictionaries* (Austin: University of Texas Press, 1954) or in Starnes and Ernest William Talbert, *Classical Myth and Legend in Renaissance Dictionaries* (Chapel Hill: University of North Carolina Press, 1955).

2. I am indebted to the excellent account of Stobaeus by Otto Hense in Pauly-Wissowy's *Real-Encyclopädie der classischen altertumswissenschaft*, 9 (1916): 2549–86, whose edition of the works, cited below, is also standard.

3. Besides the large number of editions of Stobaeus, there were many mixed editions which excerpt from him such as the *Apophthegmata* of 1517. See also *Apophthegmata Graeca regum et ducum*, Geneva, 1568, only a portion of which is Stobaeus's compilaton. There is the further complication of editions of the ' Ἐκλογαὶ φυσικαὶ καὶ ἠθικαί (the "Eclogues," or "Physical and Moral Extracts" in two books), on the one hand, and the ' Ἀνθολόγιον (the "Florilegia" or "Sermones"), on the other. The title ' Ἀνθολόγιον is often applied to each of the parts of Stobaeus, which suggests it may have been the original name for the whole. Photius gives the full title as ' Ἐκλογῶν ἀποφθεγμάτων ὑποθηκῶν βιβλία τέτταρα ("Four books of extracts, sayings and precepts"). I have not attempted a full list of the early editions of Stobaeus, but noted chiefly those which I have seen.

4. See J. E. Sandys, *A History of Classical Scholarship*, 3rd ed. (Cambridge: Cambridge University Press, 1920), 2:316.

5. See Hooker, *Of the Lawes of Ecclesiastical Polity, Books VI, VII, VIII,* in *Works of Richard Hooker,* ed. P. G. Stanwood (Cambridge, Mass.: Harvard University Press, 1981), 3:334–35, hereafter cited in the text.

6. See the best modern edition by Otto Hense, *Ioannis Stobaei Anthologium,* 3 vols. (Berlin, 1894–1912), 2 (1909): 272, *cap.* vii, 11–14 (*Florilegium* 48), whose text I follow. All citations will be to this edition. Cf. Gesner's edition (Basel, 1549), second and fullest of those which Hooker and Taylor and their contemporaries would have used (or else an edition based upon this one). I follow the older practice of referring to Stobaeus's individual sections by "sermo" (but "florilegium" in the notes).

Ecphantus was a Pythagorean from Syracuse; his treatise *On Kingship,* evidently a false attribution, has been dated variously, and some put it as late as the second century A.D. See Louis Delatte, ed., *Le Traités de la Royauté d'Ecphante, Diotogène et Sthenidas* (Liège, 1942).

7. See Hense, 2:279, *cap.* vii, 12–14 (*Flor.* 48).

8. See Hense, 2:83, *cap.* i, 1–5 (*Flor.* 43). Archytas, who flourished in the first half of the fourth century B.C., was, like Ecphantus, a Pythagorean, called the founder of mechanics.

9. See Hense, 2:86, *cap.* i, 3–6 (*Flor.* 43). On the tradition of the Pythagorean ideal of a godlike-savior ruler, see the commentary on this and the previous passage by A. S. McGrade in *Works of Richard Hooker* (Binghamton, N.Y.: Medieval & Renaissance Texts & Studies, forthcoming), vol. 6.

10. See Jeremy Taylor, *The Whole Works,* ed. R. Heber, rev. C. P. Eden (London: Longman, 1847–54), 10:451–52. Further references to this edition will be given in the text.

11. See Hense, 2:625, *cap.* xxv, no. 33 (*Flor.* 79), and cf. A. Nauck, *Tragicorum Graecorum Fragmenta,* 2nd ed. (Leipzig, 1926), Fr 5, p. 776.

12. See Hense, 2:624, *cap.* xxv, no. 28 (*Flor.* 79).

13. Ibid., no. 30, and cf. J. M. Edmonds, *Fragments of Attic Comedy,* 3 vols. (Leiden, 1957–61), 3A:92 (Fr 236A).

14. See Hense, 2:622, *cap.* xxv, no. 17 (*Flor.* 79), and cf. Edmonds, 2:624 (Fr 34): ὅστις φοβεῖται τὸν πατέρα καἰσχύνεται,
οὗτος πολίτης ἀγαθὸς ἔσται κατὰ λόγον
καὶ τοὺς πολεμίους δυνάμενος κακῶς ποιεῖν.

15. See Hense, 2:619, *cap.* xxv, no. 2 (*Flor.* 79); cf. Nauck, Fr 852, p. 637.

16. The lines are Menander's (my translation), but Taylor would have seen them in Stobaeus; see Hense, 2:496, *cap.* xxii, no. 10 (*Flor.* 67), and cf. Edmonds, 3B:812, Fr 646, and Menander, *Fragments,* ed. A. Körte (Leipzig: Teubner, 1959), 2.186, Fr 571. See Taylor, *Holy Living,* ed. P. G. Stanwood (Oxford: Clarendon Press, 1989), 155; and see further in the same edition, pp. 69 and 156, and also the discussion of Taylor's use of classical literature, pp. xliv–li, esp. p. xlviii.

17. See Hense, 2:570, *cap.* xxiii, no. 5 (*Flor.* 74), and cf. Edmonds, 3B:743, Fr 484, for the Menander; the Juvenal is not in Stobaeus.

6

Patristic and Contemporary Borrowing
in the Caroline Divines

A cold coming we had of it,
Just the worst time of the year
For a journey, and such a long journey:
The ways deep and the weather sharp,
The very dead of winter.

THE CELEBRATED OPENING of T. S. Eliot's "Journey of the Magi"
adapts a passage from Lancelot Andrewes's fifteenth sermon on the Nativity
(1622). This is well known, but less familiar may be the fact that Andrewes
himself was making free use of St. John Chrysostom's Homily VI on Matthew
2.1,2 — the scriptural text which describes the coming of the "wise men"
from the east to Jerusalem to worship Jesus. The number of wise men (once
thought to be twelve), their station in life, their origin, and the nature and
meaning of their journey were questions which gave rise to a long tradition of
patristic and later commentary on the Epiphany, as the manifestation of
Christ to the world and the commemorative feast of the church came to be
called. Chrysostom was, of course, only one among many writers on the
Epiphany, but of the Greek fathers he was one of the most regarded by the
Caroline divines and one of the most familiar to them.[1]
    The Feast of the Epiphany is of course closely related to the Nativity
of Christ, and the early church, especially of the East, observed January 6 as
Christmas Day (as the Armenian church still does). But as the commemoration of Christ's birth on December 25 became general, the Epiphany retained
its importance as a feast of the Magi, which Chrysostom sought to popu-
larize, and there were associated with it numerous legends such as the idea
that the wise men numbered three and were kings. Another, and probably
much later (and obviously western), legend is the connection of the winter
season to the feast; it is a lively metaphoric extension based upon the difficulty and inconvenience one might imagine the wise men to have undergone.
The conception may not have been Andrewes's own, but it easily reflects that
"blend of homeliness with majesty which interests him, and so affects his
style,"[2] which underscores indeed the very qualities of the Epiphany that

Chrysostom himself was eager to emphasize in his exegesis of the Gospel account.

Another point of interest is the dependence of the Caroline divines upon each other. The note in the story which helped Eliot to realize his wise man's paradoxical wish for another death has a lineage within Andrewes's own time in the sermons of John Cosin, John Hacket, and Mark Frank, all of them notable high churchmen, and all much affected both by Andrewes's theological position and his general preaching style.[3] By looking at all of these borrowings, we can discover a rather obvious truth but one that needs emphasizing for the insight it gives into seventeenth-century homiletic practice. The Caroline divines, particularly with Laudian or high church views, delight in drawing not only from original and often patristic sources, but from one another. The journey of the Magi provides one common example, and still another of considerable interest occurs both in John Donne and Cosin, the original being in St. Gregory the Great.

1

I should like first to quote from Chrysostom and then to compare the several seventeenth-century adaptations of this passage, or of those who follow Andrewes's use of it:

> For certainly had He been born in royal halls with his Father King present, in all likelihood someone would say that these men, willing to serve the Father, worshipped the born child, and in this way were setting aside for themselves beforehand much occasion of goodwill. As it is, however, neither do they expect that He will be their king but of a nation uncouth and much removed from their country, nor do they see Him already become a man. Why, then, do they make so great a journey, and bring gifts, destined also to do all these things amid dangers? For indeed on hearing these [reports] from them, both Herod was thoroughly disturbed and all the people troubled. But these men did not foresee this. Yet that would not be reasonable. For even if they had been exceedingly witless, they would not have been unaware of this, namely, that by coming into a city with a ruler, proclaiming such matters, and greeting another as King besides the one who was king at that time, they would have drawn upon themselves more than ten thousand deaths. Nevertheless, why did they worship the one in swathing bands? Now if He had been a man, someone could say that expecting support from Him they threw themselves into deliberate danger. But this would be the extreme of absurdity, that a Persian, a barbarian, and one who had nothing in common with the nation of Jews were willing, on the one

> hand, to withdraw from the family, to leave behind
> fatherland, relatives, and servants, and on the other, to sub-
> mit themselves to a second Kingdom.[4]

Andrewes preached two Christmas sermons on the text from Matthew 2.1,2.
Eliot has made the second of these, the one of 1622, well known: "It was no
summer Progress. A cold comming they had of it, at this time of the yeare, to
take a journey, and specially a long journey, in. The waies deep, the weather
sharp, the daies short, the sunn farthest of[f] *in solstitio brumali,* the very
dead of *Winter*."[5] Andrewes gives much more which is descriptive of the
hardness of the journey, and he notices, for example, "the Rocks and craggs
of both *Arabies* (specially *Petraea*) [over which] their journey lay." He also
makes explicit the moral application:

> But then, for the *distance, desolateness, tediousness,* and the
> rest, any of them were enough to marre our *Venimus* quite.
> It must be no great way (first) we must come: we love not
> that. Well fare the *Shepheards* yet, they came but hard by:
> Rather like them then the *Magi*. Nay, not like them neither.
> For, with us, *the neerer* (lightly) *the further off:* Our Proverbe
> is (you know) *The neerer the Church the further from* GOD.
>   Nor, it must not be through no *Desert,* over no *Petraea*. If
> rugged, or uneven the way; if the weather ill disposed; if any
> never so little danger, it is enough to stay us. To CHRIST we
> cannot travaile, but weather and way and all must be faire.
> If not, no journey, but sit still and see further. As indeed, all
> our Religion is rather *Vidimus,* a *Contemplation,* then
> *Venimus,* a *Motion,* or stirring to doe ought.

Andrewes's earlier Sermon 14 on the Nativity, preached in 1620, contains the
same figure, but differently enriched:

> They came a long journey, no lesse then *twelve dayes*
> together. They came an uneasy journey, for their way lay
> through *Arabia Petraea,* and the craggy rockes of it. And
> they came a dangerous journey, through *Arabia Deserta*
> (too,) and the *black tents of Kedar* there, then famous for
> their robberies, and even to this day. And they came, now,
> at the worst season of the yeare. . . . Stayed not their com-
> ming, till the opening of the yeare, till they might have bet-
> ter weather and way, and have longer dayes, and so more
> seasonable and fit to travaile in. So desirous were they to
> come with the first . . . as soone as possibly they might. . . .

John Cosin (1595–1672), the great Restoration bishop of Durham,
may have heard Andrewes preach this sermon at court; for as secretary to

Bishop Overall of Norwich (1616–19) and one whom Bishop Neile of Durham had been especially preferring, he knew the circle in which Andrewes, and Donne, too, moved. He need not have been indebted to Andrewes, however, but to the common source in Chrysostom and to his own invention—the more likely, for Cosin's first sermon on Matthew 2.1,2 is within a fortnight of Andrewes's Sermon 14. Cosin preached on January 6, 1621, the first of his sermons to have survived, at St. Edward's Church in Cambridge, and the same sermon again at Coton (Cambs) on the second Sunday in Epiphany.[6] He cites various fathers and commentators who have written on the persons and their pilgrimage – including Basil, Justin Martyr, Cyprian, Maximus, Chrysologus, Hilarius Arelatensis – and then he notes the sort of journey the wise men had: "A hard journey sure they had saith S. Chrysostome, for besides ye long way there were huge mountains and horrid deserts, great flouds and rivers to passe, wild beasts, and what is more, beastly and wild men to passe by, and yet by all these difficulties they came even from the East to Jerusalem." Cosin returned to the same text in Matthew and used this example again in his sermon at Durham House, on January 5, 1623, expanding it slightly, only making the moral application more explicitly, as Andrewes had done in his Christmas sermon for 1622. When Cosin preached once more on Matthew 2.1,2 during his Paris exile, on January 5, 1653, he considered in detail the quality and nature of the Magi, displaying considerable knowledge of the traditional sources, but he does not take up again the example about the special troublesomeness of their journey.

John Hacket (1592–1670) was another disciple of Andrewes and, like Cosin, he lived to have high office in the church. He is best known for his life of Archbishop Williams, but a folio volume of sermons also survives him.[7] *A Century of Sermons* was published posthumously (1675); the individual sermons are undated, but presumably many were preached years before their publication. Three are on Matthew 2.1,2, and the influence of Andrewes in them (and throughout his sermons) is unmistakable. In the thirteenth sermon on the Incarnation, he writes:

> There is no place in the world but hath an *Oriental* point to some horizon, and so an *Occidental* point: Every part of the world is *East* and *West* to several degrees; but commonly if you speak of the *East,* and with no more addition, it is taken for that principal part of the habitable world which respects the rising of the Sun to us, and that's *India*. . . . They [the Magi] could not come from the *East* to *Judea,* but by *Arabia Petrea,* a most rocky cumbersom Country, and by *Arabia deserta* a most thievish murdering Country: and from the heavens above they could have no better comfort at this time of the year, but either bitter frosts to travel in, or foul weather, and to continue thus for twelve days together, it was a great proof of zeal and patience, that would run

> through all difficulties to be satisfied in this one question,
> *Where is he that is born the King of the Jews?*[8]

Hacket's fifteenth sermon on the Incarnation (the third of the three on this theme and this text from Matthew) in general follows quite closely Andrewes's Sermon 15 on the Nativity with its analysis of the different qualities of the star. One brief passage near the beginning cites Chrysostom by name and notes how the wise men set out to seek Christ in the most difficult time of the year.

Mark Frank (1613–64) was a younger contemporary of both Cosin and Hacket; the influence of Andrewes is clearly at work in his sermons. Although he is little known today, his sermons deserve to be remembered: with Andrewes, Donne, and Jeremy Taylor, his work is the most striking for its literary and devotional value.[9] While being derivative, he possesses nevertheless very much his own voice and sensibility. The short passage on the Magi gives only a glimpse of his qualities:

> Many a weary step had they trod, many a fruitless question
> had they askt, many an unprofitable search had they made
> to find him; and behold yet they will not give over. Twelve
> days it had cost them to come to *Jerusalem,* through the
> *Arabian Desarts,* over the *Arabian Mountains,* both *Arabia
> Deserta & Petraea;* the difficulty of the way, through Sands,
> and Rocks; the danger of the passages, being infamous for
> Robbers, the cold and hardness of a deep Winter season,
> the hazzard and inconvenience of so long, so hard, so
> unseasonable, so dangerous, and I may say so uncertain a
> Journey, could no whit deter them from their purpose: to
> *Jerusalem* they will through all these difficulties.[10]

Frank sustains this conceit through the whole of his sermon, and in the final paragraph he urges:

> Rejoyce we ever in the light of Heaven, walk by it, make
> much of it, of all holy motions and inspirations, continue in
> it; and let neither the tediousness of the way, nor the frailty
> of our own flesh, nor any stormy or tempestuous weather,
> any cross or trouble, nor any Winter coldness of our own
> dull bosoms, nor sometime the loss even of our guides,
> (those heavenly and spiritual comforts which God some-
> times in his secret Wisdom withdraws from us) nor any
> carnal reason or interest deter us from our search after this
> Babe of Heaven, after Christ the Saviour. . . .

Again Frank turns to the difficult journey of the Magi in his third sermon on the Epiphany (Matt. 2.11), where he says of faith, "is it not a strong belief indeed, this, that can bring men out of their own Country, and that a far one too, through *Arabian* Desarts in the depth of Winter only to worship?"[11] Cosin and Andrewes go to the common source in Chrysostom, but Hacket and Frank, who might also have done this, evidently borrowed as well Andrewes's idea of the cold season. It is a good embellishment upon the traditional material, and it makes the journey seem that much more difficult.

2

I should like to point finally to another patristic source which both Donne and Cosin evidently recall and share together. St. Gregory the Great (c. 540–604) writes in his *Pastoral Care*:

> Peccatum quippe cum voce, est culpa cum actione; peccatum vero etiam cum clamore, est culpa cum libertate. At contra admonendi sunt qui accusant prava, nec tamen devitant, ut provide perpendant, quid in districto Dei iudicio pro sua excusatione dicturi sunt, qui de reatu suorum criminum etiam semetipsis iudicibus non excusantur. Hic itaque quid aliud quam praecones sunt sui? voces contra culpas proferunt, et semetipsos operibus reos tradunt.[12]

In his sermon of April 21, 1616 (on Eccl. 8.11), Donne speaks of "our good and gracious God, that though he do know our sins, as soon as they speak, as soon as they are acted, (for that's *peccatum cum voce,* says S. *Gregory,* A speaking sin, when any sinful thought is produc'd into act) yea, before they speak, as soon as they are conceiv'd; yet he will not hear of our sins. . . .[13] In his Lenten sermon "Preached to the King, at White-Hall," probably on February 11, 1627, Donne reminds us of Gregory, but now his own invention has become so elaborate that only a hint remains of the source: "Forgive me *O Lord, O Lord* forgive me my sinnes, the sinnes of my youth and my present sinnes . . . Forgive me my crying sins, and my whispering sins." Cosin, little more than three weeks later, published the first edition of his *A Collection of Private Devotions,* and it includes among the "Formes of Confession" one whose phrases Cosin may have heard Donne speak; yet Donne could as easily have borrowed from Cosin. There can be no doubt, however, that the memory of Gregory is remote: "Forgive me my sins, O Lord, forgive mee the sinnes of my youth, and the sins of mine age, the sinnes of my soule, and the sinnes of my body, my secret and my whispering sinnes, my presumptuous and my crying sins." Nevertheless, the memory of Gregory's phrase and his comments are not so distant, I think, as to be forgotten.

It is common knowledge that seventeenth-century divines like Andrewes and those of his persuasion made much use of patristic sources. But not enough is known about their specific use of them, or the ways in which Andrewes and his "school" borrow from and echo each other. The instances I have cited could no doubt be vastly multiplied; but they show a tendency which is surely typical. What is needed are well annotated editions of the most important of the Caroline divines: a start should at least be made with Andrewes and Donne who ought in every way to be treated as major writers so that we may see more fully their ways of discourse and understanding.[14]

Notes

1. See, for example, the eight sermons on the Epiphany by St. Leo the Great, esp. the first: "Epiphaniae celebritas quid insinuet, et de trium Magorum adventu ac muneribus" (*Opera . . . Coloniae Agrippinae . . .* M.D.LXIX., fols. 22–29, or J.-P. Migne, ed., *Patrologia Latina,* 54:234–37). See also Gerhard Ebeling, "Evangelische Evangelienauslegung," *Forschungen zur Geschichte und Lehre des Protestantismus,* Zehnte Reihe Bd. 1 (München, 1942), app. III: *Luthers Auslegung von Mt. 2, 1–12 auf die exegetischen Quellen zuruckgeführt.* Parallel passages are given to show how the Epiphany theme was treated by Gregory, Hilary, Jerome, and Tauler, compared with Luther.

Chrysostom (c. 347–407) was held in great esteem by the high church (or Arminian) preachers who regularly cite him in their sermons. Of all the fathers, Chrysostom's employment of rhetoric was most influential. W. Fraser Mitchell remarks that "there is an oriental richness and profusion of epithets and images noticeable in his work which mark him off from other preachers of all ages. His remained the great name; he was the 'golden-mouthed' preacher; and any luxuriance or excessive embroidery occurring in the sermons of later preachers must necessarily fall so far short of his that they were bound to appear to their composers rather to be unsuccessful strivings after an unobtainable ideal than to err by excess. . . . The unrivalled wealth of his writings became a mine from which preachers might dig" (see *English Pulpit Oratory from Andrewes to Tillotson* [1932; repr. New York: Russell and Russell, 1962], 142–44).

2. Joan Webber, "Celebration of Word and World in Lancelot Andrewes' Style," *Journal of English and Germanic Philology* 64 (1965): 263.

3. Mitchell, 164–66 and passim.

4. J.-P. Migne, ed., *Patrologia Graeca,* 57:61–65, esp. 63: Καὶ γάρ εἰ μὲν ἐν βασιλικαῖς αὐλαῖς ἐτίκτετο, καὶ πατρὸς αὐτῷ βασιλέως παρόντος, εἰκότως ἄν τις ἔφη τούτους, βουλομένους τὸν πατέρα θεραπεῦσαι, προσκυνῆσαι τὸ τεχθὲν παιδίον, καὶ ταύτῃ πολλὴν ἑαυτοῖς ὑπόθεσιν προαποθέσθαι εὐνοίας. Νυνὶ δὲ οὐδὲ αὐτῶν προσδοκῶντες ἔσεσθαι βασιλέα, ἀλλὰ ἔθνους ἀλλοκότου καὶ πολὺ τῆς αὐτῶν ἀφεστηκότος χώρας, οὔτε ἄνδρα ὁρῶντες ἤδη γενόμενον, τίνος ἕνεκεν τοσαύτην στέλλονται ἀποδημίαν, καὶ δῶρα προσφέρουσι, καὶ ταῦτα μέλλοντες μετὰ κινδύνων ἅπαντα πράττειν· Καὶ γὰρ καὶ Ἡρώδης ἀκούσας διεταράχθη, καὶ ὁ δῆμος ἅπας ἐθορυβεῖτο, ταῦτα ἀκούσαντες παρ᾽ αὐτῶν. Ἀλλ᾽ οὐ προῄδεσαν

οὗτοι ταῦτα. Ἀλλ' οὐκ ἂν ἔχοι λόγον. Εἰ γὰρ καὶ σφόδρα ἦσαν ἀνόητοι, τοῦτο οὐκ ἂν ἠγνόησαν, ὅτι εἰς πόλιν βασιλευομένην ἐλθόντες, καὶ τοιαῦτα κηρύξαντες, καὶ βασιλέα ἕτερον παρὰ τὸν τότε ὄντα δείξαντες, οὐχὶ μυρίους καθ' ἑαυτῶν ἂν ἐπεσπάσαντο θανάτους. Τί δὲ ὅλως καὶ προσεκύνουν ἐν σπαργάνοις ὄντα; Εἰ μὲν γὰρ ἀνὴρ ἦν, εἶχεν ἄν τις εἰπεῖν, ὅτι προσδοκῶντες τὴν παρ' αὐτοῦ βοήθειαν εἰς προῦπτον ἑαυτοὺς ἔρριψαν κίνδυνον, ὅπερ καὶ αὐτὸ τῆς ἐσχάτης ἀλογίας ἦν, τὸν Πέρσην, τὸν βάρβαρον, καὶ οὐδὲν κοινὸν ἔχοντα πρὸς τὸ Ἰουδαίων ἔθνος, βούλεσθαι μὲν τῆς οἰκίας ἀφίστασθαι, καὶ πατρίδα καὶ συγγενεῖς καὶ οἰκείους ἀφιέναι, ἑτέρᾳ δὲ ἑαυτοὺς ὑποβάλλειν βασιλείᾳ (translation by Professor C. W. J. Eliot). Cf. also Chrysostom's subsequent homilies on Matthew 2, esp. VII and VIII.

5. *XCVI. Sermons* (1629), 143–44. The extract from the fourteenth sermon is on p. 137. A modern edition is G. M. Story's (Oxford: Clarendon Press, 1967): see pp. xxxix–xlii, xlvi, and 99–118 (all of Andrewes's sermons were last printed in The Library of Anglo-Catholic Theology, ed. J.P. Wilson, 5 vols. [Oxford: John Henry Parker, 1841–43], vol. 1 containing the seventeen sermons on the Nativity). The copy of the first edition of Andrewes's *Sermons* from which I quote, in the University Library, Cambridge, belonged to John Hacket whose autograph signature appears on the title-page.

6. Janel M. Mueller, "A Borrowing of Donne's Christmas Sermon of 1621," *Huntington Library Quarterly* 30 (1967), 207–16. Mueller describes the extensive use Cosin made of Donne's sermon in his own Nativity sermon of 1651 (see Cosin's *Works* in The Library of Anglo-Catholic Theology, 5 vols. [Oxford: John Henry Parker, 1843], 1:276–90, and my "John Cosin as Homilist," *Anglican Theological Review* 47 [1965]: 276–89). The extract is quoted from Cosin's autograph sermons in the Chapter Library of Durham Cathedral (class mark A.IV.31), on which the printed text is based (*Works*, 1:19). For the sermon of January 5, 1623, see *Works*, 1:app.1, and for the sermon of 1653, 1:291–305.

Cosin owned both of the first folio editions of Donne's sermons, *LXXX Sermons* (1640) and *Fifty Sermons* (1649), according to the list of his books compiled by William Flower in about 1668 (in the Cosin's Library in Durham). Cosin's copy of the later edition is lost; the earlier folio, however, is still among his books in the library which he founded at Durham (1669). Cosin's extensive annotations in it show that he read the whole collection with great attention. There is a name and date at the top of the page which begins Walton's *Life*, not in Cosin's hand, "Re Jermyn June the 14 1644"; but some jottings, in French, on the last leaf of the volume, are unmistakably Cosin's. Evidently he had the first folio of Donne sermons at hand during his long exile in Paris and most probably he had the second one as well; it contains the 1621 sermon on John 1.8 for Christmas Day (no. 36), from which Cosin borrowed.

7. Hacket was Bishop of Coventry and Lichfield (from 1661 until his death). See *Scrinia Reserata: A Memorial Offer'd to the Great Deservings of John Williams . . .* (1693).

8. *A Century of Sermons,* 124–26, 136.

9. Mitchell calls his sermons "the high-water mark of Anglo-Catholic preaching" (p. 176). He was a fellow of Pembroke College, Cambridge in 1634 (where Andrewes had been a fellow and master before); he was ejected in 1644, along with Cosin who was then master of Peterhouse, but he returned at the Restoration to his fellowship and in 1662 became master of the College.

10. *LI Sermons* (1672), "The First Sermon on the Epiphany," 184, 190–91. Frank's sermons were reprinted in The Library of Anglo-Catholic Theology, 2 vols. (Oxford: John Henry Parker, 1849).

11. *LI Sermons,* 208.

12. "Pastoralis curae," in *Opera* (Paris, 1619), Pars III, Admonitio 32, III:220F, or Migne, *PL* 77:112D, and the translation by Henry Davis in *Ancient Christian Writers* 11 (Westminster, Md., 1950), 209: "For sin in words is sin in act, but sin that is cried out is sin committed with deliberation. On the other hand, those who confess their evil deeds, but do not avoid them, must be admonished to weigh betimes what they will say to excuse themselves when confronted with the strict judgment of God, seeing that they cannot excuse themselves from the guilt of their grave sins even when they are their own judges. What else, then, are these men but their own accusers? They prefer charges against their sins, and drag themselves to judgment as guilty of misdeeds." St. Gregory writes again of "peccatum cum voce" in his "Expositio secundi Psalmi poenitentialis" (i.e., Ps. 32); see *Opera* (1619), 2:933E, or Migne, *PL* 79:561A.

13. *The Sermons of John Donne,* ed. E. M. Simpson and G. R. Potter, 10 vols. (Berkeley: University of California Press, 1953–62), 1:171 and 7:361; and see also 2:113 (lines 681–85), a passage which seems to recall the same figure. For the quotation from Cosin, see my edition (Oxford: Clarendon Press, 1967), 238 and the comment on 354–55.

14. But see Janel M. Mueller's well annotated edition of *Donne's Prebend Sermons* (Cambridge, Mass.: Harvard University Press, 1971); Story's earlier edition of twelve of Andrewes's sermons (cited in n. 5) unfortunately made almost no attempt at any sort of commentary.

The beginning of John Burley's notes on Donne's sermons, in Trinity College, Dublin, MS 419, f. 72ᵛ.

7

John Donne's Sermon Notes

A RECENTLY noticed manuscript volume in Trinity College, Dublin, gives a unique record of John Donne's preaching. It contains notes made by a contemporary of two of Donne's sermons which he had heard or perhaps seen in rough copy during the last half of 1625. They let us view more clearly Donne's activities at this time, plausibly date a previously undated sermon, suggest the likely time and occasion of a series of sermons, and additionally provide the earliest manuscript notice we have so far of Donne's prose.

Of Donne's one hundred and sixty extant sermons, probably not one which we read is in the same form as when it was preached. Like most of his contemporaries, Donne spoke from notes (commonly memorized) extemporaneously. Later, if he thought the sermon worthy of publication, he wrote it out in revised and expanded form, with citations and other material more appropriate for a reader than a listener. By Donne's own testimony, we know that he worked over his sermons at two specific periods during his life. In his letter of November 25, 1625 to Thomas Roe, written from Chelsea, where he was staying with Sir John and Lady Danvers, he added a postscript:

> I have revised as many of my sermons as I had kept any note of, and I have written out a great many, and hope to do more. I am already come to the number of eight, of which my son, who, I hope, will take the same profession or some other in the world of middle understanding, may hereafter make some use.[1]

Donne was thus spending his summer and autumn in retirement in order to avoid the epidemic of plague in London. He refers again to the preparation of his sermons in the heading of an early one:

> At the Haghe, Decemb. 19, 1619. I Preached upon this Text. Since in my sicknesse at *Abrey-hatche* in Essex, 1630, revising my short notes of that sermon, I digested them into these two.[2]

Of course, Donne must have spent other times on the revision of his sermons, but the important point is that he did revise them from notes, sometimes long after he had preached the original sermon. Revision implies also review, and it is likewise obvious that Donne made selections from his notes; he did not turn everything he preached into a finished sermon, fit for publication. Indeed, his literary executor Henry King, writing in 1664, refers both to his sermons "now made publick" and to his "Sermon-Notes" and other papers.[3]

None of Donne's autograph sermon notes survive, but the contemporary manuscript volume which I found in Dublin contains notes made either from his own working papers or else from his spoken sermons. These sermon notes are in a miscellaneous academic notebook which once belonged to John Burley (now Trinity College MS 419). Burley (or Burleigh), of Devon, matriculated at Oriel College, Oxford, on November 20, 1618, as a Commoner, aged 16; he took his B.A. in 1625, and M.A. in 1628. In April 1624 Burley first went to Chelsea College, or King James's College, as it was formally known, perhaps through the influence of Matthew Sutcliffe, dean of Exeter, its founder and first provost.[4] Burley may still have been attached to it in 1650, the latest date in MS 419 (f. 76), when he describes a sermon by one "Mr Dauies the 29th of August 1650 at Chelsea." We know nothing more about Burley than what his notebook tells us, and it is quite impersonal. Besides the notes of Donne's sermons, it also includes material in Latin and English, written over a number of years, on logic, rhetoric, theology, and natural science, with commonplaces from Tacitus's *Annals*. There are 185 foliated leaves, many of them blank, measuring 19.0 cm x 14.0 cm, and the whole is bound up in parchment early in the eighteenth century.

The notes from Donne are on ff. 72^v–76^r (inclusive), very quickly written in a sprawling and often difficult secretary hand. Burley begins a theological section on f. 72^v which considers suffering and pestilence, especially from the plague; he writes, for example, that "the plague to a righteous man is as Eli[j]ahs charriot which lifted him to heauen." Shortly before the first reference to Donne (on f. 72^v), there is this statement: "Sinn is like the plague in this that it first assayleth the hart, in that it is spreading & infectious in that tis mortall" (ll. 9–10). About half-way down the page there is a short rule, and then "Dr Duns notes the 16th of October 1625 on the 6th psa v 5. or 6." The notes which follow form the skeleton, with many exact verbal similarities, of the two sermons printed by Potter and Simpson in *Sermons*, 5, nos. 18 and 19, which they are unable to date.[5] Burley's dating is surely correct. This was a Sunday, the 18th after Trinity, and probably Donne gave the sermon in Chelsea College or else in the parish church, applying the text to the time of plague – a topicality which he afterwards omitted in his revision.

Burley could have taken down these notes from hearing Donne preach; but he might also have seen the notes and written them out as he found them. He wrote them continuously, without break; thus the subsequent sermon on Colossians 1.24 (ff. 75–76), from Donne's Lincoln's Inn days,[6] is not one he could have heard unless Donne were preaching an old sermon a second or additional time.[7] But Burley probably had easy access to Donne's notes because of the enforced proximity of the two men in Chelsea for several months during the plague, and such a familiar connection is reasonable under the circumstances. The twenty-three-year-old Burley would, of course, have been eager to gather whatever knowledge he could from an eminent and learned neighbor.

The sermon notes for the penitential Psalm 6 show Donne's sense of occasion: "each knell minded us of our owne, each graue lifted us one step higher to heauen" (f. 72ᵛ, ll. 30–31); "soe now may it fall out with us, & soe to the season considering pesterd families" (f. 73ᵛ, ll. 12–13). Nothing in the finished sermon has so particular an application or is so poignant. But in his revision, Donne aimed to preach to a wider audience, to the generality of persons in need of self-examination in any sorrowful time. Since we know that Donne was writing this sermon during his Chelsea period, it is very probable that he composed, or preached, or revised the other undated sermons on Psalm 6 at the same time. He evidently conceived of them in a series, and in this sequence they appeared in *LXXX Sermons* of 1640 (as nos. 50–53 and 55).[8]

The five lines following the reference to "pesterd families" contain the ideas which Donne elaborates at the end of his completed sermon (i.e. 5, no. 19); then Burley writes "Mr Purchas," following this with a short stroke and the beginning of Ps. 91.5, "Thou shalt not be afrayd of the terour &c." What comes next (down to f. 75) is a different sermon from the one on Psalm 6, yet there is no interruption in the notes. They provide topical applications for Ps. 91.5–7, which correspond to themes raised earlier on this penitential psalm. The reference to "Mr Purchas" might mean that Burley was recording a sermon by him which he had either seen in note form or else heard. Possibly Burley is referring to Samuel Purchas, rector of St. Martin's Ludgate, the popular compiler of travel literature, who might have been another exile from the London plague. But the only extant sermon of Purchas's, preached at Paul's Cross in 1622, suggests that his style is very different from these notes, or from any sermon which could have resulted from them. Burley may have meant to indicate some kind of indebtedness to Purchas, or else to outline a different sermon which Donne preached in Chelsea but did not afterwards revise. There is enough in the notes to suggest Donne's style: "if we die our bodyes shall be but as belles new cast, they shall in the graue melloweing for the resurrection" (f. 74, ll. 8–10) — lines characteristic of Donne, or at least of someone imitating him. The final group of notes for the sermon on Colossians 1.24 is clearly set off, and there is a rule at the end, after which Burley wrote notes of the sermon by "Mr Dauies," some twenty-five years later. The notes taken from Donne, however, were obviously put down all at the same time, as if to form a set, or a "chapter" within Burley's commonplace book.

While Donne was preaching sermons at Chelsea as well as revising them, he was naturally aware of the terrible suffering so near him. Probably all of the sermons on the penitential Psalm 6 were occasioned by the plague, and if Donne preached the sermon on Colossians 1.24 for a second time, he could have made it especially suitable. At the beginning of the notes there is the statement, "Death is entred into our windows, that is into our eyes we haue seene if not tasted mortalitye" (f. 75, ll. 11–12), an appealing if somewhat mixed metaphor which does not find its way into this sermon; but it appears later, and better defined, in the sermon on Exod. 12.30, "For there was not a house where there was not one dead," preached at St. Dunstan's on January 15, 1626, "The First Sermon after Our Dispersion by the Sickness" (6, no. 18): "The windows of this House are but our eyes . . . " (p. 356, l. 266).

Most of the notes for the sermon on Colossians are echoed by, or developed in, the finished work. A few illustrative comments disappear, such as the description in the notes of one who searches after abstruse matters "like as he that undos a wood pile, should take the highest stick first, before the under matters be examind" (f. 75ᵛ, ll. 16–17). Very common is the brief note which lies behind an extended passage:

> there is a 3 fold ioye, the morall ioye common to pagans
> which may be cald onely indolency.
> the Christian ioye common which he cald true ioye.
> the consummate ioye which is of those that are sanctified.
> this ioye though neuer soe much depressed shall steel one
> up toward heaun.
> & riuett one faster to god.
>
> (f. 76, ll. 11–16)

The sermon develops these ideas:

> And of this joy in affliction, we may observe three steps, three degrees; one is indeed but halfe a joy; and that the Philosophers had; A second is a true joy, and that all Christians have; but the third is an overflowing, and aboundant joy, to which the Apostle was come, and to which by his example, hee would rouse others, that joy, of which himselfe speaks againe; *I am filled with comfort and am exceeding joyfull, in all our tribulations.* . . .
>
> (3:342, ll. 373–79)

Now Donne describes these joys by raising his discourse to that "consummate ioye." While we cannot know exactly what Donne said as opposed to what he wrote, Burley's notes do bring us nearer than we have ever been to Donne's actual preaching, to his first thoughts as contrasted with the eloquent contrivances of his later study.

APPENDIX

In the left-hand column below are three connected sections of Burley's notes compared with the corresponding passages in the published sermons, given at the right.

Dr Duns notes the 16th of October 1625 on the 6th psa v 5. or 6. Returne o Lord. deliuer my soule . . . [72ᵛ]⁹

Preached upon the Penitentiall Psalmes. Psal. 6.4,5. Returne, O Lord . . . (Potter and Simpson, 5, nos. 18 and 19)

I. Returne o Lord, wch word implyeth a former presence 2 a present absence, 3ᵈ a future residence. [72ᵛ]

First then, the first step in this Prayer, *Revertere, O Lord return,* implies first a former presence, and then a present absence, and also a confidence for the future. . . (no. 18, ll. 105–107)

By returneing is not meant a returne of prouidence for soe god is neuer from us, but in some particular grace punctually thus returneing may be eyther in remooueing iudgmentes, in vouchsafeing mercyes, or in turning us to him self.

There is no returning, without hearing, nor hearing without beleeving, nor beleeving, to be beleeved, without doing; Returning is all these. . . . So that the word which *David* receives from the Holy Ghost in this Text, being onely *Returned,* and no more, applies it selfe to all three senses, Returne thy selfe, that is, Bring backe thy Mercy; Returne thy Wrath, that is, Call backe thy Judgements, or Returne us to thee, that is, make thy meanes, and offers of grace, in thine Ordinance, powerfull, and effectuall upon us. (no. 18, ll. 201–203, 207–12)

II. Austin reports & interpretes of death as of habituall sinn in this place, & of the graue as of unpenitency which translation Ierome persues & anothr of some note who sayth tis impious to interprett it otherwaies litterally for he that remembreth god is not dead. [73ᵛ]

. . . we have another Author ancienter then S. *Augustine,* and S. *Ierome,* and so much esteemed by S. *Ierome,* as that he translated some of his Works, which is *Didymus* of Alexandria, who says, it is *Impia opinio,* not an inconvenient, or unnaturall, but an impious and irreligious opinion, to understand this verse of naturall death; because, sayes he, The dead doe much more remember God then the living doe. . . . (no. 19, ll. 256–62)

soe that dauids praire should be to this effect returne, deliuer saue &c lest I fall into sinn & impenitency, & in that graue not remember thee.

And then this reason of *Davids* Prayer here, (Doe this and this, *for in death there is no remembrance of thee*) will have this force, That God would *returne* to him in his effectuall grace, That God would *deliver* his soule in dangerous tentations, That God would *save* him in applying to him, and imprinting in him a sober, but yet confident assurance that the salvation of Christ Jesus belongs to him . . . (no. 19, ll. 277–82)

Dr Dun: Coll: 1.24. who now reioyce in my sufferings for you &c [75^r]

Preached at Lincolns Inne.
(Potter and Simpson, 3, no. 16)

III. there is 3 fold ioye, the morall ioye common to pagans which may be cald onely indolency. [76^r]

. . . of this joy in affliction, we may observe three steps, three degrees; one is indeed but halfe a joy; and that the Philosophers had; A second is a true joy, and that all Christians have; but the third is an overflowing, and aboundant joy, to which the Apostle was come, and to which by his example, hee would rouse others, that joy, of which himselfe speaks againe; *I am filled with comfort and am exceeding joyfull, in all our tribulations;* The first of these, which we call a halfe joy, is but an indolency, and a forced unsensiblenesse of those miseries which were upon them.
(ll. 373–81)

the Christian ioye common which he cald true ioye.

The second joy, which is a true joy, but common to all Christians, is that assurance, which they have in their tribulations, that God will give them the issue with the temptation . . . (ll. 388–91)

the consummate ioye which is of those that are sanctified.

But this perfect joy . . . this third joy, the joy of this text, is not a collaterall joy, that stands by us in the tribulation, and sustaines us, but it is a fundamentall joy, a radicall joy, a viscerall, a gremiall joy, that arises out of the bosome and wombe and bowels of the tribulation it selfe. . . . My calamity raises me, and makes my valley a hill, and gives me an eminency, and brings God and me nearer to one another . . . (ll. 401–10)

this ioye though neuer soe much depressed shall steel one up towards heaun. & riuett one faster to god.

My suffering: it must be unique not for me not the workes of supererogation which are anothers.

There is no joy belongs to my suffering, if I place a merit in it; *Meum non est cujus nomine nulla mihi superest actio,* says the Law; That's none of mine for which I can bring no action . . . (ll. 471–74)

meum non est cuius nulla superest actio.

we are all as clay in the potters hand, if god breake us with the hand of age &c we must be content.

Am not I *vas figuli,* a potters vessell, and that Potters vessel; and whose hand soever he imploys, the hand of sickness, the hand of poverty, the hand of justice, the hand of malice, still it is his hand that breakes the vessell, and this vessell which is his own; for, can any such vessel have a propriety in it selfe, or bee any other bodies primarily then his, from whom it hath the beeing? To recollect these, if I will have joy in suffering it must be mine, mine, and not borrowed out of an imaginary treasure of the Church . . . (ll. 481–89)

Notes

1. See *The Life and Letters of John Donne,* ed. Edmund Gosse (1889; repr. Gloucester, Mass.: Peter Smith, 1959), 2:225, and R. C. Bald, *John Donne: A Life* (Oxford: Clarendon Press, 1970), 479–81. The letter appears originally in the *State Papers Domestic.* I wish to thank the Board of Trinity College, Dublin, for their kind permission to allow me to use the manuscripts discussed herein, and to reproduce MS 419, f. 72ᵛ.

2. See *The Sermons of John Donne,* ed. G. R. Potter and E. M. Simpson (Berkeley: University of California Press, 1953–62), 2, no. 13. All subsequent references to Donne's sermons, except where otherwise noted, are to this edition.

Since Donne was actively in orders for a period of about sixteen years, he must have preached scores of sermons which he never revised. He would have spent his time on those sermons he deemed most worthy of preservation (see *Sermons,* 10:406). It was customary in the earlier seventeenth century for preachers to speak from memory, never from a written script – "extemporaneous" describes a very carefully planned address, with little left to the inspiration of the moment. See John Sparrow, "John Donne and Contemporary Preachers," *Essays and Studies by Members of the English Association* 15 (1931): 144–78, and W. Fraser Mitchell, *English Pulpit Oratory from Andrewes to Tillotson* (1932; repr. New York: Russell and Russell, 1962), 14–38.

3. *Sermons,* 1:46.

4. Burley's name does not appear in MS 419, but it does in another manuscript which also belonged to him (now Trinity College MS 446), where he records his association with Chelsea College: "Collegii Chelsie ueni 16° Aprilis an. domini 1624" (f. 151ᵛ). The other biographical details may be found in *Alumni Oxoniensis,* 1:124, and in the *Registrum Orielense,* 1:161. I am not aware of any connection between him and the Cecils, nor with the British Library Burley manuscripts.

5. See *Sermons,* 5:26–30.

6. *Sermons,* 3, no. 16. This sermon appeared in three separate manuscripts as well as in the *Fifty Sermons* of 1649; but Burley was not taking notes or making excerpts from any completed version of this or of any sermon. See the discussion of the manuscripts in 1:68.

Donne's *Sermon of Valediction,* on Eccles. 12.1, first appeared without his name in the volume called *Sapientia Clamitans* (1638); similar versions occur also in three seventeenth-century manuscripts. This text is closer to Donne's original sermon than its edition in *XXVI Sermons* (1661), which shows extensive revision; but the manuscripts and the first printed text nevertheless represent a stage of composition much in advance of Burley's notes. See E. M. Simpson's edition of the Valediction Sermon (London,

1932), and her summary comparison of the various texts in *A Study of the Prose Works of John Donne*, 2nd ed. (Oxford: Clarendon Press, 1948), 279–86.

7. The custom of making one sermon do for several occasions was common, but we have no way of knowing whether Donne did this, or, if he did, which sermons had second performances. See *Sermons*, 10:408–9. According to I. A. Shapiro, Donne must have reworked this Lincoln's Inn sermon on Colossians for his Chelsea audience, and his sermons on Psalm 6 may also have been composed before 1622, perhaps as early as 1616. See "Donne's Sermon Dates," *Review of English Studies* 31 (1980): 54–56.

8. See *Sermons*, 5, nos. 16–19, and 6, no. 1. No. 54 in *LXXX Sermons* is later and does not belong to this series, for it was preached in 1628. See *Sermons*, 8, no. 8. Burley records Ps. 6, "v 5. or 6." in his notes, which should be verses 4 and 5, as in the published sermon. Burley's error may suggest carelessness, or a faulty memory, or his own confusion about which part of Ps. 6 Donne had preached in giving this series of sermons.

The link between Donne's *Devotions Upon Emergent Occasions* (1624) and his sermons on Psalm 6 may be close, as Janel M. Mueller argues in "The Exegesis of Experience," *Journal of English and Germanic Philology* 66 (1968): 1–19, especially 8–14. But the sermons do not foreshadow the *Devotions,* as she supposes, because they probably came later. Their common topics and images really demonstrate not indebtedness but Donne's sustained interest in the same kind of material.

9. I. A. Shapiro suggests that Burley misheard Donne – transcribing, for example, "residence" for "confidence," a point which helps to confirm his presence in Donne's congregation, for the errors are evidently those of a listener. See his correspondence in *Review of English Studies* 30 (1979): 194.

8

Milton's LYCIDAS
and Earlier Seventeenth-Century Opera

FEW CLASSICAL LEGENDS have had such continuous importance and persistent appeal as the myth of Orpheus. Like his many predecessors, Milton, too, was moved by the legend of the supposed son of Apollo and Calliope, who inherits and thus embodies the power of song and verse. Ovid's extended description of the legend in books 10 and 11 of the *Metamorphoses* is perhaps the hinge that makes his whole love epic function; and a generation earlier, Vergil had told the story in the latter part of his fourth *Georgic,* the climax of that work and the culmination of even earlier traditions and folk-tales.[1]

When Eurydice, the wife of Thracian Orpheus, dies from the bite of a snake next to a river-bank as she tries to escape the pursuing Aristaeus, Orpheus laments her fate, singing to the accompaniment of his lyre. Then he goes to the underworld, gaining entrance by lulling its guards to sleep with his enchanting song, even casting a spell on Charon the boatman and on all the shades. He convinces Proserpine herself that he should have Eurydice again. With Pluto's consent, Orpheus is permitted to lead Eurydice out of hell, but only on condition that he should not look back; otherwise, he will lose Eurydice forever. But unable to keep his promise, Orpheus steals a look, and Eurydice is gone. Orpheus mourns his loss bitterly, and he weeps for seven months beneath a cliff by the river Strymon; his lamentation fascinates even the tigers and the oak trees. Since nothing can soften his sorrow, the women of the Cicones, inhabitants of Thrace and devotees of Bacchus, hideously punish him by tearing his body to pieces, throwing the flesh over the land, and allowing the severed head to float on the river Hebrus. As the water carries his head away, it calls out "Eurydice" and continues to sing. This legend has variations and numerous additions, especially in connection with Orpheus's parentage and his usually unhappy end. But the essential idea in all of these stories is that Orpheus brings harmony to all things and creatures by his inspired mingling of voice and words.[2]

Milton's earliest reference to the Orpheus legend is evidently in his elegy to Diodati (in 1629), the allusion to the one who skillfully causes the "Thracian lyre" to sound.[3] *Il Penseroso* (105–8) and *L'Allegro* (144–150) invoke the Orphean legend of "the hidden soul of harmony." In *Ad Patrem*, Milton exalts the poet who makes music with words, like Orpheus who sang not simply with his cithara but with his song, and so restrained rivers, gave ears to the oaks, stirred the ghosts of the dead to tears, and won high fame (52–55). Here is the familiar Renaissance idea that Orpheus the poet-singer subdued lower nature by causing the whole earth to listen to him in astonished wonder; Milton develops the notion substantially in the second and third invocations of *Paradise Lost*. In book 3, Milton compares his earlier description of Hell and then of Heaven with Orpheus's journey; and in book 7, he prays that "the barbarous dissonance / Of *Bacchus* and his Revellers" who destroyed Orpheus (32–33) may not also destroy him or disturb his effort to make known his "advent'rous Song" (1.13).

But it is in *Lycidas* (1638) that Milton makes most extended use of the Orpheus legend, displaying the poet-prophet-teacher's "perfect songs" which caused "even the very trees, the bushes, and the whole woods" to pull up their roots and rush to hear him.[4] The central importance of Orpheus to *Lycidas* is fundamental to the purpose of the whole poem: Milton, of course, identifies himself with Lycidas, or Edward King, in whom is realized the figure of Orpheus, controlling and organizing nature, displaying the power of recovery and creativity. In using the legend of Orpheus in *Lycidas*, Milton also uses one of the most familiar themes of the first operas, and in his "monody," he provides a literary form that parallels the *via naturale alla immitatione* of contemporary musical style.[5]

Finding the Orpheus legend so congenial, Milton must not only have read the literature but also heard or known about the music in which Orpheus figures prominently: the Italian opera of the earlier seventeenth century, with its roots even earlier in Angelo Poliziano's *Orfeo*, a work composed for the city of Mantua in about 1480, lost but still talked about when Jacopo Peri wrote his *Euridice* in 1600, and Monteverdi, influenced by both these predecessors, in his *Orfeo*, first performed in 1607. Milton's knowledge of music surely included these earliest operas, appropriately dedicated to the legendary first singer and divine patron of dramatic music. Thus, he must also have appreciated the rage for homophonic or monodic music, the so-called *stile rappresentativo* ("theatrical style"), which Giulio Caccini (c. 1545–1618) described in his *Le nuove musiche* of 1602 and illustrated in his own version of Orpheus later in the same year. Not only this legend perfectly suited the earliest music drama, but the "new music" offered an especially satisfactory way of interpreting the story. In this fashionable mode, a recitative style that sought a balance between song and speech, Milton must have discovered the usual role of Orpheus memorably redefined, and in a way also that must have seemed to him and others of his time reminiscent of ancient Greek theatre.

Milton wrote in his *Defensio secunda* (1654)[6] that after he had arrived at Venice in 1639, probably in April, he took care to have the books which he had collected during his Italian sojourn loaded on the England-bound ship. His biographer Edward Philips writes in more detail, stating that Milton

> Shipp'd up a Parcel of curious and rare Books which he had
> pick'd up in his Travels; (particularly a Chest or two of
> choice Musick-books of the best Masters flourishing about
> that time in *Italy*, namely, *Luca Marenzo, Monte Verde,
> Horatio Vecchi, Cifa,* the Prince of *Venosa* and several
> others).[7]

These all were familiar composers, important to the development of the new
music: Luca Marenzio (1553–1599) and Antonio Cifra (1584–1629) were
already well known in England, Henry Lawes (1596–1662) having made use
of the song titles and one or two performing directions from the latter's
Scherzi et arie (Venice, 1614).[8] Orazio (Tiberio) Vecchi (1550–1605) composed the popular madrigal comedy *L'Amfiparnaso* (1597), and Don Carlo
Gesualdo, prince of Venosa (c. 1561–1613), was celebrated not only for his
modernist harmonies but also for the murder of his first wife and her lover.[9]
Claudio Monteverdi, who died at the age of 76 in 1643, is today the best
remembered of this group, and the only one who was still living when Milton
visited Italy, residing in Venice when Milton was there in 1639.

Milton had obvious and ample opportunity for becoming well
acquainted with the latest fashions in Italian music. Lawes had already shown
at least a general sympathy for it in his music for *Comus* in 1634 though his
specific indebtedness may be disputed; but there is no doubt that Lawes knew
Italian music, especially of Marenzio and Monteverdi, for he had copied their
music into his partbooks, evidently as a young man.[10] But what was this new
music which could so easily be made to suit the requirements of the earliest
operas? And how did Milton adapt it to his own poetic needs?

The *camerata* centered around Giovanni de' Bardi, which was active in
Florence from 1573 to 1587, discussed the musical theories that helped lead
to the development of opera. In an effort to recover Greek music and drama,
which they presumed was entirely sung, Bardi and his colleagues studied
every source they could find. They were primarily assisted by Girolamo Mei,
the most learned theorist among them, and Vincenzo Galilei, the father of
the astronomer, and also by Caccini himself who turned particularly to Mei
for advice. Caccini set out their ideas in his influential *Nuove musichi*, already
mentioned, and he also, incidentally, dedicated his *Euridice* to Bardi. It
should be remembered that in 1581–1582 Vincenzo Galilei had written his
Dialogo della musica antica e della moderna in which he espoused the principles common to the members of the *camerata*, which they saw as necessary
steps for the appropriate development of music in their own time: (1) the
sentiments of the text ought to be expressed by the widest possible vocal
range; (2) only one melody at a time should be heard; (3) rhythm and melody
must follow the speaking voice of someone possessed by "a certain ease, a
casual affection," or *sprezzatura*, a well-used term in music as well as in
courtly conduct of the period.[11]

The elaborately polyphonic music of the sixteenth-century madrigal, customarily composed for five equal parts, gave way to madrigals written for a single voice and continuo, or else consort; the madrigal as a *concertato ensemble*, or a composition for several voices, was virtually dead by the early l630s. Thus the term "madrigal" survived as a description of a solo song, usually accompanied by a figured bass. Although "monody" was not at first applied to this kind of music, it soon became the inclusive term for all music that featured a single voice. The word appears in 1635[12] in the important *Compendio del trattato de' generi e de' modi della musica* by Giovanni Battista Doni (1594–1647), whom Milton met on March 24, 1639, in Rome, where, incidentally, he had recently – it seems very likely – heard the famous Leonora Baroni sing at Cardinal Barberini's concert. What Milton heard and the kind of music he sent back to England was evidently "monodic." At the same time, he could hardly have missed hearing what I should call "Orphean" opera with its popular recitative style.

Of the many operas on Orpheus composed during Milton's time, the best and perhaps most celebrated is Monteverdi's "Favola in Musica," *L'Orfeo* (1607). It combines a pastoral setting in a richly interwoven and symmetrically designed libretto, with a happy ending, written by Alessandro Striggio (the younger, c. 1573–1630). Above all, Monteverdi provides one of the greatest monodies in contemporary musical literature, the extraordinary aria of Orpheus, lasting nearly nine minutes in the revised edition of 1615. With "Possente spirto," Orpheus begins his song, written in *terza rima*, to Charon, at the poetic and spiritual climax of the opera. Here, indeed, is one of the first of those "strongly characterized set pieces (prayer, incantation, lament) that reappear time and again in early opera."[13] Monteverdi drew upon his great experience as a madrigalist and harmonist in what became a musical touchstone of his age. He assured for himself an even greater reputation with his next opera of 1608 to a libretto by Ottavio Rinuccini (also the author of Peri's *Euridice*): most of the music of *L'Arianna* has not survived, but the portion which Monteverdi himself described as "la più essential parte dell' opera," the lovely monodic lament, has come down to us.[14] The "Lamento d'Arianna" moved its first audience to tears and established itself in the consciousness of every music-loving Italian. For years to come, composers remembered and imitated Monteverdi's lament; and "Lasciatemi morire" and "Possente spirto" became the great and model set-pieces of the new monodic style.[15]

One musicologist calls Monteverdi's impressive achievement, especially in *Orfeo*, "a highly stylized and hieratically formalized incantation, through which a superhuman singer soothes and subjects the forces of darkness...."[16] This judgment might, I think, describe also Milton's achievement in *Lycidas*. "In this Monody," Milton writes at the beginning of *Lycidas*, "the Author bewails a learned Friend." Undoubtedly, Milton understood by "monody" the Greek literary form represented in the speeches of Andromache, Hecuba, or Helen in the *Iliad* (book 24), and elsewhere in classical literature, especially tragedy, and he was familiar with the tradition of the lamenting poet-singer. Obviously, he would have known the famous lament in Vergil's Second Eclogue and the still earlier Theocritean poems. But he must have had in mind also the current musical sense of the term; certainly, he wrote a lament essentially for one voice (with a second commenting on the whole poem in the final verse paragraph, or *commiato* to the *canzone* stanzas that precede it), making use of the central imagery of the Orpheus legend. Many commentators have ignored, or insufficiently appreciated the term "monody" at the beginning of the poem, or only briefly and inadequately described it; but I am sure it is a crucial key to understanding the poem. Some writers have discussed the "musical" qualities of *Lycidas*, and others have described its indebtedness to the madrigal.[17] But *Lycidas* is a monodic madrigal in the "modern" seventeenth-century sense; it has nothing in common with the old-fashioned five-part songs, or the polyphonal harmonies of earlier composers. Written just before Milton went on his Italian journey, *Lycidas* is a remarkable testament not only to Italian poetic form in its *canzone* structure and rhyme scheme, but also to Italian opera.

Monteverdi, of course, did not write the libretto of *Orfeo*; that was the younger Striggio's work, which, in the early years of opera, implied something more than collaboration. Because the new monodic music had as its principal intention the wringing of a deeper meaning from the texts, the poet often became more important than the musician in operatic collaborations. In this unequal partnership, "the words came to be regarded as the design and the music the colour."[18] While some libretti were naive and awkwardly written, others, and certainly Striggio's among them, possess commendable clarity and literary power. Orpheus's long monody in act 3 begins with the appearance of "Speranza," or Hope.[19] She quotes Dante's famous line from the *Inferno* (3.9), part of the inscription on the lintel of the gate of Hell: "Lasciate ogni speranza, voi ch'entrate" ("Abandon all hope, ye that enter"). Vergil, of course, is the ultimate source, as he writes of the Sybil who warns away Aeneas's companions just as he is about to enter the underworld: "Procul O, procul este, profani / conclamat vates" ("O away, stand away, the Sybil cried, you uninitiated ones" [*Aeneid* 6.258–59]). The boldness of the journey is justified by the heaviness of the loss or the overwhelming desire to learn the wisdom of the dead and find some prospect for the future. While Milton, as the "uncouth swain," does not similarly enter the underworld to visit Lycidas, he compares his dead friend with Orpheus, eventually also seeing himself in them, and managing to turn his poem into a metaphorical journey not only to the place of the dead but, at the last, of the living.

Like Orpheus rising from the place of death to life once more, "So *Lycidas*, sunk low, but mounted high . . . hears the unexpressive nuptial Song" (172, 176). In Striggio / Monteverdi's version, this new life is achieved through the intervention of Apollo, who ascends with Orpheus to Heaven, "Dove ha virtù verace / Degno premio di sè, diletto e pace" ("Where true virtue has its just rewards, joy and peace"). For Milton the apotheosis comes "Through the dear might of him that walk'd the waves." Striggio has given Orpheus a happy end, unusual for this legend, but it incidentally anticipates

Milton's Christian resolution of his poem, and it also reinforces the strongly moral direction both of his Orpheus and of Milton's *Lycidas*. At the conclusion of act 4 of Monteverdi's opera, as Eurydice vanishes after her brief moments with Orpheus, the chorus explains what went wrong:

> Orfeo vinse l'Inferno e vinto poi
> Fu da gli affetti suoi.
> Degno d'eterna gloria
> Fia sol colui ch'avrà di sè vittoria.

> Orpheus conquered Hell, but then was conquered by his passions. Worthy of eternal fame shall be only he who has victory over himself.

The sentiment is a sound Renaissance interpretation of the Orpheus legend; but it is also a good description of Milton's abiding belief, implicit in the honest virtue that exalts *Lycidas*, the "spare Temperance" that preserves the Lady in *Comus*, and above all the Love that "hath his seat / In Reason," an idea fundamental to *Paradise Lost*, and further elaborated in Raphael's parting advice to Adam to "take heed lest Passion sway / Thy Judgment to do aught, which else free Will / Would not admit" (8.635–37).[20] Milton could be moved by the Orphean monody, especially when the words of the song helped to expel "the grim Wolf with privy paw" (129).

Milton's most important use of the Orpheus legend occurs in *Lycidas*, his own monody, a lament that recalls the style of Monteverdi, Peri, Caccini, and others. The poem is testimony to Milton's appreciation of the new music; but his sonnet to Henry Lawes (of 1646) provides one more instance of his knowledge and approval of this kind of music; for Lawes's "well measur'd Song / First taught our English Music how to span / Words with just note and accent"; he, too, knew how to "honor" verse by fitting the music to the sense of the words, as his *Ariadne*, Milton indirectly says, happily proved. Although certainly less skillful than its model, Lawes's "O Theseus, hark! but yet in vain" is an obvious descendent of "Lasciatemi morire." Milton saw in Lawes's composition a noble achievement, and in lauding it, he implicitly compliments also the musical tradition from which it grew, remembering, one may suppose, his own indebtedness to the monodies of the earliest Italian opera.

Notes

1. See the collection edited by John Warden, *Orpheus: The Metamorphoses of a Myth* (Toronto: University of Toronto Press, 1982), especially the essays by Emmet Robbins, "Famous Orpheus," 3–23, and by W. S. Anderson, "The Orpheus of Virgil and Ovid: *flebile nescio quid*," 25–50.

2. Because he journeyed to the underworld and emerged alive, he is also identified with the Prince of Peace, the Messianic king mentioned in Isaiah 9.6. See Eleanor Irwin, "The Songs of Orpheus and the New Song of Christ," in *Orpheus: The Metamorphoses of a Myth*, ed. Warden, esp. 58–59; and Patricia Vicari, "*Sparagmos:* Orpheus among the Christians," 63–83. For further background, see also John Block Friedman, *Orpheus in the Middle Ages* (Cambridge, Mass.: Harvard University Press, 1970), esp. chap. 3, "Orpheus-Christus in the Art of Late Antiquity."

3. Except where indicated, quotations from Milton are taken from the edition by Merritt Y. Hughes, *Complete Poems and Major Prose* (New York: Odyssey Press, 1957), afterwards cited as "Hughes."

4. See Prolusion 7, about 1632 (Hughes, 629).

5. The "natural way of imitation" attempted a style midway between song and speech, emphasizing the solo voice. See Nigel Fortune, "Italian Secular Monody from 1600 to 1635: An Introductory Survey," *Musical Quarterly* 39 (1953): 171–95, and also the more detailed study by Gary Tomlinson, "Madrigal, Monody, and Monteverdi's 'via naturale alla immitatione,'" *Journal of the American Musicological Society* 34 (1981): 60–108. See also Tomlinson's *Monteverdi and the End of the Renaissance* (Berkeley: University of California Press, 1987), esp. chap. 5, "Guarini, Rinuccini, and the Ideal of Musical Speech"; and Walther Dürr, "Sprachliche und musikalische Determinanten in der Monodie: Beobachtungen an Monteverdis 'Orfeo,'" in *Claudio Monteverdi: Festschrift Reinhold Hammerstein*, ed. Ludwig Finscher ([Heidelberg:] Laaber-Verlag, 1986), 151–62. Of course, Milton's Italian journey of 1638–39 followed his writing of *Lycidas*; but what he was to hear and learn of "the new music" made his understanding of it more compelling.

6. See Hughes, 830 (in the 1654 edition, p. 86).

7. See *Life*, 1694, xvi, in Helen Darbishire, ed., *The Early Lives of Milton* (London: Constable, 1932), 59. Cf. Anthony à Wood's sketch: "After he had taken the degrees in Arts, he left the University of his own accord. . . . Whereupon retiring to his Fathers house in the Country, he spent some time in turning over Latin and Greek Authors, and now and then made excursions into the great City to buy books, to the end that he might be instructed in Mathematicks and Musick, in which last he became excellent, and by the help of his Mathematicks could compose a Song or Lesson" (Darbishire, 36).

8. See under "Cifra" and "Lawes, Henry" in *The New Grove Dictionary of Music and Musicians*, ed. Stanley Sadie, 20 vols. (London: Macmillan, 1980), hereafter cited as *New Grove*. Henry Lawes dedicated his first book of *Ayres and Dialogues* (1653) to the daughters of the earl of Bridgewater, "most of them being Composed when I was employed by Your ever Honour'd Parents to attend Your Ladishipp's Education in Musick," that is, about twenty years earlier, or near the time of *Comus*, which Lawes wrote for Bridgewater's inauguration as Lord President of Wales. For Henry Lawes's connection with contemporary Italian music, see Willa McClung Evans, *Henry Lawes: Musician and Friend of Poets* (New York: Modern Language

Association, 1941), 16–32. From 1612 (and perhaps earlier), Lawes was learning "of the fashionable world of court musicians, a world in which Coperario's influence swayed musical thinking, in which Campion was well established, and in which Ferrabosco was enjoying the height of his success" (21). Giovanni Coperario (that is, the Englishman John Cooper), it should be recalled, had returned from his visit to Italy sometime between 1604 and 1608, bringing with him the new methods of composition.

9. Gesualdo surprised his wife and her lover Fabrizio Carafra, duke of Andria, "in flagrante delicto di fragrante peccato." See Lorenzo Bianconi, "Gesualdo," in *New Grove*.

10. See Evans, 19–21, and the article in *New Grove*. See also Harris F. Fletcher, *The Intellectual Development of John Milton*, 2 vols. (Urbana: University of Illinois Press, 1956–61), esp. 1, chap. 21, "Music in the Grammar School Period" and 2, chap. 19, "Music." Cf. Walter L. Woodfill, *Musicians in English Society from Elizabeth to Charles I* (Princeton: Princeton University Press, 1953).

11. Castiglione is the first to write of *sprezzatura* in his *Il Cortegiano* (1528), well known in the English translation by Thomas Hoby (1561). But Caccini is the first to apply the term to music, in his preface to *Euridice* (1600), where he insists "that by means of it I approach that much closer to the essence of speech." He writes in his *Le nuove musiche* of "negligently" (that is, naturally) introducing dissonances in order to approach "speaking" tones. See Nigel Fortune, "Sprezzatura," in *New Grove*. On Caccini's personal rivalry as well as his musical differences with Peri, see Nino Pirrotta and Elena Povoledo, *Music and Theatre from Poliziano to Monteverdi*, trans. Karen Eales (Cambridge: Cambridge University Press, 1982), 238–57. (First published as *Li due Orfei* [1969]). – Vincenzo Galilei's *Dialogo* appeared in facsimile, ed. Fabio Fano (Rome, 1934); and several related documents, with introductions and annotations, appear in *The Florentine Camerata: Documentary Studies and Translations,* ed. Claude V. Palisca (New Haven: Yale University Press, 1989).

12. Francesco Patrizi (1529–1597) was first to use the term "monodia" in Italian, in his *Della poetica* (Ferrara, 1586), ed. D. Aguzzi Barbagli (Florence, 1969–70), 1:382, discovering the word in Plato's *Laws*, 764D. "Dico monodia, non per lo canto di un solo de' coreuti, che con questo nome dicemmo che fu detto, né per la monodia lamentevale di Saffo, ma per quella monodia la quale Platone distinse contro alla corodia, la quale dicemmo essere canto di tutto il coro, in quelle parole che di suo adducemmo in questa sentenza." ("By monody I mean, not the song of only one member of the chorus, which was called by that name, nor the sorrowful monody of Sappho, but that monody which Plato distinguishes from choral song [*corodia*], which we define as being sung by the entire chorus, in those words of his which we quote in this context.") In his *Compendio* (Rome, 1635), Doni writes: "Dove mi son proposto solamente di alcuni miei pensieri intorno le musiche a una voce sola (che anticamente si dicevano monodie, o semplici ch'elle fussero o accompagnate con l'instrumento) e quelle che di più voci si compongono"

(2:96) ("Therefore, I have only put forward some of my thoughts about musical pieces for one voice [which in antiquity were called monodies, either because they were 'simple' or accompanied by the instrument] and those musical pieces that are carried through by several voices").

13. See Iain Fenlon, "The Mantuan Stage Works," in *The New Monteverdi Companion*, ed. Denis Arnold and Nigel Fortune (London: Faber and Faber, 1985), 275.

14. See letter of March 21, 1620, quoted in Hans Ferdinand Redlich, *Claudio Monteverdi: Life and Works*, trans. Kathleen Dale (Westport, Conn.: Greenwood Press, 1952), 101, and also *The Letters of Claudio Monteverdi*, trans. Denis Stevens (London: Faber and Faber, 1980), 197–98. Quotations from Striggio's libretto are taken from the 1615 text edited by Nigel Rogers for the London Baroque performance (on EMI Angel 4D2X–3964, London, 1984).

15. Cf. Henry Lawes's *Ariadne* (1653, but composed perhaps in the late 1640s), and the comments at the end of the present essay. See Evans, 161–66.

16. See Pirrotta and Povoledo, *Music and Theatre from Poliziano to Monteverdi*, 277.

17. See, for example, "The Minor English Poems," in *A Variorum Commentary on the Poems of John Milton*, ed. A. S. P. Woodhouse and Douglas Bush (New York: Columbia University Press, 1972), 2:637. See also Gretchen Finney, "A Musical Background for 'Lycidas,'" *Huntington Library Quarterly* 15 (1951–52): 325–50; Joseph A. Wittreich, "Milton's 'Destin'd Urn': The Art of *Lycidas*," *PMLA* 84 (1969): 60–70; Mortimer H. Frank, "Milton's Knowledge of Music: Some Speculations," in *Milton and the Art of Sacred Song*, ed. J. Max Patrick and R. H. Sundell (Madison: University of Wisconsin Press, 1979), 83–98.

18. Simon Towneley Worsthorne, *Venetian Opera in the Seventeenth Century* (Oxford: Clarendon Press, 1954), 117.

19. In Rinuccini's text for Peri's setting of *Euridice* (1600), Venus escorts Orpheus on his journey to the underworld. On the relationship of Rinuccini and Peri with Striggio and Monteverdi, see Tomlinson, "From *L'Euridice* to *Orfeo*," in *Monteverdi and the End of the Renaissance*, 131–41.

20. Compare the final scene of the opera with Milton's "Tomorrow to fresh Woods, and Pastures new." Milton's quiet and harmonious resolution of his poem refers, of course, to the swain who must survive in the world without Lycidas. Yet Lycidas, like Orpheus, continues to live, the one through Christian immortality, the other through an Apollonian eternity. As Apollo ascends with Orpheus, the chorus sings reassuringly of him: "Così va chi non s'arretra, / Al chiamar di Nume eterno, / Così grazia in ciel impetra / Chi quaggiù provo l'Inferno / E chi semina fra doglie / D'ogni grazia il frutto coglie" ("Thus goes he who does not hesitate at the call of an everlasting god; thus he obtains grace in Heaven, who here below tasted the infernal. And he who sows in sorrow shall reap the fruits of all grace"). Striggio's original ending of *Orfeo* in his libretto of 1607 provides a Bacchanalian chorus which anticipates the death and dismemberment of Orpheus, a conclusion in close

accord with Vergil and Ovid. F. W. Sternfeld argues that Monteverdi himself changed Striggio's sad ending for the happy one of his opera, sometime before 1609, the date of the first published score. See his "The Orpheus Myth and the Libretto of 'Orfeo,'" in *Claudio Monteverdi: Orfeo*, ed. John Whenham, "Cambridge Opera Handbooks" (Cambridge: Cambridge University Press, 1986), 20–33. Whenham gives Striggio's original version, 35–41.

III

THREE CAMBRIDGE DIVINES

9

John Cosin and His Devotions

1

JOHN COSIN was born in Norwich on November 30, 1595,[1] of a wealthy father, probably a merchant, and a mother who came of a landed family. Educated at the Grammar School at Norwich, Cosin was selected at the age of fiteen to fill one of the scholarships reserved for the school at Gonville and Caius College, Cambridge, then under the mastership of William Branthwaite.[2] He took his B.A. in 1614 and M.A. in 1617; his D.D. was conferred in 1630. Little is known of Cosin's life while at Caius, either as an undergraduate, or, from 1620 to 1624, as a junior fellow. He evidently showed remarkable ability, since in 1616 he attracted the attention of two eminent churchmen: both Lancelot Andrewes, then bishop of Ely, and John Overall, bishop of Lichfield, offered him a position as episcopal librarian and secretary. On the advice of his tutor, Cosin decided in favor of Overall, remaining in his service until May 1619, when Overall died at Norwich, to which episcopal see he had only a few months previously been translated. This short period probably marked the beginning of Cosin's association with the "Arminians," that party of the church most vigorously opposed to the "Puritans."[3] Whatever influence Overall had — and it was likely very considerable — there can be no doubt of Cosin's lasting fondness for his memory, for years later, in 1669, he erected a handsome memorial to him in the cathedral church of Norwich.

After an interval of four years at Caius, during which time he was rhetoric praelector (1620–21) and university preacher (1622), Cosin was called by Bishop Neile of Durham to be one of his domestic chaplains. He received immediate preferment to the mastership of Greatham Hospital, a position he soon resigned in favor of a prebendal stall at Durham and the rectory of Elwick. In 1625, his second year at Durham, he was made archdeacon of the East Riding, and finally in 1626 rector of Brancepeth, a living which he seems to have particularly enjoyed and often occupied. Cosin must have spent much time, however, with Bishop Neile at Durham House in London, which had become a center for discussion of theology and the current problems of the church. They were often joined there by many of the most important churchmen of the day, such as William Laud, Francis White,

Richard Mountague, and John Buckeridge. Cosin's early biographer, Thomas
Smith, wrote concerning the year 1626:

> *Londini* in aedibus D. *Neli, Dunelmensis* Episcopi, tanquam
> in Collegio & sacro consessu, venerabiles viri, D.D.D.
> *Laudus,* Episcopus *Bathoniensis & Wellensis, Whitus,* mox
> Episcopus *Carleolensis, Richardus Montacutus,* aliique
> pietate, doctrina, & flagranti Ecclesiae *Anglicanae* contra
> tum Pontificiorum, tum Puritanorum insidias & impetus
> tuendaë zelo insignes, de rebus ad Ecclesiam & religionem
> spectantibus consultaturi, convenire soliti erant: quorum
> colloquiis *Cosinus,* licet annis & dignitate longe inferior,
> praesens aderat.[4]
> (At London there were gathered in the house of Dr Neile,
> bishop of Durham, as if in a college and sacred council, the
> eminent men, Dr Laud, bishop of Bath and Wells, Dr
> White, soon to be bishop of Carlyle, Dr Richard
> Mountague, and others outstanding for their devotion, doc-
> trine, and burning zeal to protect the English church against
> the wiles and attacks both of the papists and of the puritans,
> for the purpose of consulting about matters relating to the
> church and religion. Cosin was present in the meetings of
> this company although he was by far the least in years and
> in rank.)

These meetings of church leaders at Durham House may have provided inspiration for one of the most important controversial books of the
time, *Appello Caesarem* (1625), by Richard Mountague, canon of Windsor
and later bishop of Chichester. Mountague knew Cosin at Durham House
and, though by many years the older man, came especially to trust in his judgment. He submitted his book to Cosin, instructing him to alter it in any way
that he saw fit. *Appello Caesarem* sets out a part of the Arminian position —
that the Church of Rome is a true church though in error — and it naturally
brought down a storm of abuse from the puritans in the House of Commons
as soon as it appeared, for it substantiated all too well their worst fears of the
leadership of the church. Mountague had already written polemical works —
especially, *A Gagg for the new Gospell? No: A New Gagg for an Old Goose*
(1624) — so the puritans now regarded him with extreme disfavor. Another
response to Mountague's books was a conference at York House, in London,
at which arguments for and against his theology were heard, with Cosin
acting as secretary and also speaking in his defence.[5]
    Cosin defended Mountague (and had perhaps even written some of
the *Appello*) because he believed the Anglican tradition was best expressed as
a way of finding the mean between the "excesses" of Geneva and Rome,
while yet retaining catholicity, with "Antiquity [as] the best Expositer of
Faith." From the first, then, Cosin declared himself the friend of those who

understood the English church to be a sound branch of the Catholic church, purged of the corruptions of Rome on the one side, and Calvinism on the other. Like Hooker, he appealed to the authority of the early church, the fathers and the first general councils, in order to vindicate the church of the *via media,* Catholic and reformed, a church "which ever held firm (and we are able to make it good) in a continued line of succession from former known bishops, and so from this very mission of the Apostles."[6] This is a theme that runs through Cosin's thought, and we see it well expressed in one of his early sermons spoken at the consecration of the bishop of Carlisle, Dr. Francis White, a friend and regular visitor at Durham House. The text was from John 20.21,22: "As my father sent me, even so send I you":

> We demand . . . How was Christ sent? And He was sent for two ends. The first, to be the Redeemer of our souls, and to reconcile God unto men, which He did by His death; the second, to be the Bishop of our souls, and to reconcile men unto God, which He did by leaving us a Gospel, His life and doctrine, in a Church behind Him. In the first sense the Apostles were not sent, they were to be no redeemers nor mediators neither. For it cost more to redeem men's souls, and both they and their successors must let that *sicut* alone for ever. And yet there is a *sicut similitudinis* in it for all that, though there be no *sicut aequalitatis,* there is some likeness in their sendings this way. He, sent by His Father to be a Mediator for mankind, and to reconcile the world by His death and sacrifice upon the cross. They, sent by Him, to mediate and to pray for the people, to be ministers of the reconciliation, as St. Paul speaks, and in a manner, to be sacrificers too, representers at the Altar here, and appliers of the Sacrifice once made for all; without which last act, the first will do us no good.[7]

At the same time, Cosin would probably have agreed with Mountague's assertion, "I professe my selfe none of those furious ones in point of difference now-a-dayes, whose profession and resolution is, That the farther in any thing from communion with the Church of *Rome,* the neerer unto GOD and Truth . . . the Church of *Rome* is a *true,* though not a *sound* Church of CHRIST, as well since, as before the Councell of *Trent;* a part of the Catholick, though not the Catholick Church."[8] Since Cosin had been identifying himself from the outset of his career with these principles and the party that most keenly espoused them, he was himself destined to become the butt of considerable puritan abuse.

The appearance of Cosin's *Devotions* in the first part of 1627 aroused immediate opposition, for the disagreements between Charles and the high churchmen, on the one hand, and the puritans, sustained by the majority of the House of Commons, on the other, were growing increasingly acute and bitter. The hard words over Mountague, whom the king had advanced to a bishopric, surely had not been forgotten, nor had Cosin's connection with him. To the puritans the *Devotions* seemed one more effort to advance "popery," with Cosin a champion of the Arminian position. In 1628 William Prynne and Henry Burton wrote fierce pamphlets about it, apparently to attract the attention of the Parliament then sitting. In the same year Cosin upset one Peter Smart, a fellow prebend at Durham, who on July 27 preached in the cathedral an extraordinarily abusive sermon, directed principally against him: *The Vanitie & Downe-fall of Superstitious Popish Ceremonies.* Cosin, in keeping with the high churchmen's desire to enrich the liturgy by splendid ceremonial, had supported the reform of services at Durham Cathedral — though it is likely that the services had been "reformed" even before his arrival: he may have extended only what was already begun. Smart's attack reflects numerous puritan dislikes: there is a passing, slighting reference to the *Devotions* in the preface to the printed version of the sermon, but the sermon itself is concerned with such things as music in the church, the wearing of copes, the placing of the altar in the east end with the font at the west entrance, bowing to the altar, the use of candles. It was, of course, the theological implications of these things that troubled the puritans. Thus, Smart says, "Now indeed the originall cause of most of our superstitious Ceremonies, is that Popish opinion, that Christs Church hath yet Priests Sacrifices and Altars: when as indeed Christ was sent of God to be the last priest, which should offer the last sacrifice upon the last Altar, that ever the world should have."[9] Because Cosin could not agree, he had no peace.

The next Parliament saw in Cosin a menacing figure. The king had followed his general forgiveness of Mountague, Cosin, Sibthorpe, and Mainwaring — all of whom had outspokenly offended the puritans — with a proclamation issued on January 17, 1629, calling in Mountague's book, an action meant to put an end to discussion of it. Soon after the opening of this Parliament a petition of February 4 was preferred against Cosin, "with articles annexed thereunto, tending to the introduction of Popish doctrine and Popish ceremonies [at Durham]."[10] Cosin was also ordered to answer to the Commons on February 23. On the 24th the famous "Head and Articles Agreed upon by the House" was put forward, and in it Cosin was particularly named. Religion, it was declared, struggled sadly in a troubled state, for not only did books supporting Arminianism flourish, but also services were being established full of popish imitation. Cosin must obviously fall on both points, with appropriate condemnation. It was recommended that the books of Mountague and Cosin, including the *Devotions,* described as his "Horary," be burned, and "that such as have been authors or abettors of those Popish and Arminian innovations in doctrine may be condignly punished."[11] Only the Royal intervention, adjourning and then dissolving Parliament, saved Cosin from the implementation of these proposals. The "Eleven Years' Tyranny" which followed gave him a respite from the attacks of the puritans, but they renewed them in 1640. Peter Smart laid a set of charges against him, and although his responsibility for the *Devotions* was not discussed again, his other offences confirmed the puritans in that opposition to him which finally forced him into years of voluntary exile.[12]

In 1634 Bishop White, lately translated from Carlisle to Ely, doubtless remembering his earlier association with Cosin and his approval of his views, preferred him from the nominations of the fellows to the vacant mastership of Peterhouse, Cambridge. At the same time, Cosin retained his Durham appointments — although his patron, Neile, had been elected to Winchester (1627) and the archbishopric of York (1631) — and his post as chaplain-in-ordinary to the king, which he had been given in 1627. When he came to Peterhouse, Cosin set out to enforce the high church attitudes he discovered there. The college was already known for the high churchmanship of the two previous masters, Leonard Mawe and Matthew Wren. Mawe and Wren were both known to the court and had enjoyed preferment: they had both accompanied the Prince to Spain on behalf of the ill-fated marriage settlement with the Infanta, and Wren had left Peterhouse for the bishopric of Hereford.

In Tudor and Stuart times, crown and church constantly interfered with the universities. Both masters and fellows were frequently intruded by royal proclamation, "local statutes notwithstanding"; appointment to college office was a common way of rewarding a favorite, or someone with suitable views. James had thus intruded Matthew Wren into the mastership. Although Cosin's appointment to the mastership appears to have followed the usual, legal custom, he was nevertheless enjoying the benefits of faithful service to the established order. As master of Peterhouse he could be securely counted on to promote the doctrine and welfare of the church and king in the university — an obviously important area of influence.

At Peterhouse, Cosin applied his love of ceremony and his devotion to "the ordered past." He enriched the chapel, begun under Wren, with lavish decorations, introducing an elaborate ritual, which included incense, and possibly, if Prynne's subsequent allegation is correct, the use of the canonical hours from his *Devotions*. He further enforced an exacting discipline on the scholars, requiring fines, for example, for absence from prayers.[13] In generally puritan Cambridge, Peterhouse was pre-eminently loyalist. It was first among the colleges to forward its silver to the Royal Mint in July 1642,[14] while Cosin, as principal in all its affairs, early fell victim to the new Parliament. He had been vice-chancellor of the university in 1639–40, and, since the end of 1640, dean of Peterborough, an office to which the king preferred him.[15] As vice-chancellor, Cosin instituted into the university church of Great St. Mary's "innovations" which recalled his activities at Peterhouse and the ceremonies Smart had criticized at Durham.

Such regular practices could not be tolerated by the Commons; they sent for Cosin on November 21, 1640 as a "Delinquent." In the following year, on March 11, he was impeached, being held unfit to hold any office. It is not certain just when he left Cambridge — he could not have remained long in safety — but he had surely set off well before the visitation by the earl of

Manchester in March 1644 with his order from the Long Parliament to "regulate the Universities."[16]

Before leaving England, Cosin perhaps spent some time with friends, in hiding to avoid Parliamentary arrest. We next know of him in Paris, but not until 1645. There he passed the long period until the Restoration as chaplain to the little group of Anglican royalists, preaching encouragement to them, conducting English services at Faubourg St. Germain in the old Laudian way with ceremony and dignity, and writing defences of the English church and her doctrines – of these there were the *Regni Angliae Religio Catholica* (1652) and *History of Popish Transubstantiation* (1655). He was in difficult circumstances, living on gifts from friends and a small pension from the French government, but all the while under Queen Henrietta Maria's cold neglect. Yet Cosin remained strong within the English church, "the Atlas of the Protestant Religion," proving his faith to be based on more than political or economic expediency.[17] He enjoyed small comfort for his loyalty now, nor, when fortunes were so low, could he have looked forward to any ease later.

At the Restoration, Cosin returned to his mastership at Peterhouse, while as dean of Peterborough he resumed services there; soon, however, in October 1660, he was elected to the see of Durham, being consecrated on December 2. At Durham, until his death on January 15, 1672, he proved an energetic bishop, improving and enriching the diocese with lavish building and gifts; he attended as well to the details of diocesan business with watchful interest. Because Cosin was one of the chief survivors of the Laudian regime, he exercised also an important role at the Savoy Conference and at the Convocation for revising the Book of Common Prayer – not since Cranmer had a single man exercised so much influence on the English liturgy.[18]

It has been suggested that Cosin returned from his exile less of a high churchman than he had been in his younger days,[19] but there is little evidence for this. If the *Devotions* gives us a reliable picture, then Cosin's position in 1627 was in fact a good deal more moderate than the clamor of his puritan opponents would lead us to expect, while a consideration of his work for the revision of the Book of Common Prayer leads to the conclusion that in 1661 he wanted to go on from where he had left off twenty years before.[20] Varied and long as Cosin's life was, it reveals a consistency of doctrine and purpose.

His early love for the *Ecclesia Anglicana* finds comparable expression in his later years; his last will reveals him, as we should expect, as firm and unequivocal with respect to Rome as he had always been:

> I am now, and have ever been from my youth, altogether
> free and averse from the corruptions and impertinent new-
> fangled or papistical (so commonly called) superstitions and
> doctrines, and new superadditions to the ancient and primi-
> tive religion and Faith of the most commended, so
> orthodox, and Catholic Church, long since introduced, con-

trary to the Holy Scripture, and the rules and customs of the ancient Fathers.[21]

Equally, his last will reveals his continuing distaste for

> the separatists, the anabaptists, and their followers, (alas) too too many, but also the new independents and pres- byterians of our country, a kind of men hurried away with the spirit of malice, disobedience, and sedition, who by a disloyal attempt (the like whereof was never heard since the world began) have of late committed so many great and execrable crimes, to the contempt and despite of religion and the Christian Faith.[22]

His contacts with the continental reformed churches during his exile left him, if sympathetic, firmly persuaded of their inferiority to the Church of England, which he saw as, of all the reformed churches, "both for doctrine and dis- cipline, the most eminent, and the most pure, the most agreeable to Scripture and antiquity of all others."[23] He could, as in his last will, rise above the divisive issues of the day and state:

> I take it to be my duty, and of all my brethren, especially the Bishops and Ministers of the Church of God, to do our utmost endeavours, according to the measure of grace which is given to every one of us, that at last an end may be put to the differences of religion, or at least that they may be lessened, and that we may "follow peace with all men, and holiness."[24]

Yet here also his lifelong love for the English church finds expression as he confesses himself "most addicted to the symbols, synods, and confessions of the Church of England, or rather the Catholic Church."[25]

With an abiding sense of the majesty and holiness of God, Cosin loved liturgical order and beauty in religion, and devoted much of his life and ability to the advancement of these ideals; to this end he offered the splendid chapel at Auckland Castle − the residence of the bishops of Durham − where he caused his tomb to be inscribed: "In non morituram memoriam Joannis Cosini, Episcopi Dunelmensis."

2

The *Devotions* is properly described as a primer, and belongs, therefore, to an old tradition of Christian devotion, while the provision it makes for the observance of the canonical hours of prayer associates it with an even older and more universal tradition.[26]

The observance of the canonical hours can be traced back to the time of the early fathers, Clement of Alexandria, Origen, Tertullian, and Cyprian, when it was a matter of purely private devotion. By the sixth century in the west, however, as the *Regula* of St. Bernard implies, the daily offices at the canonical hours had become public services, for the lay people and secular clergy as well as the ascetics. Bernard's elaboration of the existing Roman scheme provides for a daily recitation of matins and lauds, prime, terce, sext, none, vespers, and compline. Such a scheme of public observances constituted the Divine Office, which, in various forms, was to be used throughout the west for many centuries.

The individual offices said at the hours followed a general pattern, with an invocation, psalms preceded or followed by a hymn, antiphons, one or more lessons, responsories, and prayers. Such offices would vary according to the liturgical season as well as the time of day. In the course of time, however, the Breviary, the book in which the various divisions of the Divine Office were collected, became so complicated, with its continually varying texts, that in England in the Middle Ages its use had become restricted almost exclusively to the clergy. Lay observance of the canonical hours of the Divine Office had so much declined by the late fourteenth century that Langland might refer in *Piers Plowman* to "the lawe of holy churche":

> And up-on sonedays to cesse · godes seruyce to huyre,
> Boþe matyns and messe · and, after mete, in churches
> To huyre here evesong · every man ouhte.
> ("C" Text, ed. Skeat, 10.227–29)

In place of the Divine Office, popular devotion in the Middle Ages found expression in the prayers of the Primer. The origin of the Primer lies in a series of devotions supplementary to the Divine Office, devised as early as the ninth century by the piety of individuals in the Carolingian monasteries. These devotions were gradually and voluntarily adopted in the course of two or three centuries by the secular clergy in many parts of the western church, so that by the fourteenth century they had come to be regarded as obligatory, and almost a part of the public daily office itself. They included six basic divisions: offices of the dead, and of the Blessed Virgin Mary (the latter known as the Little Office), three groups of Psalms (penitential, gradual, and the commendations), and the Litany. The *Ancrene Riwle,* an anonymous early thirteenth-century work, gives interesting testimony to the growing importance of these supplementary devotions: the author bases the devotional scheme for his three anchoresses entirely on these devotions while making no provision for the use of the Divine Office itself.

Such devotions formed the basis of the book known as the Primer (apparently from the Latin word *primarium,* for prime) which we first find towards the end of the thirteenth century. The central feature of the early primers is the Little Office, an invariable form which modified the seven hours of the Divine Office by the frequent use of the Ave Maria, with a choice of other material − canticles, hymns, little chapters − appropriate to the Blessed Virgin (hence the name by which the medieval Primer was most often known, *Horae Beatissimae Virginis Mariae*). The Primer thus continued to provide for the observance of the canonical hours of prayer; frequently, however, a certain amount of other matter came to be included along with the Little Office and the other basic parts, such as an almanac or table to find the date of Easter, a calendar of saints' days, the Paternoster, the Creed, and the Ten Commandments, with brief expositions, one or more edifying treatises, any number of approved special prayers and graces, a form for the confession of sins. Invariably, however, the hours of the Blessed Virgin, and usually some of the other basic constituents, recur in all the primers of the period. The Primer, in Latin or English or both, could therefore be used to follow at least some of the services recited in Latin in the church, if not the Divine Office itself. In fact, however, it was probably more often regarded and used as a book of private devotion. Whichever way it was used, the Primer established itself as the prayer book of the English lay people in the Middle Ages, becoming the most widely known book among all classes of people. It was the book upon which oaths were sworn, as one of the *Paston Letters,* of 1460, indicates: "My Maister Fastolf, . . . by his othe made on his Primer ther, grauntted and promitted to me" (ed. Gairdner, 1:539).

During the upheavals of the sixteenth century, the Primer enjoyed an extensive popularity: more than 180 editions appeared during the crucial years from 1525 to 1560, most of them in English (although after 1549, when the Book of Common Prayer first appeared, they can have been useful only for private devotion). Several of these were officially authorized, by Henry VIII, Edward VI, Mary, and Elizabeth I, who clearly intended to use them to help establish and protect current theological positions. They reveal the shifting theological emphases of the Reformation. By the time we come to the Elizabethan primers, for example, the Little Office could in no sense be described as "of the Blessed Virgin Mary." Elizabeth put forth her first primer in 1559, and it appeared in a Latin version, the *Orarium,* in the following year; it is this 1560 Primer that Cosin notes on his title-page and obviously used as a model. The *Orarium* provides for the observance of the seven canonical hours, drawing material from the Breviary and the Prayer Book as well as from the Little Office of the earlier primers, and includes two other basic features of the Primer, the Penitential Psalms and the Litany. Cosin's second acknowledged source is the Primer authorized by Elizabeth in 1564, *Preces Privatae,* which appeared again in 1568 and, with revisions and additions, in 1573. Here no midday hours appear at all, but only matins and vespers. Both of these Elizabethan primers include, like many of their predecessors, a large amount of that extra devotional material which made the Primer a means of touching a wide variety of personal and daily requirements.

The growing ascendancy of the Book of Common Prayer during this period, with the accompanying development of private devotions of a more informal, non-liturgical type, helps to explain the virtual disappearance of the Primer after 1564, the few to appear being based on the *Preces Privatae* and the other Elizabethan primers. Cosin's *Devotions* represents a Caroline revival, the classical Anglican version of the Primer and of the canonical hours of prayer.

Cosin's book must have seemed curious to the well-intentioned and literate layman of the time, brought up to approve a less traditional style of devotion. Nothing like it, apart from various unreformed primers for the use of recusants, had been published in England for almost fifty years. The new type of Elizabethan prayer book, such as Thomas Becon's *The Flower of Godly Prayers* (1551) and *The Pomaunder of Prayer* (1558), John Bradford's *Private Prayers and Meditations* (1559) and *Godly Meditations upon the Lordes Prayer* (1562), and John Day's *A Booke of Christian Prayers* (1578), had stirred the popular spirit. These writers offered their wisdom to meet ordinary, everyday needs. Becon, for example, in *The Flower of Godly Prayers,* provides prayers which are like little homilies: "A Prayer against the temptations of the Devil, the World, and the Flesh," "A Prayer against Whoredom," "A Prayer against Slandering and Backbiting." Bradford's *Godly Meditations* relates practical life to the familiar Christian material, the Lord's Prayer and the Commandments, and gives instruction in Christian life, as in "A Meditation for the exercise of true mortification." Often prayers are provided, as in many of the primers, to see one through the day; thus Day's *Booke* has "A Prayer to be said at our first waking," "A Prayer at our uprising," "A Prayer at the putting on of our clothes," and so on, to "A Prayer when we be ready to sleep."

The considerable popularity of this type of book accounts to some extent for the failure of the *Devotions* to win such acclaim as one might expect from an age that took new religious books so eagerly to heart. Sought after and admired in a comparatively small circle, it never won anything like the popularity of a contemporary devotional work, Lewis Bayly's *The Practice of Piety,* which first appeared in 1612, reached its eleventh edition by 1619, and was destined for a fifty-eighth by 1734. Bayly's book (which Bunyan called his favorite) appealed in a different way from Cosin's; Bayly looked back to the popular Tudor books with their prayers fitting many occasions, their meditations on the faith and directives for pious living, while also providing direction and instruction in prayer but not regular prayers at the traditional intervals. Cosin's *Devotions,* standing in the ancient tradition of the Primer, was a very different matter. In a small way it does recall the interests of these newer devotional manuals, with their ample provision of occasional prayers: two at least of Cosin's "Prayers and Thanksgivings for Sundry Purposes" derive from Becon's *Pomaunder of Prayer,* and a few other prayers are similar in type; yet the *Devotions* remains essentially and unmistakably a primer, a somewhat isolated phenomenon in relation to the popular devotional literature of the time.

The *Devotions* is not, however, fully understood when we have seen its important place in the history of the Primer and its tenuous relationship to popular contemporary devotional literature. It needs to be seen also against the background of Laudian churchmanship which Cosin supported. In describing the character of Laudian devotion, one must recognize a dominant and a minor attitude, a more and a less representative form, though both forms may occur together, in varying proportions, within the same work. In its less representative form, Laudian devotion looked towards contemporary Rome, showing an interest in recusant publications such as *A Christian Directorie* (1582) by the Jesuit Robert Persons, and in the translations of continental Roman Catholic writers such as St. François de Sâles, St. Teresa of Avila, and Luis de Granada. This interest generally involved no doctrinal infidelity, and borrowings from Roman Catholic sources were in the spirit of Hooker's distinction:

> Where Rome keepeth that which is ancienter and better;
> others whome we much more affect leavinge it for newer,
> and changinge it for worse, we had rather followe the per-
> fections of them whome we like not, then in defects resem-
> ble them whome we love.[27]

Sometimes, however, doctrines which the Church of England had repudiated at the Reformation were either asserted or implied, as in, to cite perhaps the most extravagant example, Anthony Stafford's *The Femall Glory: or, The Life, and Death of our Blessed Lady, the holy Virgin Mary, Gods owne immaculate Mother* (1635).[28]

In its more characteristic form, however, Laudian devotion paid little attention to contemporary Rome. Deriving to a large extent from Hooker, with Andrewes and Overall as something like the "fathers" of the movement, the more typical Laudian churchmanship sought to express, in worship and prayer and liturgy, that essentially reformed Catholicism which many increasingly recognized as the distinctive development of the English church, and which made it for them, in the words of Cosin's later friend, Sancroft, "the most glorious Church upon earth." A frequently wide and profound acquaintance with the early fathers, an intense sacramentalism, and a firm stress on the liturgical life as provided for in the Book of Common Prayer marked the ethos of this more typical Laudian devotion. Within this ethos Andrewes and Donne preached their sermons, the former framed his *Preces Privatae* (1648), George Herbert wrote *The Temple* (1633) and his manual for *A Priest to the Temple* (that is, *The Country Parson,* published posthumously in 1652), Nicholas Ferrar evolved the community at Little Gidding, and Laud sought to establish "decency and an orderly settlement of the external worship of God in the Church."[29]

Among these men there were of course those whose devotional life was not unaffected by contemporary Roman Catholicism, but always the doctrinal norm was that of the Church of England as they understood it, and the liturgical background that provided by the Book of Common Prayer. While celibacy finds a renewed esteem in Andrewes's praise in his *Preces Privatae* for "the beauty of virgins," while his deep sacramentalism shows itself in reference to "the power of the thrice holy keys and the mysteries in Thy

Church," and while his highest aspiration is "in the holy and catholic Church to have my own calling, and holiness, and portion, and a fellowship of her sacred rites, [and] prayers," there is nevertheless no doubt − the position he took in the controversy with Bellarmine can leave us in no doubt − that such Catholic devotion was for Andrewes part of a full and loyal membership in the Church of England. Likewise with the community at Little Gidding: part of the household's rule possibly derived from that of the Oratories of St. Philip Neri, Nicholas Ferrar could translate a moral treatise by the Belgian Jesuit, Lessius, as well as the "Divine Considerations" of the Spaniard, Valdez, and the sisters bind a copy of the *Introduction to the Devout Life* of St. François de Sâles, yet the whole life of the community was conducted in such a manner as was "agreeable to the Doctrine of the Church of England."[30] Even Laud, who felt able to give official approval to Stafford's floridly Mariolatrous book, was proud to assert that he had lived and should be willing to die "in the faith of Christ, . . . as it is professed in the present Church of England."[31] He appealed constantly to the English articles and canons, to the Prayer Book and the Bible, and he went about his improvements to the conduct and setting of public worship with the moderate conviction that, with regard to externals,

> too many overburden the service of God, and too few leave
> it naked. And scarce anything hath hurt religion more in
> these broken times than an opinion in too many men, that
> because Rome hath thrust some unnecessary and many
> superstitious ceremonies upon the Church, therefore the
> Reformation must have none at all; not considering there-
> while, that ceremonies are the hedge that fence the sub-
> stance of religion from all the indignities which profaneness
> and sacrilege too commonly put upon it. And a great weak-
> ness it is, not to see the strength which ceremonies, −
> things weak enough in themselves, God knows, − add even
> to religion itself.[32]

With much about it that is redolent of older ways, then, the more typical Laudian devotion is yet unequivocally Protestant and shares many of the insights and attitudes of the Reformation.

Within this setting Cosin's *Devotions* is best understood. He does not hesitate to quote some of the later Catholic theologians, to borrow and adapt from the Sarum liturgical texts, to make use of a little recusant book of prayers, *A Manual of Prayers newly gathered out of many . . . authours . . .* (1583); but his work is, from a doctrinal point of view, firmly in the tradition of the Book of Common Prayer. Cosin emphasizes those features of Christian spirituality most strongly reminiscent of the Catholic ethos, and yet he was convinced that his was a position of complete, even especial, loyalty to the Church of England.

One finds in the *Devotions* many of the most characteristic attitudes of the seventeenth-century high churchmen. Cosin reveals a wide and sympathetic knowledge of the teaching and practice of the primitive church "before Popery." Besides adducing the testimony of scripture on many points, he refers with great frequency to the early fathers and councils, and to "the ancient Discipline and religious custome of the Church." He also draws upon the formularies of the reformed Church of England, and implies throughout that the Church of England is a true and sound branch of "*Christs Catholicke Church.*" At the same time we get hints of his understanding of the Reformation in England as a wise and moderate one, and of his disapproval of the unseemliness of puritan worship and of the corruptions of the Church of Rome. Essentially for Cosin, as for most of the sixteenth-century reformers, and for Hooker, Andrewes, and Laud, the English church's choice of "the middle way" is a positive option for primitive and Catholic Christianity.

Cosin shares with his Laudian contemporaries, moreover, a deep reverence for the sacraments, because "they have Gods marke upon them, being set apart and dedicated to the service of his most Holy and fearfull Name." He is careful to distinguish between the two "principall, and truly so called," and the other five which have "not the like nature" — the puritan jibe, whereby he was "Cossens, the 7 sacramentary man," was typically unfair.[33] The frequent references to baptism show that Cosin's attitude is strongly objective: he speaks of it as "the first regeneration." In the Holy Eucharist he understands Christ's most blessed Passion and Sacrifice to be "represented before" God. Cosin also lays great stress upon the liturgy and upon the details of the liturgical year. His "Precepts of the Church," for example, imply a corporate, organic notion of life in the church, a life centered upon the liturgy.[34] In various places he makes it clear that the *Devotions* is to be regarded not as a substitute for, but as a complement to, common prayer; and, in fact, one of the most impressive features of his book is the way in which what it provides interlocks with the Book of Common Prayer.

There are many less prominent features which identify Cosin's *Devotions* as typically Laudian. Among these should be noticed the emphasis on worship and adoration, the "heavenly duty of performing [one's] *Daily & Christian Devotions* to Almighty God," in which we have "a perpetuall *Communion* with the *Saints* triumphant" (urged in the preface to the whole book); the recommendation that such worship should be "with the lowly reverence, even of our Bodies also"; the encouragement to auricular or sacramental confession, "especially before the receiving of Christs blessed Sacrament"; the belief in the Real Presence in the Eucharist (the communicant is advised to say "Amen" after the words of administration); the evident attraction of the 1549 Prayer Book; the strongly *affirmative* character of the prayers. Cosin also shows his close kinship with the Laudians in his citation of the Visitation Articles of Andrewes and Overall, the prefatory refutation of "the common conceit of most Recusant Papists," the attack upon the Sabbatarianism of the puritans, who on the Lord's Day, "under a pretence of serving God more strictly than others (especially for hearing and meditating of Sermons,) doe by their Fasts, and certaine Judaizing observations, condemne the joyfull Festivitie of this High & Holy day";[35] the attitude of reverence to the king, to "his sacred power, and his Soveraigne Authoritie over us." In all of these ways, and in many others, Cosin's *Devotions* belongs essentially in the Laudian setting.

Cosin also reveals many personal qualities in his *Devotions*. The stress upon the Passion, its "extreme sorrow and anguish," but the much greater emphasis upon the goodness and bounty of God and the joyful potentialities of life, "the blessings of Heaven above, and the blessings of the earth beneath," indicate something of the character of his faith — a faith reminiscent, in this respect, of his near contemporary, Thomas Traherne. The evidence of his knowledge of the patristic writings demonstrates his considerable learning. The care with which he quotes so many authorities, and, in controversial matters, specifically Anglican ones, points to the importance to him of orthodoxy. His literary ability is also marked in both prayers and prefaces. An analysis of his prayers reveals a variety of structure, rhythm, and language similar to that of the prayers of the Book of Common Prayer, while the frequent scriptural allusions give an additional richness. From the delicate beauty of the brief prayer "At the washing of our hands," or the Ember prayers "For the health of our Bodies" and "In the time of Advent," to the long and splendid "Prayer and Thanksgiving for the Whole Estate of Christs Catholike Church," Cosin manifests notable skill as a composer and reviser of prayers.[36] His many introductory and explanatory passages — something of an innovation in the Primer — form a distinguished series of lucid expositions on a number of topics, in a prose at once concise, dignified, and pleasing. Many of the earlier primers were untidily put together, often containing matter of little relevance to normal devotional requirements; but the *Devotions,* with its few rubrical directions precise and useful, its neatness of arrangement and comparative economy of content, is an encouragement to an ordered and unburdened devotional life, and reveals an orderly and practical mind in its compiler.

Finally, we may discover in the relationship of the *Devotions* to the Book of Common Prayer, to one aspect of which — that of its complementary quality — I have already briefly referred, its most distinctive contribution to devotional literature and to the development of Anglican liturgy. Cosin was not alone of his time in commending the hours of prayer. For example, Andrewes does this in his *Preces Privatae* and Jeremy Taylor in *A Collection of Offices, Or Forms of Prayer in Cases Ordinary and Extraordinary* (1658), while Laud's *Summarie of Devotions* (1667) gives several prayers at the hours for each day of the week. Cosin's is the fullest Anglican version of the hours in Caroline times, but this is not its only distinction. Cosin's particular achievement lies in providing a series of private devotions which are linked to the medieval offices and are alternative (in certain circumstances prescribed in the preface) to the public prayers of the church which derive from the same medieval sources. Cosin frequently looked back beyond the Prayer Book of 1549: the offices for matins and vespers in the *Devotions,* for example, are close to those in the Book of Common Prayer because Cosin and Cranmer drew upon common sources, the Primer and the Breviary. The *Devotions* thus provides an integral and homogeneous *private* complement to the *common* prayer of the church. That Cosin's compilation should have had a creative influence upon subsequent revision of the Book of Common Prayer is a natural consequence of its unique character.

3

There are two contemporary descriptions of the occasion of Cosin's coming to compile the *Devotions.* John Evelyn, in an entry in his *Diary* dated October 1, 1651, records a story he says he heard from Cosin himself:

> At the first coming over of the *Queene* into *England* she, & her *French* Ladys, were often up-braiding our Religion, that had neither appointed, nor set forth, any *Houres* of Prayer, or *Breviaries,* which Ladies & Courtie[r]s (that have much spare time) might edifie by, & be in devotion, as they had: Our Protestant Ladys scandaliz'd it seemes at this, moved the matter to the *King,* whereupon his Majestie, presently call'd *Bishop White* to him, and asked his thoughts of it, & whither there might not be found some formes of Prayer, proper on such occasions, collected out of some already approved formes? that so the Court-Ladys &c. (who spend much time in trifling) might at least appear as devout, and be so too, as the new-come-over *French* Ladys, who tooke occasion to reproch our want of zeale, & Religion: Upon which the *Bish[o]p* told his Majestie that it might be don easily, & was very necessary: Whereupon the K. commanded him to employ some Person of the *Cleargy* to compile such a Work, & presently the *Bishop* naming *Dr. Cosin:* & the King injoynes him to charge the Doctor in his name to set about it immediately: which *Mr. Deane* told me he did, & 3 monethes after bringing the book to the *King,* he commanded the *Bishop* of *London* to reade it over, & make his report: which was so well liked; that (contrary to former customs) he would needes give it a warrant under his owne hand.[37]

The second report occurs in Peter Heylyn's biography of Laud:

> [There] came out a Book entituled, *A Collection of Private Devotions, or the Hours of Prayer,* composed by *Cozens* one of the *Prebends* of *Durham,* at the Request, and for the

> Satisfaction, as it was then generally believed, of the
> Countess of *Denbigh,* the only Sister of the Duke, and then
> supposed to be unsettled in the Religion here established, if
> not warping from it.[38]

A wave of fashionable conversions to Rome was taking place at the court early in the reign of Charles I. They were, for the most part, sponsored by Endymion Porter's wife, Olivia, and were almost invariably feminine. The Countess of Denbigh was one of the ladies of the court — she became the first lady of the bedchamber to Henrietta Maria — and she may well have been "warping from" the "Religion established" at this time, for she was notoriously unstable in her ecclesiastical allegiance, and did in fact become a Roman Catholic later in life.[39] Probably the countess was one of the "Protestant ladys" who, according to Evelyn, complained to the king. It seems that Charles and his advisers hoped that a book of devotion such as that envisaged might help to sustain some of the ladies in their loyalty to the Church of England.

Evelyn's and Heylyn's accounts, of course, complement each other, but neither of them supports Prynne's later assertion that Cosin had already prepared his collection of devotions quite independently *"for his owne private use,"* nor is there any other evidence for Prynne's statement.[40] Cosin's interests certainly lay in this direction, and he would naturally have felt moved to do such a work, his own interest coinciding with the royal pleasure. Most likely Cosin began his work on the *Devotions* in November or December 1626; working in considerable haste, he had the book licensed on February 22, 1626, and entered in the Stationers' Register on March 1, 1627, to Robert Young.[41]

Although the *Devotions* did not bear the name of the compiler — Cosin's name does not appear until the ninth edition of 1676, the first edition after his death — there was evidently no secret about his part in it.[42] For the group with whom Cosin was associated it was "a Jewel of great Price and value" but to the puritans it was, in Peter Smart's words, a "base begotten bratt . . . that painted fardle."[43] The puritan reaction, which was especially noisy and outspoken, seems to have affected the second edition of 1627. Cosin altered several controversial points and included a piece entitled "The Printer to the Reader" in which he explained that the troublesome points were due to "the Printers haste, or the Correctors oversight," but that these had now been emended. Still later, in September of the same year, "Observatons upon Dr. Cosin's Book" were delivered by Sir Francis Nethersole to the Secretary of State, Lord Conway, who passed them on to the king. This concern demonstrates the effectiveness of puritan criticism — the authorities were at least sensitive to it.[44]

The full force of the puritan attack is best evident in the two pamplets by Prynne and Burton, published between March and June 1628, presumably with the hope of eliciting support from the new Parliament. Prynne, who was to become one of the principal pamphleteers in the puritan cause, wrote *A*

Briefe Survay and Censure of Mr Cozens His Couzening Devotions. Proving both the forme and matter of Mr Cozens his Booke of Private Devotions, or the Houres of Prayer, lately published, be meerely Popish. Burton, who was already involved as a pamphleteer for the puritans, produced *A Tryall of Private Devotions, or a Diall for the Houres of Prayer.*[45] Prynne's pamphlet is a good example of his work, extremely laborious, without a trace of humor, loaded with learned but often irrelevant notes citing Cosin's "Popish" sources; Burton's is notable for its naive, racy, and often rather scurrilous style. The fundamental puritan objection to the *Devotions* becomes clear in these two works. Both complain first of all of the title-page, which, with its "IHS" motif, is "Jesuitical."[46] There are many other offensive points in Cosin's book: the use of the canonical hours; the inclusion of prayers for the dead; references to the ministry of angels; an apparently unsatisfactory distinction made between the two dominical sacraments and the five "somtimes called" sacraments; the use of words like "devotion" or "Catholic," and besides these, many extremely trivial and doctrinally indifferent points.[47]

Prynne and Burton are hardly representative puritans, for the former was an extreme eccentric by any standards, and the latter was embittered by his dismissal from a court appointment; but in their attitude towards the *Devotions* they are typical of the puritans of that time, "Puritans," that is, in religion and church policy, who felt that the Reformation in England had not gone far enough and who wished for further reform of the church from within. The *Devotions,* with its highly traditional appearance, and in its origins associated with the court of Charles I, naturally aroused suspicion among such men. They already regarded the court as virtually papist because of the presence of Henrietta Maria and her entourage and the papal agents, and feared the great influence at court of "Laud's faction." There were grounds, it at least seemed, for fearing an English Counter-Reformation. Looking neither closely nor fairly at the *Devotions,* some saw in it confirmatory evidence of such an "Apostacie from Christ to antichrist," and could charge Cosin (and his friend Mountague) with "Mountebanke Arminianisme and Cozening Poperie." Prynne and Burton illustrate well the radical attitude of the religious puritans. To Burton, trying to put things into some sort of perspective, the King's Primer of 1545 appeared "in the dawning of the Gospell in England," while the Elizabethan primers were further measures in the process of reformation, but showing "a tender regard . . . of the weaknesse of the time," the last of them, the 1573 edition, being "yet more exact . . . as the more distant still from the Horarium" (the 1560 edition). Cosin's Primer, on the other hand, appearing unexpectedly and subversively in "our aged and noontide seasons of the Gospell," was no less than a step on the way *back* to Popery, the provision for the observance of the canonical hours importing nothing else "but a necessitie of bringing in Monkerie and so of erecting cells again." To Prynne the danger implicit in the publication of the *Devotions* was equally real, for he saw it as a threat to the state. He thereby reminds us of how puritanism in religion and church policy almost inevitably merged with political puritanism: "Our State

Enemies, are no other but our Church Enemies; our State greivances, are but the fruites and issues of our Church annoyances (sig. A4ʳ). However ill-founded the fears of Prynne and Burton and of many persons more reasonable than they, it is easy to understand how, at a time of growing mistrust, when the tensions which finally found expression in the civil war were mounting, a book like the *Devotions* should arouse such hostility.

In spite of the vigor of the puritan attack upon the *Devotions* and its compiler, the book achieved an immediate popularity in a much wider circle than that offered by the ladies of the court. The first edition was a small one, perhaps between 150 and 250, but the second and third editions of later 1627 were both much larger, estimates giving 1,000 and 1,500.[48] Interest persisted in the *Devotions*, with five more editions appearing in Cosin's lifetime. After the twelfth edition of 1719, there followed a long period during which acquaintance with the book was evidently very slight, until 1838, when a further edition was published. This renewed interest is to be attributed to the Tractarians' early intention of continuing and reviving the churchmanship of the Caroline divines; to this aspect of the Anglican revival in the nineteenth century we may attribute the publication of a further four editions up to that of 1867 — the seventeenth and last before my Oxford edition of 1967.

There are other evidences of the persistent appeal of the *Devotions*. Cosin's version of the canonical hours was used by at least one of the early English sisterhoods of the nineteenth century, the Church of England Sisterhood of Mercy of Devonport and Plymouth, while in Bishop Wilberforce's experiment of a retreat at Cuddesdon in 1860 it was again used.[49] There have been borrowings from the *Devotions*, from the seventeenth century to our own time, in other books of private devotion; and the revisions of the Book of Common Prayer, both in 1662, and, in various churches of the Anglican Communion, in this century, have been influenced by Cosin's compilation.[50]

The long series of editions through which *A Collection of Private Devotions* has gone is testimony to its persisting appeal. It is also a work of considerable interest in several other respects. It stands firmly within an ancient tradition of devotional literature, and is yet in many ways a fresh and individual contribution to that tradition. Its material, as written and revised by Cosin, has for the most part an intrinsic excellence, with its own historical interest: the situation in the court of Charles I which occasioned its compilation, and the character of the puritan reaction to its publication, provide useful illustrations of the tensions and controversies of the times. It is a fruit of that distinctive English spirituality, Catholic and reformed, of which the Book of Common Prayer is the corporate, liturgical expression, and it provides, in particular, a wide-ranging illustration of the nature of Laudian or Caroline churchmanship and devotion, so exact an illustration, in fact, that we might describe it as the typical Laudian text. Essentially of its time, Cosin's *Devotions* remains a fine witness to

> that true *Devotion*, wherwith God is more delighted, and a
> good soule more inflamed and comforted, than with all the

> busie subtilties of the world. In which sense S. AUSTIN was
> wont to say, that *The pious and devout, though unlearned,*
> *went to heaven, whiles other men, trusting to their learning,*
> *disputed it quite away.*[51]

Notes

1. The *DNB* gives 1594, evidently an error. Cosin, in a letter to his
secretary Miles Stapleton, of January 2, 1671/2, remarks that he is "76 yeares
at St. Andrews day last past." The letter is one of several, all to Stapleton,
formerly in the library of Peterhouse, Cambridge, now in the Cosin's Library,
University of Durham. See A. I. Doyle, "John Cosin (1595–1672) as a
Library Maker," *The Book Collector* 40 (1991): 335–57.

   Cosin's various writings were collected in the nineteenth century in
The Library of Anglo-Catholic Theology as *The Works of . . . John Cosin*, 5
vols. (Oxford: John Henry Parker, 1843–55). Much of his correspondence,
"illustrative of his life and times," was published for the Surtees Society
under the editorship of George Ornsby (Durham, 1869–72). Both collections,
but particularly the latter, contain biographical notices based especially on
the seventeenth-century life by Cosin's domestic chaplain and preacher at his
funeral, Isaac Basire, *The Dead Man's Real Speech* (London, 1673); and also
on Thomas Smith's *Vita . . . Joannis Cosini,* included in his *Vitae Quorundam*
Eruditissimorum et Illustrium Virorum (London, 1707). There are of course
many contemporary notices of Cosin, especially by his opponents such as
William Prynne, in *Canterburies Doome* (1646), but also by Thomas Fuller in
The Church History (1655) and in *The History of the Worthies of England*
(1662). The Durham antiquarian Robert Surtees mentions Cosin in his *His-*
tory of Durham (1843) and the long notice of him in the *DNB* is by J. H.
Overton. But the most recent biographical study, and the only one that
attempts fullness, is *A Life of John Cosin* by P. H. Osmond (London: A. R.
Mowbray, 1913), an unimaginative history which mainly summarizes Cosin's
published *Works* and *Correspondence.* But more recently, G. J. Cuming
prefaced his edition of *The Durham Book* (London: Oxford University Press,
1961) with a detailed description of Cosin's importance to the liturgical conferences at the Restoration, while in *A History of Anglican Liturgy* (London:
Macmillan, 1969), Cuming provides a general narrative of "The Grand
Debate"; and John G. Hoffman has written on "John Cosin . . . Champion of
the Caroline Church" (Ph.D. diss., University of Wisconsin, 1977), and published several articles, including "The Arminian and the Iconoclast: The Dispute between John Cosin and Peter Smart," *Historical Magazine of the*
Protestant Episcopal Church 48 (1979), 274–301. Robert S. Bosher, *The*
Making of the Restoration Settlement: The Influence of the Laudians
1649–1662 (London: Dacre Press, 1951), gives an illuminating view of Cosin's
situation, along with the other Laudians, during the Paris exile. H. Boone

Porter, Jr. contributed a valuable discussion of the *Devotions* to *Theology* 56 (1953): 54–58, "Cosin's Hours of Prayer: A Liturgical Review." L. W. Hanson's bibliographical study of the first three editions is indispensable: "John Cosin's *Collection of Private Devotions,* 1627," *The Library* 13 (1958): 282–87. On Cosin's architectural achievements, see Nikolaus Pevsner's *County Durham* in the Penguin Series of The Buildings of England (1953), esp. 31–33, and John Cornforth, "Auckland Castle, Co. Durham," an illustrated series that appeared in *Country Life,* January 27, 1972 (pp. 198–202), February 3, 1972 (pp. 266–70), and February 10, 1972 (pp. 334–37).

I am indebted to the Reverend Daniel O'Connor of the College of the Ascension, Birmingham (UK) for his collaborative help with this study, which originally appeared in the introduction of my edition of John Cosin's *A Collection of Private Devotions* (Oxford: Clarendon Press, 1967). The present version is slightly revised.

2. He was "admitted to the scholars' table, March 25, 1610." His tutor was John Browne, a fellow of the college. Cf. *Biographical History of Gonville and Caius College,* compiled by John Venn (Cambridge, 1897), 1:207.

3. Overall, who had been Regius Professor of Divinity at Cambridge (from 1595 to 1607), was a particularly influential figure in the development of that movement which Nicholas Tyacke describes in his important book, *Anti-Calvinists: The Rise of English Arminianism c. 1590–1640* (1987; repr. Oxford: Clarendon Press, 1990), cited also in chap. 2, n. 2.

4. Smith, *Vita,* 4. See Tyacke, *Anti-Calvinists,* 106–24, on "Bishop Neile and the Durham House group." I am well aware of the general difficulty of using the designation "puritan," and of those recent historians, who, like Tyacke, would, quite properly, abandon the term altogether or at least be discerning in their use of it.

5. See "The Sum and Substance of the Conferences Lately Had at York House concerning Mr. Mountague's Books," in Cosin's *Works,* 2:17–81; and see Tyacke, *Anti-Calvinists,* 125–80.

6. Cosin, *Works,* 1:93. The expression *via media* is, of course, an invention of the Tractarians. I do not believe that Hooker and his earlier seventeenth-century descendants in fact regarded the English church as a "mean" or as a compromise between "extremes," though it is easy for us to have this impression. The essential point of Cosin, of Mountague, and others like them, is their belief in the truth of *their* church, and that its polity reflects primitive and traditional discipline. This idea helps to explain George Herbert's "The British Church": "I Joy, deare Mother, when I view / Thy perfect lineaments and hue / Both sweet and bright."

7. Ibid. 1:94, Sermon 6: "Dominica Prima Adventus, Decembris 3, 1616 . . . in Durham House Chapel, in London." White had taken part in the first two "conferences" with Fisher in 1622 – Laud met Fisher in the celebrated third and last. For a discussion of Cosin's sermons, see my "John Cosin as Homilist," *Anglican Theological Review* 47 (1965): 276–89.

8. *Appello Caesarem,* 112–13.

9. Smart, *Popish Ceremonies,* 6.
10. See *Commons Debates for 1629,* ed. W. Notestein and F. H. Relf, University of Minnesota Studies in the Social Sciences, 10 (Minneapolis, 1921), 36.
11. Ibid., 100.
12. Smart's petition dated "Novemb. 3. 1640" was read in the House only a week later.
13. Exactly what the ritual at Peterhouse consisted of is not clear; one must rely on reports given often secondhand and then by those most opposed to Cosin's practices. Prynne alleges that Cosin had introduced the observance of the canonical hours into Peterhouse, based evidently upon his *Devotions,* "as was attested upon Oath by Mr. *Le Greese* and others" (*Canterburies Doome,* 208). Prynne, in an earlier passage (p. 74), styles this observer "Master *Nicholas le Greise* (late Student in Cambridge)," but he is otherwise unidentified.

Most of what is known about the Peterhouse chapel in Cosin's time is described by R. Willis and J. W. Clark, *The Architectural History of the University of Cambridge* (Cambridge, 1886), vol. 1, part 1, "Peterhouse," and chap. 6, "History of the Chapel," 45–46, and by Sir Herbert Butterfield, late master, in the *Victoria County History of Cambridge and the Isle of Ely* (1959), 3: "The City and University of Cambridge," 334–40, esp. 337. Allan Pritchard discovered a more detailed – though puritan – description of Cosin's Cambridge. He discusses Harley MS 7019 (in the British Library) in the *Times Literary Supplement* (July 2, 1964): "Puritan Charges Against Crashaw and Beaumont." T. A. Walker, the Peterhouse historian, relates a few of the details of college life during Cosin's mastership in *Peterhouse* (Cambridge: W. Heffer, 1935), 56. See John G. Hoffman, "The Puritan Revolution and the 'Beauty of Holiness' at Cambridge," *Proceedings of the Cambridge Antiquarian Society* 72 (1984): 93–105.

The dominant sympathy of Peterhouse lay with the royalists, but the college did lodge some notable puritans of whom the best known was John Hutchinson (1615–64), the "Regicide." His *Life,* written by his widow and first published in 1806, describes his five years at Peterhouse from which "he came away . . . untainted with those [Arminian] principles or practises" taught by Wren and Cosin. See *Memoirs of the Life of Colonel Hutchinson . . . Written by His Widow Lucy,* 3rd ed. (London, 1810), 1:78.
14. Cosin's signature is on a college order, now in the treasury, dated July 2, 1642, for sending plate to the king. On the forwarding of the plate, see J. B. Mullinger, *The University of Cambridge . . .* (1911), 3:231–37, 267–68.
15. Cosin was instituted dean of Peterborough on November 7, 1640. Laud had written to Thomas Morton, bishop of Durham, on July 18, 1639: "I have received your letters of July the 3rd, by the hands of Dr. Cosin; and I heartily thank your Lordship for them. For the Doctor, I do very well know his deserts are great, and his means not so. But his Majesty hath a very good opinion of him; and that will, I doubt not, in good time mend his fortunes" (*The Works of William Laud,* in The Library of Anglo-Catholic Theology

[Oxford: Parker, 1847–62], 6:567). Among the charges against Laud which Prynne notices in *Canterburies Doome* there is his habit of promoting "popish" and "superstitious" men, including Cosin (p. 532). But Laud defends himself before this particular accusation (p. 356): "I presented four of his Majesties Chaplaines in ordinary to his Majestie for the Deanery of Peterborough: His Majesty pitched upon Doctor Cosin in regard his meanes lying in the Bishoprick of Durham was in the Scots hands, and nothing left to maintain him, his wife and children, but a poor Headship worth 40 l. per annum; And out of the same consideration, and no other, did I put his name with his Majesty" (Laud, *Works,* 4:293–94).

16. The iconoclast William Dowsing made his famous visit to Peterhouse on December 21, 1643, but he makes no mention of Cosin. It is very likely that Cosin had already left by then.

17. The source of these comments is of course a friendly one. See Fuller, *The Worthies of England:* "Whilest he remained in *France,* he was the *Atlas* of the *Protestant Religion,* supporting the same with his Piety and Learning, confirming the wavering therein, yea dayly adding *Proselytes . . .* thereunto" (295). Cosin in fact seems to have felt more sympathetic toward the reformed churches as his exile drew on; at least the French Protestants showed more friendliness than the Roman Catholics. In a letter to Richard Watson, dated June 19, 1646, and first printed in 1684 as "The Right Reverend Doctor John Cosin . . . His Opinion . . . for Communicating rather with Geneva than Rome," Cosin says: "It is far less safe to joyn with these men [i.e. the Roman Catholics], that alter the *Credenda,* the *Vitals* of Religion, than with those that meddle only with the *Agenda* and *Rules* of Religion, if they meddle no farther. . . " (3). The letter is republished in Cosin's *Works,* 4:385–86. Cosin's only son caused his father some sadness by leaving the Church of England for Rome in 1652. He became a Jesuit priest while in residence at the English College in Rome, and in 1659 he was sent as a missionary to England.

18. "With [Matthew] Wren, the most copious contributor to the Prayer Book since Archbishop Cranmer" (*The Durham Book,* xv). Cf. Cuming's summary description of Cosin's influence in *A History of Anglican Liturgy,* chap. 7, "The Grand Debate," cited in n. 1, above.

19. The suggestion is made by Osmond, *Life,* 320, who gives a certain amount of rather flimsy evidence in support of this view, and by Cuming, *Durham Book,* xv, who does not attempt to substantiate it.

20. This is Cuming's estimate in *The English Prayer Book 1549–1662,* ed. A. M. Ramsey, et al. (London, 1963), 110.

21. Cosin, *Works,* 4:527. This is Basire's translation of Cosin's *Ultimum Testamentum* which he published in *The Dead Man's Real Speech.*

22. Ibid.

23. Ibid., 5:526 ("On Confirmation").

24. Ibid., 4:527.

25. Cosin, *Works,* 4:526–27.

26. The following discussion is indebted to several authorities: E. Bishop, *Liturgica Historica* (Oxford, 1918); C. C. Butterworth, *The English Primers, 1529–1545* (Philadelphia, 1953); E. Hoskins, *Horae Beatae Mariae Virginis* (London, 1901); E. C. Ratcliff, "The Choir Offices," in *Liturgy and Worship,* ed. W. K. Lowther Clarke (London, 1932); H. C. White, *The Tudor Books of Private Devotion* (Madison, Wisc., 1951), esp. chaps. 3 and 4; C. Wordsworth and H. Littlehales, *The Old Service Books of the English Church* (London, 1904).

27. See *Of the Lawes of Ecclesiastical Polity,* 5.28.1 in *Works of Richard Hooker,* ed. W. Speed Hill (Cambridge, Mass.: Harvard University Press, 1977), 2:121.

28. Stafford gives a florid description of the Virgin's life: her prudence, her beauty are evoked; her Conception, her Purification, her Assumption are imaginatively detailed. In the preface "To the Masculine Reader," however, he declared: "if I have swerved in any the least point from the tenents received in the English Church, I shall bee most ready to acknowledge my selfe a true Penitent" (sig. C3^r). Stafford's enraptured *Life* apparently found many friends, for he received the official approval of the Primate and of Bishop Juxon.

29. Laud, "Epistle Dedicatory" to *Conference with Fisher,* in *Works,* 2:xvi.

30. B. Blackstone, ed., *The Ferrar Papers* (Cambridge: Cambridge University Press, 1938), 55.

31. Laud, *Conference with Fisher,* in *Works,* 2:373.

32. Ibid., "Epistle Dedicatory" to *Conference with Fisher,* 2:xvi–xvii.

33. *Acts of the High Commission Court within the Diocese of Durham* (Surtees Society, 1857), 34:200. Cosin's careful distinction is in marked contrast with the way in which Robert Shelford, an old alumnus of Peterhouse, in his *Five Pious and Learned Discourses* (Cambridge, 1635), makes an undifferentiated seven of them: "Which way soever you turn you, here you shall finde the saying of our Saviour fulfilled, *Thus it becometh us to fulfill all righteousnesse.* Desire you new life? here is Baptisme to give it. Are you gone from it? here is the Baptisme of tears and penance to restore it. Want you weapons for the spirituall warre? here is the Catechisme, and Confirmation. Need you food for the new life? here is the bread and wine of Christs body and bloud. Want you supply of vertuous young souldiers? here is Matrimonie and Christian education. Need you leaders and governours? here are Christs Ministers. Want you provision for the journey to the high Jerusalem? here is the *viaticum* of the heavenly Manna expressed in the Communion of the sick" (35). The contrast of this with Cosin's entry on "The Sacraments of the Church" points to the difference between what I have called the less and the more representative forms of Laudian devotion. Cosin writes simply: "The principall, and truly so called, (as generally necessary to salvation) are *Baptisme* and *The Lords Supper.* The other five . . . though they be somtimes called, & have the name of Sacraments, yet have they not the like nature that the Two principall and true Sacraments have" (*Devotions,* ed. Stanwood, 54).

34. "To observe the *Festivals* and Holy dayes appointed. 2 To keep the *Fasting dayes* with devotion and abstinence. 3 To observe the *Ecclesiastical Customes* and *Ceremonies* established . . . 4 To repaire unto the publike Service of the Church for *Mattens* and *Evensong* . . . 5 To receive the *Blessed Sacrament* of the *Body* and *Blood* of Christ with frequent devotion" (*Devotions,* 53–54). For some illuminating observations on Cosin's Precepts, see Martin Thornton, *English Spirituality* (London: SPCK, 1963), 263–64.

35. See "Offenders against the fourth Commandement," *Devotions,* 47; the important reference to Andrewes's and Overall's Visitation Articles occurs on p. 54, in which they particularly commend auricular confession.

36. *At the washing of our hands:* "Cleanse me, O God, by the bright fountaine of thy mercy, and water me with the dew of thine abundant grace, that being purified from my sinnes, I may grow up in good workes, truly serving thee in holines and righteousnes all the dayes of my life (*Devotions,* 66)."

For the health of our Bodies: "O God the Father of Lights, from whom commeth downe every good and perfect gift, mercifully looke upon our frailtie and infirmitie, and grant us such health of Body, as thou knowest to be needfull for us: that both in our Bodies and Soules we may evermore serve thee with all our strength and might, through Jesus Christ our Lord" (261).

In the time of Advent: "Grant we most humbly beseech thee, O heavenly Father, that with holy *Simeon,* and *Anna,* and all thy devout servants, who waited for the consolation of Israel, we may at this time so serve thee with fasting and prayer: that by the celebration of the Advent and Birth of our blessed Redeemer, we may with them be filled with true joy and consolation, through the same Jesus Christ our Lord" (262).

Prayer and Thanksgiving for the Whole Estate of Christs Catholike Church: "Almighty God, who by thy holy Apostle hast taught us to make Prayers & Supplications for all men: we humbly beseech thee most mercifully to receive these our prayers, which wee offer unto thy divine Majestie for all men in generall: and more especially for thine owne people, the holy Catholik Church, the Mother of us all that beare the Name of Christ: beseeching thee to inspire it continually with the Spirit of truth, unitie, and concord: and grant that all they who doe confesse thy holy Name, may agree in the truth of thy holy Word, and live in unitie and godly love, being one Fold, under one Shepheard, Jesus Christ our Lord. And here forasmuch as we be not onely taught to pray, but to give Thanks also for all men, we doe offer up unto thee most high laud, and heartie thanks for all thy wonderfull Graces and Vertues, which thou hast declared in all thy Saints, and by them bestowed upon thy holy Church from the beginning of the world: and chiefly in the glorious and most blessed Virgin MARIE, the Mother of thy Sonne Jesus Christ our Lord: as also in the blessed Angels of Heaven: & in all other holy persons upon earth, who by their Lives and Labours have shined forth as Lights in the severall generations of the World: such as were the holy Patriarchs, Prophets, Apostles, and Martyrs, whom we remember with honour, and commemorate with joy: and for whom, as also for all other thy happie Servants our Fathers and Brethren, who have departed this life with the seale of Faith, and doe now rest in the sleepe of peace, wee prayse and magnifie thy glorious Name: most humbly desiring, that wee may still continue in their holy Communion, and enjoy the comfort thereof while we are on earth, following with a glad will and mind their holy examples of godly living and stedfastnes in thy Faith: and that at the last day we with them, and they with us may attaine to the resurrection of the just, and have our perfect consummation both of soule and body in the Kingdome of heaven. For these, and for all other things that Thou, O God, wouldst have us to pray, and to praise thy great Name, we are bold to call upon thee, and say as Christ our Lord hath taught us. *Our Father, &c.*" (284–85). While the basis of this last prayer is the Prayer for the Church in the Order of Holy Communion (from the Book of Common Prayer, 1549), Cosin has freely adapted it here.

37. See *The Diary of John Evelyn*, ed. E. S. de Beer (Oxford: Clarendon Press, 1955), 3:45–46. There is a second version, in all essentials like this one, but dated wrongly (October 12) and apparently written long after the actual occurrence. Cf. Appendix A, 634–36.

38. See *Cyprianus Anglicus* (London, 1668), 173. Jeremy Collier follows Heylyn in his *An Ecclesiastical History of Great Britain* (London, 1714), 2:714.

39. Susan, first Countess of Denbigh, was the sister of Sir George Villiers, Duke of Buckingham. The earl (William Feilding) died during Prince Rupert's attack on Nottingham in 1643. Richard Crashaw addressed a verse epistle to the Countess of Denbigh "the Noblest & best of Ladyes, . . . Perswading her to Resolution in Religion" (published for the first time in 1652, and again, in a much altered version, in 1653). See *The Poems English Latin and Greek of Richard Crashaw*, ed. L. C. Martin, 2nd ed. (Oxford: Clarendon Press, 1957), xxxi–xxxiii, 236–38, 347–50.

40. C. J. Stranks, *Anglican Devotion* (London, 1961), 67, makes the same suggestion, but without reference to Prynne. Cf. Prynne, *A Briefe Survay and Censure of Mr Cozens His Couzening Devotions* (1628), 26.

41. There are a number of indications that Cosin did his work in some haste. He told Evelyn that it was done in three months; Prynne says in *A Briefe Survay* (92) that "the Printer had his written Coppy but by peecemeale, sheete by sheete, and not compleate together." Prynne also hints at irregularities in the licensing of the *Devotions*, as does Burton in *A Tryall of Private Devotions* (1628).

42. It was first attributed to Cosin in a newsletter to Joseph Mead dated May 16, 1627. See T. Birch, *Court and Times of Charles I* (London, 1848), 1:227, quoted in Cosin's *Correspondence*, 1:126.

43. See Heylyn, 174, and also "Articles . . . to be exhibited by his Majestie's Heigh Commissioners, against Mr. John Cosin," in Cosin's *Correspondence*, 1:195.

44. Ibid. 1:125–26. Cf. "Observations upon Dr. Cosin's Book, Entitled The Hours of Prayers," *State Papers Domestic* 78:19 (Charles I.1627: Sept. 13).

45. Heylyn describes Prynne's attack in some detail but says nothing specifically about Burton, of whose work "there was but little notice taken,"

although Smart gives equal credit to the two pamphleteers. He says: "This pedler's pack, going under the name of John Cosin, hath been layd open to the vew of the world by many, but chiefly by 2 very excellent writers, Mr. Burton and Mr. Prinn, who have so wel discovered the hidden cosenage of the false wares, cunningly couched togeather in that painted fardle, that now theare is little danger that any but very ideotts should be deceived therwith" (Cosin, *Correspondence,* 1:195). Cosin himself seems to have regarded them as equally troublesome, referring to them in a letter to Laud as "these two barking libellers" (*Correspondence,* 1:139).

46. According to Thomas B. Stroup, the imagery and design of the title-page of the *Devotions* may have influenced George Herbert's "The Altar." See "'A Reasonable, Holy, and Living Sacrifice': Herbert's 'The Altar,'" *Essays in Literature* (Macomb, Ill.) 2:149–63.

47. Cosin's answers to many of these charges can be seen in a paper entitled "The Objections which some have been pleased to make against a Booke intituled the Houres of Praier: with briefe Answeres thereunto," included in the *Correspondence,* 1:127–36. It is endorsed in Cosin's hand, "For ye R^t. R^d. and my honorable good Lord, The Lord Bishop of Durham," and marked, among the *State Papers Domestic* 65:72 (1627: May?); but this date must be in error since Cosin evidently takes account of the pamphlets of Prynne and Burton which appeared between March and June of 1628. It is therefore likely that Cosin sent this paper not to Bishop Neile, as Ornsby (the editor of the *Correspondence*) assumes, but to Bishop Mountain who had licensed the *Devotions.* Mountain was nominated bishop of Durham, in succession to Neile, on February 15, 1628, although he was further nominated to York on June 4, probably before the Durham appointment was confirmed.

48. See L. W. Hanson, "John Cosin's *Collection of Private Devotions, 1627," The Library* 13 (1958): 284. In a letter to Cosin, dated July 2 [1627], Mountague writes: "We did in the country talk strangly of your booke before it was commen. But now, for ought I heare, σεσίγηται. What they say att London οὐκ ἔχω φράσαι, only this, you left order I should have 3, and I could scarce gett one" (Cosin, *Correspondence,* 1:124).

49. The *Devotions* may well have been used at Peterhouse (see n. 12), and at Little Gidding, though there is little evidence for justifying either suggestion. A scurrilous anonymous pamphlet, *The Arminian Nunnery* (1641), suggests, though not with much conviction, that the *Devotions* may have been used by the community at Little Gidding for their night offices: "They have promiscuous private Prayers all the night long by nightly turnes, just like as the English *Nunnes* at Saint *Omers* and other Popish places: which private Prayers are (as it seemes) taken out of *John Cozens* his *Cozening* Devotions, (as they are rightly discovered to be by Orthodox men) and extracted out of divers Popish *Prayer-Bookes*" (sig. B2^r). The author may, however, have been merely embellishing his account with appropriately lurid speculations, since his pamphlet is known to have been based on a letter written by one Edward Lenton in 1634, describing a recent visit to Little Gidding, in which he makes

no reference to the *Devotions.* See Alan Maycock, *Chronicles of Little Gid-ding* (London: SPCK, 1954), 41. Cf. Hugh Trevor-Roper, *Catholics, Anglicans and Puritans: Seventeenth-century essays* (1987; repr. London: Fontana Press, 1989), esp. chap. 2, "Laudianism and Political Power," *passim.* In giving easy credence to Cosin's detractors, Trevor-Roper draws a generally unfavorable (and consequently unfair) portrait of him.

50. For a detailed list of borrowings, see my edition of the *Devotions,* preface, li–liii, and also the commentary on the calendar, 323–25.

51. *Devotions,* 14.

10

A Portrait of Stuart
Orthodoxy

OF THE SMALL group of writers, both poets and priests, who rallied about what we should now style the High Church Movement in seventeenth-century Cambridge, Richard Crashaw is best known, and his history most familiar. But Joseph Beaumont (1616–99)[1] may be more typical because less original and inspired, a minor figure of an age who more greatly receives than shapes its tendencies; for, with straightforward and steady vision, he clearly reveals many of the same influences that Crashaw knew but may have stated less explicitly. Associated at Peterhouse before the outbreak of the civil war, they shared many of the same interests, especially in the "divinely established" monarchy and episcopacy with its high church discipline and worship, and in the introduction of Catholic and devotional themes into English religious poetry. Beaumont has never attracted much attention, however, perhaps because of the formidable extent and diffuseness of his works – his allegorical epic on the soul's pilgrimage with its nearly 40,000 lines easily exceeds in length *The Faerie Queene* – perhaps, and more probably, because of the homage paid to his greater contemporary Crashaw.

 The general circumstances of an age certainly help to form a person's mind, but not necessarily to force it, for one has a special sensibility and independence to act upon, and, in a great measure, to do with as desire may urge. Beaumont was a man of his age, to be sure, but he also possessed an intelligence of his own. In this account of him, I should wish to suggest what events made the man, but also what sense he gave to them. Herein will be a contribution to the history of the times, a history broadly typical of the Caroline divine who dabbled in the arts, and whose own fate paralleled the rise and decline of influence and rise again to power of the seventeenth-century Anglican clergy.

 In addition to what Beaumont's life shows of its times, it offers interest for its own sake. Yet biographies of Beaumont are few, and these range either from the merest sketch, like the entry in the *Dictionary of National Biography,* or they reflect private whims, like the eccentric interpretation by A. B. Grosart in the introduction to his edition in "The Chertsey Worthies' Library" of *The Complete Poems of Joseph Beaumont,* 2 vols. (Edinburgh,

1880). There is need now for a life of Beaumont sympathetic to his special qualities and full enough to show his true significance.

1

In the earlier seventeenth century, Peterhouse became closely identified with the royalist and episcopal cause. Under the guidance of several masters who espoused royalism and, inseparably, the established church, Peterhouse came to have an academic regimen, firmly fixed by Beaumont's time, that reflected the obedience, unity, and order enjoined by the church, especially by the liturgical reforms of William Laud, from 1633 archbishop of Canterbury. John Cosin, who accepted the mastership of Peterhouse in 1634, was one of Laud's most faithful and important clergymen. Having already proved himself an active and able apologist for Laudian church reform, he was one of the high church party most actively opposed to the puritans and the reforming protestants. He had, in 1626, defended the outspoken Richard Mountague, whose *Appello Caesarem* (1625) gave offense to the Calvinist leaders of the church. He had assembled a book of devotions at the request of Charles I; and he had while prebendary of Durham Cathedral introduced elaborate forms of worship of the kind which later he would bring to the chapel at Peterhouse − at Durham they drew him into a quarrel with the puritan prebendary, Peter Smart.[2]

At Peterhouse, Cosin's high church sympathies found a friendly circle. His watchful care in preserving the proprieties of religion elicited the kindest response, for the college was already accustomed to the high churchmanship of two previous masters, Matthew Wren and Leonard Mawe, who, as chaplains to Prince Charles, had joined the Prince in Spain in 1623 to help arrange the Spanish marriage. Cosin supported this loyalist tradition. The puritan polemicist William Prynne, who had attacked him for his "Catholic" book of devotions, later reported in his well known animadversions on popery at Cambridge − in colorfully exaggerated terms − the supposed customs of Peterhouse chapel: "There was a glorious new *Altar* set up, & mounted on steps, to which the Master, Fellowes, Schollers bowed, & were enjoyned to bow by Doctor *Cosens* the Master, who set it up; . . . there were Basons, Candlestickes, Tapers standing on it, and a great Crucifix hanging over it." He quotes, with yet more horror, one Nicholas le Greise, "late Student in *Cambridge*," who is said to have witnessed upon oath

> that in Peter House there was . . . a carved Crosse at the
> end of every seat, and on the Altar a Pot, which they usually
> called the incense pot: that the Master, Fellows, and Schollers of that house at their entring into, & going out of the
> Chappell, made a low obeysance to the Altar, being
> enjoyned by Doctor *Cosens* under a penalty (as they
> reported) to doe it; and none of them might turne their
> backs towards the Altar going in nor out of the Chappell:

> That divers Schollers of other houses usually resorted
> thither, some out of Curiosity only to behold, others to
> learne and practise the Popish Ceremonies and Orders used
> in that Chappell.[3]

Cosin nourished royalist and high church sympathies with some success, for
he was not only deprived of his ecclesiastical benefices early in 1640 by vote
of the Commons but also ejected from the mastership in the general parliamentary order for "regulating" the universities in March 1644.

The events of Joseph Beaumont's early years prepared him to move
easily into the company of Peterhouse and find a congenial place there. His
father, John Beaumont, an espouser of high church principles, was a cloth
merchant of Hadleigh (Suffolk), and several times mayor of that town.
Observing in his son an unusual ability at learning, he may have considered
sending him to Westminster; but he determined that his son should remain at
home in Hadleigh and attend the grammar school there. Grosart, in his
idiosyncratic introduction to *The Complete Poems,* calls this an unhappy deci-
sion; at Westminster he would have learned better Latin, and he would have
become less provincial.[4] Such a judgment overlooks an important emphasis
on locality; for it was customary in Caroline England, at least in East Anglia,
that the local school, usually conducted by the resident clergy, should provide
education for the parish youth. The young Beaumont would naturally enough
have been directed toward it.[5]

Beaumont's opportunities for going to the university were not
diminished during these early years. While at home he was beginning to
esteem tradition – both in moral instruction, through the guidance of the
established church, and in intellectual training, through the discipline of the
grammar school – he was, in fact, being excellently readied for the milieu in
which he would soon live, and to which he proved to be so well suited. For in
1631, at the age of sixteen, in the same year that Richard Crashaw entered
Pembroke, Joseph Beaumont was admitted into Peterhouse.[6]

An agreeable life, these years at Peterhouse. Heartened by its
ceremony and tradition; surrounded by friends of like spirit, among them
Richard Crashaw, from 1635 a fellow of Peterhouse;[7] guided by the order,
watchful and strict, of Cosin, Beaumont flourished. He must have enjoyed his
work and his contemplation, peacefully pursued. When, a few years later, as
fellow and tutor,[8] he no longer could carry on his studies in the unbroken way
which he had formerly enjoyed, Beaumont complained in a letter to his father:
"When I was a Beginner, under tuition, I enjoyed that freedom of spending
days and weeks without interruption upon my private studies. But now the
case is altered."[9] Beaumont was perhaps recalling his ambitious program of
reading, in which he had made himself acquainted with the scriptures in their
original languages and had examined "the state of Christianity from its foun-
tain, through the successive ages of the Church down to his own [age]," and
had written, for his private use, a calendar of saints and an essay on the
miracles.[10]

Beaumont's wide reading in traditional writers is not so unusual as his study of contemporary authors. He read not merely Hebrew, Latin, and Greek, but Italian, Spanish, and French as well. He displays this knowledge perhaps most plainly in a speech at Cambridge which he gave *in scholis publicis,* in 1638.[11] His plan is to describe philosophy, rhetoric, and literature, adding an historical remark to each area, and suggesting how each should be taught. This is an important speech for Beaumont. He is advising students, on the one hand, but he is also flattering and impressing his academic superiors, on the other. He courts approval by supporting accepted educational practice and, at the same time, proving how much he himself has benefited from it. He tells his audience: "It is not the sign of ignorance to be wise on the side of serious men, to dispute on the side of authority, to pursue philosophy along with your mother academy. For in truth this fashion does not suppress free minds, but sees to it that public differences of opinion are being handled according to one standard and that the unyielding revilings of the sects are being confined." Beaumont was twenty-two when he espoused these principles. His eagerness to remain steadfast before the ruling authority and his readiness to support tradition were principles he had learned well during his early years at Hadleigh, and then practiced at Peterhouse. These attitudes of mind, appropriate to a member of the high church party, remained with him all his years, and governed his whole view of life. Having bound himself to this creed, he might let his mind range freely within the coherent rule of apostolic and historical faith. So Beaumont read whatever was new as well as old: he extols Cicero and Vergil and Homer, but also Bacon; he recalls his excitement in reading Marino and Tasso; of the French, he judges Caussin "summis laudibus prosequendum"; he tells affectionately of the Spanish mystics, and most fondly of St. Teresa, "her whose pen, filled with divine dew, dripped I know not what sweeter than sweetness itself, and bathed the whole heaven."[12]

When the earl of Manchester came with an ordinance from the Long Parliament to "regulate" the university, Peterhouse, because of its well-known royalist sympathies, was one of the first colleges to be "reformed." Beaumont, along with Crashaw, was ejected from his fellowship in 1644, although he must have left Cambridge some months before the parliamentary visit. Little of Beaumont's writing survives from this time besides the one Latin speech. He is said to have delivered an oration before the university on November 5, 1640, and also to have made a parallel between the Roman Empire of Theodosius and his two sons to contemporary England (1641), the intention being to show the evils of his time. A few short poems appeared in five separate collections of Cambridge poets, printed between 1635 and 1641. A majority of these are commemorative verses, in Latin, and most are uninspired and lifeless. One is interesting, not so much for its own sake — although it is the only elegiac verse Beaumont seems ever to have written — but because it appears in the same volume with *Lycidas*. Beaumont, like Milton, was one of the sorrowing friends of Edward King of Christ's College.[13]

There is little more to record of Beaumont's life at Peterhouse prior to the outbreak of the civil war. He was undoubtedly busy with his students and his own studies. Fearful of the approaching conflict, he must have been fully conscious of his dangerous position at Peterhouse; for the college would obviously be among the first to fall before puritan wrath. Very few Peterhouse men embraced the puritan cause — not even one of Beaumont's scholars — and in the year following the initial ejection, only one of the old fellows remained.

Beaumont next appears at home, in Hadleigh, a place more congenial to him now than disordered Cambridge. These years in Hadleigh were active, the time filled by writing; almost all the poetry Beaumont wrote in his long life comes from this period of enforced leisure. There were two volumes of short poems, although only one survives in full.[14] But most important, he wrote *Psyche: or Loves Mysterie* (1648), his chief work. This he began at least by 1645 and had finished before the spring of 1648. Even by the early part of 1647, Beaumont must have completed a substantial part of it. Henry Molle, the university orator, from whom Beaumont had solicited criticism of *Psyche,* had written to him in February, offering so much praise that Beaumont put no trust in his judgment. But Edward Martin, the ejected president of Queen's College, Cambridge, and once a chaplain to Laud, likewise declared in a letter to Beaumont (January 14, 1648) his full approval of *Psyche.* These letters, in the Peterhouse treasury, also urge Beaumont to abandon his fears about publishing his poem; because he thought *Psyche* was too topical and dealt too harshly with the puritans, he seems to have considered publishing it anonymously. Certainly, Beaumont's fear of interference must have made him cautious; it is notable how much more violent are his attacks on the puritans in the second edition of *Psyche,* published posthumously more than forty years later, in 1702.

Except for this short period, from about 1644 to 1652, Beaumont wrote very little poetry; for he turned to poetry when he was not busy with his theological studies and college duties, "that I might not live in mere Idleness." He wrote poetry "when I was stormed from my books and had not so much as one Book with me, but Marino and only his Adoring."[15] In fact, the obvious concern of his writing during the years away from Cambridge, from the ejection until the return in 1662, was theological, not poetic: two enormous *Annotationes Criticae,* written in this period, one on Ecclesiastes, the other on the Pentateuch, are ample testimony to his theological interests.[16]

Psyche is a more useful guide to Beaumont's thought by far than his scriptural exegeses; for the many enthusiasms of his life find expression in his capacious epic. There are not many poems in English longer than this one, nor subject to more digressions. Besides describing the vicissitudes of the soul which longs for union with God — the presumed subject of the poem — Beaumont writes as well a history of Christ's life in heaven and on earth, and relates by the way his Harrowing of Hell, with some passing consideration of the Incarnation, of the Holy Eucharist, of persecution, and of martyrdom; he reviews and rebukes ancient and modern heretics, but singles out the puritans for special attention; he eulogizes his deceased wife; he praises poets old and new — Horace and Crashaw, Homer, Vergil, and Spenser. Everything finds its place in *Psyche,* and the very range of subjects, so randomly chosen, gives bizarre charm and variety to Beaumont's poem.

2

Royalists and Arminians passed from poor times to worse; the wonder is that so many could have survived the war and the hardship of a long dispossession. That many did return to power with the Restoration, unchanged in doctrine, convinced as before of the divine nature of kingship and episcopacy, Beaumont himself attests. But now there was no more struggle to maintain high church belief; it could be held with little anxiety, comfortably. Now there was a new, liberal climate where most opinions could flourish; yet Beaumont and his party, as before, naturally excluded enthusiasts, sectarians, and "heretics" from their system, and where once they felt resistance, they now could live and worship uninterruptedly, with the same order and rule as in the days of Laud.

Like the other old upholders of religion, lately returned to power, Beaumont's mind had not been altered save by hardening and inflexibility, for he could say: "Their saucy arguments are many ages ago confuted, who magnify democracy, oligarchy, poliarchy, or any form of government, but that of monarchy." These were the sentiments Beaumont expressed in a sermon in Peterhouse chapel, delivered on the commemoration of the restoration of Charles II (that is, May 29), in 1664, based on the text, "Blessed art thou, O land, when thy king is the son of nobles" (Eccles. 10.17).[17] He speaks of many examples of properly constituted monarchies, classic and biblical, "whence we may well collect that the dint of majesty is so strongly divine, that for my part, I think the Loyalist hearts can better feel than express it." Of episcopal government, Beaumont says:

> The ecclesiastic government will not be administered with
> less, but rather with more exactness than the civil, as being
> of more precious concernment. For under such a king (so
> long as his power is not ravished from him by a torrent of
> wild and frantic disloyalty), [there is] no fear that sects and
> heresies should have uncontrolled liberty to spawn; that
> profaneness and sacrilege should grow rampant; that zeal
> and reformation should be made the stakes to rapine and
> tyranny; that sobriety should be trampled down, and
> ignorant boldness set up as pure spiritual devotion; that the
> horridest works of darkness should be ushered in by new
> lights, that men in mere conscience should turn assassinates
> and devils; that undigested, impertinent, erroneous,
> blasphemous fancies should be fathered upon the Holy

Ghost; that Christ should be set upon his throne by pulling down his sacred vice-regents; that God should be solemnly blest for fortunate villainy, and made the author and patron of what Himself forbids and abhors; that were Christ to be born again, He might find a stable and a manger in His temple; that where the Bread of Heaven was provided for Christians, the only provision should be provender for horses. No fear, I say, of such prodigies in religion; for besides his pious edicts, the very life of a king who is thus the *Son of Nobles* will be of authoritative influence.

Appending to this sermon an application suitable for the day of Charles's martyrdom, January 30, Beaumont asks:

And was not the land most blessed in him [Charles]? In civil respects: was it not the paradise where peace, plenty, and honor securely flourished, whilst they were nipped and blasted in other nations? Was not this the object of the world's envy, and yet so secured, as all that envy could not endanger it? In ecclesiastical respects: was it not the only sanctuary of the truly Catholic and Apostolic faith and discipline? Was not God's service amongst us happily protected from supersition on one hand, and from profaneness on the other? Was ever this, or any other nation enriched with so ample a stock of learned and expert champions of the reformed profession? Join both respects together, and were not the forged prerogatives of the Golden Age, I say not copied, but really transcended by our felicity under this government?

While the ideas are conventional, the vigor and passion of Beaumont's convictions cannot be doubted, nor can any difference between the Beaumont of the Restoration and the Beaumont of Cosin's Peterhouse be detected. There was no difference, and that is the most cogent truth of Beaumont's whole career. He remained the same throughout his life, tenaciously holding to an intellectual golden age that was orderly and regulated. When this world seemed once more to come alive as Cromwell's rule decayed, Beaumont and his friends might have felt vindicated; for now victorious, they could again enjoy their appropriate prerogatives. That they really entered their old offices in another and reformed age never clearly occurred to many of them.

The restoration years were indeed fortunate for Beaumont's ecclesiastical and academic affairs. Like many other earnest adherents of king and church, he now gathered richly. Primarily through the patronage of bishop Wren of Ely, Beaumont came into possession of numerous preferments. In his episcopal capacity as visitor of Peterhouse, Wren, in 1663, intruded Beaumont as master, setting aside the nominations of the fellows. Beaumont succeeded to this office, which he held until his death, after resigning the mastership of Jesus College to which Wren (who also exercised visitorial rights there) had appointed him in the preceding year.[18]

But the restoration years were less happy for Beaumont's literary life. During his exile, he had never wearied of translating the devotional ideals of the European Counter Reformation into English. He had filled his poetry, both epic and lyric, with admiring awe of the Holy Virgin's breasts, and with ecstatic wonder of the Incarnation; he had celebrated such saints as Mary Magdalene, Gregory of Nazianzen, Simon Stylites, with exuberance and warmth. In a poetry where hearts quiver and wounds bleed, where angels hover near devotées who cry for death from the seering dart of Love, Beaumont had begged, again and again, for spiritual vision and annihilation of the senses. Frequently, he had exhorted Love to visit him, and fervidly he had longed for mystical union.[19] Beaumont's labors went now, in this Restoration age, to performing the duties of his mastership which involved him in tiresome disputes with the fellows, and to managing the business of his widely separated livings and an increasing amount of property, including farms, houses, and estates. The stubborn resistance to regulation of college and worldly affairs must have annoyed a man so fond of order in all things; Beaumont, in consequence, expended most of his energy in managing the trivial offices of daily life.[20] The old love for the "true and ordered" religion was turned into an eager desire for producing sensible politics; the Beaumont of the Restoration had become secularized with hardly a wish for higher vision.

With the appointment to the Regius Professorship of Divinity, an office, endowed by Trinity College, to which he was admitted on March 30, 1674, Beaumont's theological interests could flower, while his poetic creativeness seems to have been confined to revising and expanding of his *Psyche*. Most attention went to his regular bi-weekly Latin sermons, which have survived. Lifeless but craftsmanlike, they seem endlessly to have emanated from Beaumont's study. They came easily, all reflecting the tenets of an intellectual faith. Of these several hundred sermons, hardly one is really worth remembering.[21] Perhaps Beaumont himself realized how mechanical his sermons were; for in his will, he forbade that any of them be published. Nor is the extended contention with Henry More over his *Mystery of Godliness* edifying; it is, rather, litigious and unliterary. Beaumont again was cavilling, as he was, in these restoration years, so accustomed to do.[22] But he was faithful to his duties — his sermons, like his account books, run until the last month of his life: only the handwriting became infirm; the mind was resolute, as ever.

Joseph Beaumont's long life ended on November 23, 1699, not many days after his last sermon. He was buried in the ante-chapel of Peterhouse. The marble slab over his grave bears his handsome coat of arms; and on the north wall, a memorial plaque tells of his illustrious life as *poeta, orator, theologus praestantissime.*

Beaumont's life after the Restoration does not rouse the imagination. Worldly and crabbed, he carried the culture of one age into another, without change; the enthusiasm that he once felt for it had now degenerated into perpetual bickering. The years at Cosin's Peterhouse were his most attractive, and they bore their best fruit in the short period of intensive poetic activity after his ejection. His most natural communication was the sermon, the lecture, the tract; but his poetry, the most memorable of all his work, was perhaps a happy accident; in his poetry, he was at leisure, less self-consciously disputative, and most informal. As soon as he could, he corrected himself.

Notes

1. Descended from the Leicestershire Beaumonts, Joseph Beaumont was laterally related to the famous dramatist and also to the poet of *Bosworth Field*. See Edward T. Beaumont, "The Beaumonts in History, A.D. 850–1850" (1929), an unpublished typescript copy in the University Library, Cambridge.

2. See *A Collection of Private Devotions,* ed. P. G. Stanwood (Oxford: Clarendon Press, 1967), discussed in the previous chapter, with an account of the circumstances of its publication.

3. William Prynne, *Canterburies Doome* (1640), 73–74. Prynne, of course, is an unreliable witness; nevertheless, we may infer from his hostile account that Peterhouse employed *some* sort of formal and embellished liturgy. For an excellent recent description of Cosin's Peterhouse, based especially on documents in the University of Cambridge archives, see Hilton Kelliher, "Crashaw at Cambridge," in *New Perspectives on the Life and Art of Richard Crashaw,* ed. John R. Roberts (Columbia, Mo.: University of Missouri Press, 1990), 180–214.

4. See *The Complete Poems of Joseph Beaumont,* ed. Alexander B. Grosart (Edinburgh, 1880), 1:xii.

5. See David Mathew, *The Social Structure in Caroline England* (Oxford, 1948), 64. A document in the Peterhouse treasury, a single sheet, unsigned and undated, describes a number of the principal events of Beaumont's life. He is here declared actually to have been sent to Westminster but afterwards "recovered to Hadleigh to be under the superintendence of his father."

6. See T. A. Walker, compiler, *Admissions to Peterhouse* (Cambridge: Cambridge University Press, 1912), 42–43. The entry in the Admission Book reads: "Apr. 26, 1631. Josephus Beaumont Suffolk. admissus pensionarius sub custodia M^{ri} Horne."

7. Beaumont commemorated his friendship with Crashaw in canto 4 of his epic poem, *Psyche: or Loves Mysterie* (1648), sts. 93–95. There he complains of Crashaw's absence from England and the poetic advice he consequently misses: "Fair had my Psyche been, had she at first / By thy kinde-censuring hand been dress'd and nurst" (95). There can be no doubt that the

friendship between Crashaw and Beaumont was a productive one; it is impossible to say how much one influenced the other. But it would seem that the greater poet had more to teach the lesser. There is not, in Crashaw's poetry any mention of indebtedness to Beaumont, yet many obvious similarities appear in their poems. See L. C. Martin's introduction to *The Poems English Latin and Greek of Richard Crashaw*, 2nd ed. (Oxford: Clarendon Press, 1957), xci, and his commentary. See also Eloise Robinson's introduction to *The Minor Poems of Joseph Beaumont* (London: Constable, 1914), where many echoes of Crashaw are pointed out. Elsie Elizabeth Duncan-Jones argues persuasively that Crashaw addressed his Leyden letter of February 20, 1644 to Beaumont, which would demonstrate the closeness of their relationship. See her essay in *New Perspectives on the Life and Art of Richard Crashaw*, 174–79.

8. Beaumont was elected a fellow of Peterhouse in his twentieth year, on November 20, 1636, and made a tutor four years later. He took the M.A. degree in 1638.

9. Quoted from a letter in the Peterhouse treasury, dated January 30, 1640.

10. According to John Gee, who edited Beaumont's *Original Poems . . . to which is prefixed An Account of his Life and Writings* (Cambridge, 1749). Apparently none of the documents mentioned in the text above has survived.

11. This speech, with six other autograph Latin addresses by Beaumont, is included in a small unbound volume with the title-page written by his son, Charles: "A Collection of my R[ev]. Father's Latin Speeches" (Peterhouse MS 459). Two of the addresses included in this collection are dated: the one to which I refer, second in the volume, bears the date 1638; the other, seventh or last in order of the volume, 1674. The heading of the 1638 address reads, "Habui in Scholis pub[licis]. Cantab[rigiensibus]." It is very likely that Beaumont gave this oration as an academic exercise to demonstrate his rhetorical proficiency. Such declamations were common in seventeenth-century Cambridge; they were given either privately, or, as this one, publicly, on this occasion *in scholis,* in the Old Schools of the University. I translate from the Latin in the quotations which follow. Cf. the following chapter on Beaumont's *Psyche,* esp. n. 3 (and the accompanying discussion).

12. The allusions Beaumont makes to continental authors are interesting, especially for their contemporaneity. His reference to Teresa of Avila seems to be the first public mention of her by any English writer. See Austin Warren, "Crashaw and St. Teresa," *TLS,* August 25, 1932, where Warren discusses the relevance of this allusion to Crashaw's interest in St. Teresa. Nicholas Caussin, confessor of Louis XIII, known chiefly for *The Holy Court* [*La Cour sainte*] . . . *Written in French, & translated into English by T. H.* [Thomas Hawkins], 2 vols. (Paris, 1628), still was living when Beaumont spoke — he died in 1651. Cf. chap. 11, esp. n. 7.

13. This anthology is in two parts: the first, *Justa Edovardo King naufrago* (Cambridge, 1638), contains verse entirely in Latin, with one poem, signed "J. B.," evidently by Joseph Beaumont. The second part, and bound

with the first, titled *Obsequies to the memorie of Mr Edward King,* contains Beaumont's elegy, signed "Joseph Beaumont," and Milton's *Lycidas.* See Ruth Wallerstein, *Studies in Seventeenth Century Poetic* (Madison: University of Wisconsin Press, 1950), who reprints Beaumont's poem and comments on it. T. A. Walker gives a register of Beaumont's known works and a list also of volumes in which his verse appears in *A Peterhouse Bibliography* (Cambridge: Cambridge University Press, 1924), 12–13.

14. The first volume of poems, edited by Eloise Robinson in 1914, was begun in early 1644; the latest poem of the collection was written before the end of June 1652. The second book of poems was titled *Cathemerina,* after Prudentius' fourth century *Cathemerinon;* it was written, according to Gee (in his introduction to the *Original Poems*), between May 17 and September 3, 1652. Some of the poems in this volume survived the manuscript, now lost, and appear in Gee's 1749 edition. Gee says Beaumont wrote no more poetry after 1652, but it seems more probable that he wrote some, even if very little. Many of the revisions to *Psyche* would have occupied part of his time after this.

15. Beaumont, in an undated letter, but presumably of late 1647, to an unnamed correspondent, asks criticism of his poem. Since he seems to intend a title for Marino's book and not a description of it, "Adoring" must be a mistake for "L'Adone." The letter, from which the quotations are taken, is in the Peterhouse treasury.

16. Both of these works survive in the Peterhouse library in the autograph. The commentary on Ecclesiastes is dated "Julii 7. A.D. 1655."

17. The quotations come from the fourth sermon of seven, collected and bound in an autograph copy in the Peterhouse library (MS 448); these are the only English sermons of Beaumont known to me. The only one dated is this one from which I quote, but they would seem to have been written in the first years of the Restoration.

18. The friendship between Wren and Beaumont began when Beaumont first went up to the university, while Wren was master of Peterhouse. During the civil war and the Interregnum, while he was imprisoned in the Tower, Wren entrusted his two sons to Beaumont's tutelage in Hadleigh. Beaumont was married to Elizabeth Brownrigg, the daughter of Wren's wife by a former marriage, on May 7, 1650. Six children were born to them, three of whom lived into adulthood. Beaumont's wife died in 1662.

Charles II made Beaumont D.D. by a *mandamus,* on July 28, 1660, and appointed him a royal chaplain. Beaumont proceeded also to the degree of S.T.P. on August 18, 1660. He had long before this time taken Orders, probably in Februry 1648, as one of his minor poems would suggest: "Paulo post Ordinationem," written on the occasion of his ordination, bears the date "Febr. 27" [1648]. See Robinson, *Minor Poems,* 329–30.

19. I give a more detailed description of Beaumont's poetry in the next chapter.

20. For typical incidents during his mastership, see Beaumont's diary, "Memoriae ergo . . . ," in the Peterhouse treasury, an almost continuous daily

record of the business of the mastership from the date of his admission until September 28, 1666.

21. None of these sermons survive in the original. But together with some other theological writings of Beaumont, they were copied from the autograph by Thomas Richardson, Beaumont's successor to the mastership, and fill twenty-five large folio volumes in the Peterhouse library.

22. One of the Cambridge Platonists, More published *An Explanation of the Grand Mystery of Godliness* in 1660. Beaumont criticizes this work in *Some Observations upon the Apologie of Dr Henry More for his Mystery of Godliness* (Cambridge, 1665). A paper controversy between More and Beaumont ensued and it continued through many years, turning later to the "correct" interpretation of Daniel and the Apocalypse. Cf. John Twigg, *The University of Cambridge and the English Revolution 1625–1688,* The History of the University of Cambridge: Texts and Studies, vol. 1 (Woodbridge, Suffolk: Boydell Press, 1990), 255–58, and chap. 12 below.

11

St. Teresa and Joseph Beaumont's

PSYCHE: OR LOVES MYSTERIE

WHEN JOSEPH BEAUMONT set himself the task of writing his vast epic, he recalled the lessons he had learned at Peterhouse, Cambridge.[1] There, as we have seen, he had profited from the attention of John Cosin, who like his immediate predecessors in the mastership, had enjoined the society of the college to a love for discipline and order, in life both scholarly and ecclesiastical.[2] At Peterhouse, Beaumont had joined his wide and catholic reading in the classics and in contemporary continental writers with the dogmatic orthodoxy of tradition, propriety of worship, and "correct" belief. These he would expend, during the years of the civil war, upon his overflowing *Psyche*. Ejected from his fellowship in 1643 along with Richard Crashaw and others who had outspokenly supported the King and the Laudian episcopacy, Beaumont retired to his home in East Anglia, in Hadleigh, Suffolk; and there he undertook the most important labor of his life, a poem about the soul which longs for union with God.

Perhaps there is no other poet of the 1640s who reflected so much of the culture of his age: himself no innovator, Beaumont was, rather, a mind that accepted tradition in poetry, as in politics and religion, or at least followed what had been well tried before. He admired Ariosto, and relied heavily on Tasso for the prototype of his Christian hero.[3] He adopted the allegorical method of Spenser and his followers, especially Giles and Phineas Fletcher. He drew, furthermore, on Marino, and on the great sixteeenth-century Spanish mystic, St. Teresa of Avila. These would not be unusual sources for an English poet of the mid-seventeenth century; but in Beaumont, they all merge, deliberately, self-consciously, uniquely, to form an extraordinary poem, at once fashionable, topical, and learned.

Beaumont clearly was writing firmly within the epic tradition, as he and his contemporaries understood it: liberally employing biblical allegory and Christian motifs, he aimed at being largely didactic.[4] But this purpose embraced as well a *devotional* end. For if Beaumont wrote, on the one hand, an allegorical epic in the Spenserian tradition, displaying the martial conflict between good and evil, Christ and Satan, he also brought to the epic, on the other hand, an ecclesiastical tradition nurtured by the devotion of the

Laudian church, matured by a literature sometimes exuberantly passionate and polemical, but nearly always appealing to the authority of the universal church.

Beaumont's *Psyche* is not just one more Renaissance epic, a mere echo of *The Faerie Queene,* although it is partly that: *Psyche* is unique in English literature because it contains in Spenserian epic form the further religious, indeed, devotional interests of the high church. Revering the historic and ecumenical church, these followers of the English church formed a sympathetic audience for the "enrichment" of the liturgy, as well as for the numerous guides to the devout life.[5] Beaumont, who eagerly followed the Catholic practices of his college, was obviously one of those who most warmly responded to such pieties. While his college stood encouragingly by to support and mediate, Beaumont's sense of belonging to the historic and apostolic church increased and flourished.

Among English writers of the period, Crashaw and Beaumont, perhaps more than any others, defended the church by emphasizing in their poetry what protestant, and mostly Calvinist maligners would particularly disparage, by emphasizing, in fact, the most important themes emerging from continental, Catholic literature and art: vision and ecstasy, legends of the Blessed Virgin and the saints, the sacraments, the paradoxes of death and martyrdom. Like the Tridentine artists, they sought to render doctrine immediate and articulate, and, perhaps, sensational or strident. Both poets thus used vocabulary, tone, and theme that would realize the visual and tactile impact of language, not literally but symbolically perceived.[6]

To study and admire the assault of language on the senses, where better might one have turned than to St. Teresa − St. Teresa who, in her *Life* and in *The Mansions,* beautifully represented the mystic way by describing the struggle of the soul to escape mortal limitations, and displayed in her life as in her works her rapturous longing for divine consummation? She had touched Beaumont's liveliest sensibilities when he had first read her, she who had not written "with human sweetness only." He had been profoundly moved by her "whose pen, filled with divine dew, dripped I know not what sweeter than sweetness itself, and bathed the whole heaven . . . O how least a death would it be, in her writings to die!"[7]

Crashaw honored this saint in several poems, Beaumont in all of *Psyche;* for though he mentions her name not even once in it, his intention is clear: *Psyche* is Beaumont's abstraction of St. Teresa herself, and of her mystical experiences. The real *form* of Beaumont's poem, therefore, belongs no more to the epic than to the religious and devotional tradition of the Counter Reformation, so well manifested by St. Teresa, and so congenial to the high church temperament.[8] But transcending any particular tradition is universal and timeless mysticism. Beaumont's attraction to the devotional intensity of Spanish mysticism would not have been so great had any real doctrinal association been required of him. Though still of the English church, and firmly avoiding the persuasions of Rome, he might with impunity often pray in their style.

1

The minor poems of Beaumont, which he was writing at the same time as his long poem, well introduce *Psyche;* for these, most of which remained in manuscript until this century, are akin to the "epic" poem, though most of them are under sixty lines, and some, indeed, are briefly epigrammatic.[9] They deal with recurrent subjects: some, distinctly topical, reveal Beaumont's attitude toward the civil war. When he writes his birthday poem for 1649, not quite two months after Charles's death, he turns his outrage into a metaphorical description of his own heart's battle:

> Though I have seen our wretched Britain made
> The Isle of Monsters; though the onely Trade
>   Our England drives be Frensy, and
>   Rebellious Desperation; Yet
>   I finde a more enormous Band
>   Of Rebells in my Bosome mett:
> Rebells, whose furious stomach dares disdain
> Not *Britains Monarch,* but *Heavns Soverain.*
>
> The Lower House, the Commons of my Breast,
> My traiterous Passions, speciously drest
>   In Liberties bewitching cloke;
>   First trampling down my Will & Reason
>   As useless Peers, in triumph broke
>   Into the gulfe of deepest Treason,
> And murdered their *royal Lord* again,
> Whose guilt was nothing but his Gentle Reign.

("Γενεθλιακόν, March 13. 1649," sts. 3 and 4, pp. 378–79)

There are also poems which deal specifically with the absence of "sensible devotion":

> Falln on my knees, I had no lesse then leave
>   To supplicate My God & King.
> Alas, a thousand wants my Soule did greive,
>   I had to ask Him many a Thing.
>
> Up went my hands & Eyes: so should my Heart,
>   And so a little while it did:
> But as my craving Tongue performed her part,
>   I knew not how, my Mind was fled.

("Dull Devotion," sts. 4 and 5, p. 36)

Here is Beaumont's typical mood, substituting already the memory of desire for desire itself. How gratefully, indeed, he finds in the saints and mystics of the church the grace for which he himself so often longs, with which he seems usually out of touch. He fondly celebrates the devotion which their deeds and their lives afforded.

Mary Magdalene is one Catholic saint about whom Beaumont writes: on the fire of love, her tears of sacramental penance fall, the flames of love complementing the contrition shown by her tears. Her grace and absolution may thus be twice observed:

> *Marie's* on fire: and such stout Fire as fears
> > No ocean streams
> > To check its flames,
> Which burnes amidst a Sea of brinie Tears.

> These Waters, & those Flames in Her brave Eyes
> > Both have their Place,
> > Both have their grace,
> And stoutly strive which should the higher rise.

("S. Mary Magdalen's Ointment," sts. 3 and 4, p. 250[10])

The minor poems contain many other hagiologies, some of which have few parallels in English literature. Beaumont wrote of such un-English saints as Simeon Stylites, anticipating Tennyson's similarly titled but quite different poem. Beaumont's poem, "Lemniscus ad Columnam S. Simeonis Stylitae appensus," is interesting because it so generously conveys his own attitude toward the ascetic life. It opens with praise for St. Simeon's pillar, then for his humility; finally, there follows a description of his profound struggle:

> His treacherous Flesh quickly fell downe,
> All his false Friends away were blowne,
> His Lusts grew tame, & every Passion
> To his brave Will it selfe did fashion.

Heaven called him to show publicly his devotion. He mounted the pillar, and there he remained until he seemed no longer alive. Though his flesh was mortifying,

> Sure Simeon feels no blow
> Nor wound, but those, wch LOVE'S sweet Darts
> Bestow on Saints Delicious Hearts.

At last, Simeon unites with Love; through fasting, through diligence, through prayer, he finally wins peace in God:

Thou
Shalt be exalted, & above
In ye warme bosome of thy LOVE
Be payd for thy cold Station heer.
Farewell, Brave Soule, & though thy Sphear
Be too high for Us, & our
Poor Songs to reach, yet will we poure
Them on ye noble Place of thy
Dear feet, & heap our Prayses high
To crowne thy Column, or to be
Crowned by its Nobilitie.

(255, 258–59)

Beaumont's respect for the painful victory of the spirit over the flesh underlines his own heart's desire; the whole group of saints' poems persistently reflects his admiration of spiritual qualities which he confesses himself so little to own. But he is comforted by the promise of eternal life won through acts of devotion and by the rapturous vision of God which the saints obtained. For the Blessed Virgin, who expresses the paradox of the Incarnate God, Beaumont reserved some of his most sensuous poetry. He writes of Mary with the intimacy of Catholic awe; his "Jesus inter Ubera Maria[e]" trembles with ecstatic amazement:

In ye coolnesse of ye day
The old Worlds Even, *God* all undrest went downe
Without His Roab, without His Crowne,
Into His private garden, there to lay
On spicey Bed
His Sweeter Head.

There He found two Beds of Spice,
A double Mount of Lillies, in whose Top
Two milkie Fountaines bubled up.
He soon resolv'd: & well I like, He cries,
My table spread
Upon my Bed.[11]

Three more stanzas and a "Chorus" follow; throughout the whole poem, angels move about protectingly; sweet odors of paradisal fragrance spread over Christ's garden — the effect is violent, palpable, emblematic.

Little change in mood ever accompanies a change of subject in these poems; though their intensity varies, they taste all of the same sweet flavor. Whether he is honoring the saints, praising Christian wonders, or describing his spiritual state, Beaumont writes as fervently as he can; and that is what makes his poems all sound so much alike. Having sprung from the same source, they mostly stream toward the same end. Beaumont's wish to make his poetry pictorial and emblematic demonstrates his understanding of a certain kind of Catholic piety; devotion thus lives within his sight, and in him it grows with the further influence of the mystical way.[12]

Vision and mystical ecstasy — artistic interpreters of the Catholic Reformation — these are the most characteristic motifs in Beaumont's poetry. He writes of spiritual annihilation, so regularly, indeed, that one distrusts Beaumont's own ability to be moved by more than an intellectually realized ideal. He frequently exhorts Love to visit him, making, for example, this fervid and rhetorical wish for mystical union:

> How dead am I
> Sweet Master of Heavns Archerie,
> Because I am not slaine by Thee!
> Helpe Mee to die,
> Lest dangerous Death
> Suck up my breath
> Before I live: My Heart
> Will need a speciall Dart:
> Yet make no stay,
> Look but this way,
> Thy potent Eyes my Soule will quickly slay.

("Love," st. 11, p. 25)

Beaumont never wearies of writing in this fashion: his poetry is filled by the description of Love's sweetness, of its mysterious and purifying joy. Hearts quiver, wounds bleed, angels hover near their victims who cry for death from the searing dart of Love. The poetry explodes with metamorphosis, while, again and again, as at the end of "The Relapse," Beaumont begs for spiritual vision:

> O mighty Soverain
> Of Pittie, Loe my prostrate Heart
> Lies trembling once again
> Under thy Dart:
> Strike, strike, & pierce it by
> LOVES healing cruelty;
> That by that blessed Wound my Soule may be
> Sett ope, & bleed out every thing but Thee.

(353)

2

Although the minor poems are like *Psyche* in their religious and personal sentiments, they do not, collectively or individually, explore a single scheme of thought systematically or thoroughly. This is the task of the long poem, and, while, the same tendencies described in these lyric effusions are still present, they contain, rather than outline, *Psyche*. These modes of religious experience provide the thread on which the whole is strung.[13]

Beaumont needed a heroine who might alone embrace the themes of the minor poetry; but such a figure must be dramatic, not a static embodiment of religious fervor, for she would have to undergo spiritual movement in order to display convincingly Catholic devotional practice. St. Teresa was able to answer these requirements; the religious way she knew was, in spite of its unpredictable ecstasies, an orderly and sensible pilgrimage Godward, and Beaumont found in her life the pattern, *par excellence,* of the mystic traveler whom he translated into his heroine — Psyche.

Beaumont intended his heroine to advance according to a tried program. She does proceed, indeed, along the three time-honored mystical ways: the Purgative, the Illuminative, the Unitive. But within these divisions, Psyche passes through four distinct climaxes, the four degrees of the contemplative life which St. Teresa calls "waters," and describes in her *Life*. The first degree is for "beginners in prayer." "The beginner must think of himself as of one setting out to make a garden in which the Lord is to take His delight, yet in soil most unfruitful and full of weeds." The soil must be nurtured, and the garden, once planted, must be watered:

> It seems to me that the garden can be watered in four ways: taking the water from a well, which costs us great labour; or by a water-wheel and buckets, when the water is drawn by a windlass . . . ; or by a stream or a brook, which waters the ground much better, for it saturates it more thoroughly and there is less need to water it often, so that the gardener's labour is much less; or by heavy rain, when the Lord waters it with no labour of ours, a way incomparably better than any of those which have been described.[14]

Thus, with the first degree, the soul must toil and set out to collect its own strength; with the second degree, the soul need not work exclusive of God's grace, divine favors now being granted; the third degree discovers the soul lost in wonder, passively accepting God's gifts and the will in union with Him; the fourth degree is like the third, except now the soul is completely dead and senseless: "There is no feeling, but only rejoicing, unaccompanied by any understanding of the thing in which the soul is rejoicing" (1:105).

These four degrees of spiritual progress, or "waters," then, describe the preparation of the soul (*Purgation:* the First and Second Waters) for the higher enjoyment of God (*Illumination:* the Third Water); and if God is willing to grant the highest favor of all, he permits the soul to join Him, while still it remains on earth (*Union:* the Fourth Water). St. Teresa distinguishes further between the Prayer of Recollection and the Prayer of Quiet. In the Prayer of Quiet, one may feel effortlessly the divine presence without calling up pictures of it. This "imageless prayer" is, of course, the more perfect kind; but the other, occurring in the first degree of contemplation, is more important to Beaumont's *Psyche:* as St. Teresa would recommend, Beaumont's heroine images Christian scenes. St. Teresa writes of the Prayer of Recollection:

> I would try to make pictures of Christ inwardly; and I used to think I felt better when I dwelt on those parts of His life when He was most often alone. It seemed to me that His being alone and afflicted, like a person in need, made it possible for me to approach Him. . . . I was particularly attached to the prayer in the Garden, where I would go to keep Him company. I would think of the sweat and of the affliction He endured there. I wished I could have wiped that grievous sweat from His face, but I remember that I never dared to do so, for the gravity of my sins stood in the way. I used to remain with Him there for as long as my thoughts permitted it.   (1:54–55)

The cantos of Beaumont's poem telling of the life of Christ, upon which Psyche must look and think, serve the uses of this Prayer of Recollection. These long narrative sections are perhaps more hortatory than truly meditative, yet Psyche does seem to benefit spiritually from seeing and thinking about the life of Christ, if only to feel her privation more acutely, and to swoon more frequently.

These four stages of prayer have corresponding degrees in St. Teresa's later work, *The Mansions, or Interior Castle;* there are in it seven degrees of prayer, or "mansions." The first three of them which are subsumed under the first degree, the First Water, of the *Life,* describe the duties of the awakening soul in greater detail, including humility, practice of recollective prayer, meditation, and an exemplary life. The soul proceeds to the Fourth Mansion, which can be identified with the Prayer of Quiet, or the Second Water; the Fifth Mansion corresponds to the Third Water; the Sixth and the Seventh, different chiefly in the intensity of experience, correspond to the Fourth Water. The mystical scheme of *The Mansions,* though more elaborately stated than that of the *Life,* seems little different from it. The most striking refinement of *The Mansions,* perhaps, is St. Teresa's introduction of mystic marriage, the Heavenly Wedding, which the earthly analogy adumbrates. But the soul's wish for divine union, a desire which passes from the enamored, through the betrothed, to the married state, although analogous to common life, is, in fact, ineffable. Beaumont, of course, did not need to be solely inspired by St. Teresa in his use of these terms of the courtship and marriage of the soul, nor was the saint original in her use of them: the Canticles long ago provided this symbol of the mystic search for the divine spouse.

The bride seeking her groom, a search that extends painfully from the first moment of love until its consummation, requires, at least on the divine scale, all the ardor of a pilgrimage. So with Beaumont's heroine who sets out on a way exceedingly difficult, with dangerous detours; she has a guardian angel – appropriately named Phylax (φύλαξ = guard or sentinel) – to help her over many depressions, but frequently she must by herself resist the enticements of Satan. Beaumont at once introduces these two forces that struggle, throughout the whole poem, to win Psyche's faith. Both Satan and Phylax appear in canto 1, and in the next canto, they do battle.

Satan approaches Psyche disguised as a courtly lover, really Lust, or Aphrodisius. She is sorely tempted, but with her guardian's help, she overcomes the devil's art at the moment of succumbing to it. Phylax casts the hissing serpents from Psyche's heart so that she may see them, "roll'd about the floor."[1] Though wrung with guilt and sorrow for having entertained False Love, Psyche has, nevertheless, attained some spiritual growth; now, with Lust conquered, she is at the beginning of her search for her true Love. Falling asleep, she dreams of a stately procession; above her watchful position stands the House of Chastity. When Christ himself appears as the King of Chastity, Psyche looks,

> But as He forth was issuing,
> Intolerable Beams from His did fly
> Upon her face: she started at the stroke,
> And rubb'd her dazeled eyes, and so awoke.
> (2.172)

Thus Psyche's first vision of Christ, climactically placed at the end of her first struggle to win perfection, rewards her victory over sensuality. She has entered the Purgative Way: she has begun to fetch water, that the garden of her soul might someday grow strong enough to know God.

Psyche must continue in the elementary part of her spiritual course, however, until she has subdued the main cause of her separation from God – Pride. St. Teresa is most clear about the primary importance of humility; without the purgation of pride, nothing can be achieved. Yet Psyche has already advanced enough to receive the favor of divine encouragement. In canto 3, through the intercession of Phylax, she receives a "Love Token," or girdle, a gift from Christ, on which rich embroidery depicts the life of St. John the Baptist. As soon as she puts on the girdle, Psyche is at once seized by "matchless Throws and Pangs," but before the girdle fits well, her Grief must expel the heavy Disillusionment she feels for her unworthiness:

> Imperfect Embryo's, unformed *Lust,*
> Pin-fethered *Fancies,* and halfe-shap'd *Desires,*
> Dim Dawns of *Fondnesse,* doubtfull seeds of *Rust,*
> Glimmering Embers of corruptive Fires,
>   Scarce something, and yet *more than Nothing,* was
>   That mystick *Chaos,* that dead-living *Masse.*

> O how tormenting is the Parturition
> Of tender souls, when they unload themselves

> Of their blinde night-conceiv'd Bratts of Perdition!
> How doe the peevish and reluctant Elves
> (Mad with their own birth,) viperously contend
> The labouring bowells of the Heart to rend!
>   (3.176–77)

Psyche has reached the Second Water; however, she has received divine favor, and now she can perform more zealously the tasks remaining to be done before she may join her spouse. Still she has to subdue Pride, its hand-maidens, the Passions, or Senses, and its eventual partisans, the Reason, and the Will, before she can advance to the next degree of her spiritual way.

Because Psyche adopts a way of life so ascetic, her senses rebel. Each of them, Opsis (Seeing), Ophresis (Smelling), Geusis (Tasting), Acoë (Hearing), and Haphe (Touching), reproach Psyche for her stern life. She appeals to Logos, her Reason, who speaks eloquently to the rebels, but they take him prisoner. Only Thelema, the Will, remains to protect Psyche, but it, too, finally supports the rebel passions. Now Psyche is given "pretties," and a mirror for gazing at herself; with a fine coach, Psyche, overweening and disdainful, goes on a progress to show off her loveliness. But Phylax, who has been temporarily absent from Psyche's side so that she might alone test her strength, returns suddenly to save his ward from her contumely; he destroys her coach and helps to restore her to propriety and penitence. Psyche is, indeed, remorseful, and she cries out:

> O selfe-deluded
> And justly wretched soul, that mine own Fist
> (And heer she stroke) could pierce this treacherous
>   breast.
>
> A noble Stroke it was; and broke its way,
> Its happy Way, quite through unto her heart.
> Forth-with a cole-black Stream, which swelling lay
> And balking there, took warning to depart:
>   Out flew the Poyson reaking on the ground,
>   Which splitting, to its Hell its way it found.
>   (6.89–90)

Psyche calls for her best dress, made of haircloth:

> Come trusty Hair-cloths you did never yet
> Foole me of my selfe by garish Pride:
> Come honest Rope, thou never yet didst let
> Ambition blister me, but gird'st my side
>   Close to my heart, and left'st no Room between
>   For puffing strutting Thoughts to harbour in.
>   (6.94)

Now Phylax, to encourage her ward's devotion, expounds the scheme of the redemption, from the creation of the world and man, through his temptation and fall, to the coming of Christ, with an account of His life and death, His Resurrection and Ascension, and the outpouring of the Holy Ghost at Pentecost. Psyche is further enjoined to beware of the sins of heresy, and to mark well the Real Presence in the Holy Eucharist. At frequent points in Phylax's narrative, Psyche expresses her desire for immediate union with Christ, and paradoxically, her anxiety lest she be unable to receive it:

> O LOVE, how how shall finite I
> Contain thy ravishing Immensity![16]

Again to strengthen Psyche's faith, which had suffered much from the batterings of Heresy, Phylax takes her to visit Ecclesia, or Holy Church. The entrance is narrow and mean, but at the second, much nobler gate, Penance is seated:

> Her pensive Eyes so overladen were
> With *constant clouds,* that downward to the earth
> They always look'd: the *weather* ne're was clear
> With Her, but when one *Tempest* had broke forth,
>   Another crowded on; or rather one
>   *Continual flood* did from her Fountains run.[17]
>   (16.64)

Penance permits Psyche to enter the court of Ecclesia, where she sees the trophies victory has won over error. Especially displayed is the "Presbyterian God," or Covenant. The great Queen of Ecclesia herself appears, attended by Unity, Sanctity, Temperance, and Virginity. Psyche is struck with "dainty ecstasy," and as she stands before Truth,

> She felt her inward *mystick Day* arise,
> Which gently flourish's through her wondering Eys.
>   (16.209)

Through continued mortification, through the admonition of her guardian, through prayer and penance, Psyche has put her passions in rein at last and secured her "Cinque-Ports." Moreover, she holds her reason in proper check, deprecating it, and its servant, the Memory, for easily leading the soul into dangerous folly:

> (What are the busy *Scholes,* but a perplex'd
> And implicated *Maze,* in whose Meander
> With thousand knotty scrupulous By-paths vex'd
> The ever-doubling *Student*'s forced to wander?

> *Learning* her Self's a *Circle,* and the Soule
> Can finde no rest where it must always *roule.*)
>   (17.283)

Now, that she may be well prepared to continue to the next stage on her mystic way, Psyche begins a course of meditation on the attributes of God:

> A noble *Week of Attributes* she chose
> In the vast Treasures of the *Deitie;*
> And prest her *seav'n Dayes* to attend on those
> Each in his order; by which practise she
>   Knew how *Time* went, not by the posting *Sun,*
>   But her own *Contemplations Motion.*[18]
>   (17.309)

At the conclusion of her devotions, she sacrifices her will to God, and, at once, another Will from Him is put in its place. The Will is now held captive:

> And now her Soule, like a new weaned *Childe*
> Which wholly hangs upon its *Nurses* Will,
> It self not by it self did move and weild,
> But absolutely resting on the skill
>   And care of her dear *Lord who tutor'd it,*
>   Was carried wheresoever *he* thought fit.
>   (17.388)

Psyche is admitted now to the Third Water. This exchange of wills has completed her purgative experience; she is now betrothed to Christ; having reached the Illuminative state, she may rest passively in it. She need no longer fetch, by her own toil, water for the garden:

> On *God,* and onely him her joyes did feast;
> *His* royall Pleasure was her pretious Blisse:
> So well did all *his* Laws and Statutes taste
> To her Hearts palate, that the Pleasantness
>   Both of the Honey and the Honey-comb
>   Had in her approbation no room.
>
> What grated hardest on her Soul before,
> *Wrongs, Slanders, Pains, Distresse, Calamities,*
> *Mishaps,* and *Sicknesse;* tortur'd her no more:
> For by her *Spouses Will* she fix'd her Eyes,
>   And still embraced as the best, what he
>   Did either order, or permit to be.

> This kindled such a Bonfire of Delight
> Throughout her Breast, that had she been invited
> Ev'n by all *Paradise,* to yeild her right
> In this Possession, she would have sleighted
>   The mighty Bait, and triumph'd still to be
>   The *Holocaust* of *Loves Extremitie.*
>   (17.390–92)

Psyche is able to withstand any further attacks from Satan; she endures all subsequent persecution with composure and patience, while still longing ardently for marriage to her spouse.

But now, once so close to Christ, Psyche can enjoy nothing without Him; she finds herself derelict, alone; and this state, this position between heavenly consummation and abject deprivation, "The Dereliction" canto describes. Psyche must undergo "the dark night," the aridity every advanced mystic traveler has known. St. Teresa says of it in her *Life:*

> I used to remember some words of Saint Paul, about his being crucified to the world. I do not say that this is true of me — indeed, I know it is not — but I think it is true of the soul when no comfort comes to it from Heaven, and it is not in Heaven, and when it desires no earthly comfort, and is not on either, but is, as it were, crucified between Heaven and earth; and it suffers greatly, for no help comes to it either from the one hand or from the other. For the help which comes to it from Heaven is, as I have said, a knowledge of God so wonderful, and so far above all that we can desire, that it brings with it greater torment; for its desire grows in such a way that I believe its great distress sometimes robs it of consciousness.[19]   (1:123)

Beaumont understands the saint's meaning well, for he pours into this canto of Psyche's desolation as much understanding as if he were himself a fellow sufferer. His intellectual comprehension of this state of the soul is profound, and also his realization of its necessity to the mystic pilgrimage. For in the final canto of *Psyche,* Beaumont can at last see his heroine, purged of all evil attributes, desires, and aridities, experience divine ecstasy:

> For lo, the sullen *Clouds* which heretofore
> Had damm'd the way to her rejected sight,
> Drown'd in repentant Tears, themselves did poure,
> And dash in sunder, to lay ope a bright
>   And undisturbed Passage to that Sphear
>   Where *Psyche's* Jewels all enshrined were.
>
> In bounteous Beams of royall Influence

> Her *open Sun* bestow'd himself upon her:
> And this awak'd her long astonish'd sence
> To finde and feel the sweets of this dear Honor;
> > This swell'd her Bosom with such Ravishment
> > That through her Lips she hast's to give it vent.
>
> And now, o my *delicious Lord,* said she,
> I thank thee for that *Famine* I endured:
> I little dream'd that this Felicitie
> Could by this torturing anguish be procured:
> > But in the Wisdome of thy Love didst thou
> > Then make me *Fast,* the more to *Feast* me now.
> > > (20.41–43)

Psyche has reached the Fourth Water; and this, the final and highest climax of her wish for mystic marriage to Christ, admits her to the Unitive Way, the end of her spiritual pilgrimage. Her soul, "sacrificed to Ecstasy," is ravished by the fire of Love: her own candle merges with its more "delicious flame":

> Then, having bid unto the Earth adieu,
> And firmly fix'd her loving longing Eye
> Upon the Heav'ns, to keep *her Aim* in view;
> Her Flames triumphant Tempest swell'd so high,
> > That She, unable to contain its Tide,
> > With a deep Sigh, cri'd out, O LOVE, and di'd.
> > > (20.219)

Psyche has reached the conclusion of her mystic pilgrimage. Having proceeded over a difficult course, filled with so many disillusionments, she at last achieves the union she has sought since the first moment of her divine awakening.

3

Although Beaumont writes as if he might have fancied himself a mystic, he does not, in the way of the great mystics, tell of his own spiritual experiences, except occasionally to remark how little he has had to do with them. But rather, he reports an intellectual understanding of mysticism; the plan of his epic poem, as we have seen, is good proof of that. It is one thing to call Beaumont a mystical poet, but another to name him a mystic; sympathetic to the mystical way, as to the Catholic themes which he joined with it, Beaumont was able to discover a manner of expression that suited well his dogmatic mind.

Imagistic, picture-minded mysticism, with its raptures, its visions, its supersensory phenomena — well represented by St. Teresa — merges with a cerebral understanding in Beaumont: he has consciously used St. Teresa in order to construct his *Psyche,* but he has restrained his heroine by schematizing her faith. It is no matter that Psyche's adventures are stirred with palpable ardor; they are, but because Beaumont knows they ought to be. Never does he permit his heroine to try an unplanned course; he knows that her activities must be circumscribed, and her devotion kept systematic. More generous is the Spanish saint, who, however practical, does not enjoin an exact, formularized belief.

We ought, then, to understand Beaumont as one who knows how he should feel, but has not himself felt. When he wrote *Psyche,* he was closest to the passions of the civil war, and this fact may have urged him to some intellectual enthusiasm by forcing him to defend his doctrinal beliefs. *Psyche* was born in restless times; yet characteristically, Beaumont settled himself comfortably in Hadleigh with his family and friends, where he could watch the world peacefully, himself remaining undisturbed by the inconvenient clatter of outside struggles. For a religious apologist and reporter, this may have been the best of possible circumstances.

Psyche repeats a mystical system rather than gives birth to one; but it is, nevertheless, a mystical poem. The fact that Beaumont so little reflects the immediacy and uniqueness of the true mystic's spiritual vision does not keep him from joining hands with others far more endowed with the mystic understanding; for we should not think that the only mystics are the original ones. Religious literature is filled with the outpourings of little inspired souls; and second-hand utterances − of Beaumont's kind − are far more commonly found than the extraordinary expressions of St. Teresa or of Crashaw. Beaumont is, as much as they, a religious and mystical writer, but one who understood his task much better than he could do it.

Notes

1. The circumstances of Beaumont's life (1616–99) are given in the preceding chapter.

2. Leonard Mawe was master, 1617–25, Matthew Wren, 1626–34; both were royalist, of high church sympathies; both had been in Spain in 1623 to assist with the ultimately unsuccessful negotiations for the marriage of the Infanta to Prince Charles.

3. In his public lecture in 1638 (briefly mentioned in the preceding chapter, p. 128, and n. 11, *In Scholis pub[licis]. Cantab[rigiensibus].,* Beaumont reviews both ancient and modern learning. He is particularly lavish in his praise of Tasso; he is the most faultless of Italian poets, and among epic writers of all ages, he is peerless: "Boccacium et Sannazarum video soluta oratione purissimos, Ariostum sola fictae materiae levitate infaelicem, Petrarchum incredibili amoris suavitate modulantem, Marinum in Epigrammate argutum, in Adonite heroicum in Innocentibus splendidum, in

singulis Lauro dignum: At cum in Torquatum Tassonem oculos conjicio, nec Pindarum miror amplius; nec Horatium, nec Homerum cum stupore lego, nec Maronem; quicquid enim ad Epigrammatum festivitatem concinnum, quicquid ad Lyricorum puritatem elimatum, quicquid ad Heroici operis celsitudinem illustre putatur, id in illo uberrimum video, minime tamen (quod est laudabilius) affectatum. Tanto autem Torquatus Tasso Maronem superat, quanto fortissimus Godfredus Aeneam transfugum, tanto Homerum praecedit, quanto Jerusalem liberata clarior Troja perdita" (Peterhouse MS 459, ff. 9–10). ("I see Boccaccio and Sanazzaro most faultless with inartificial language, Ariosto felicitous in all except the invention of his material, Petrarch modulating with the unbelievable sweetness of love, Marino artful in the *Epigrammata,* heroic in *L'Adone,* splendid in *Innocenti,* worthy for the laurel in each. But when I turn my eyes on Torquato Tasso, I do not admire Pindarus more, nor do I read Horace, nor Homer, nor Maro with greater amazement; indeed, whatever is considered illustrious for the height of heroic work, I see that most fully in him, yet (what is worthier) least affected. Torquato Tasso outstrips Maro by so much as the most strong Godfredus outstrips the deserted Aeneas; he surpasses Homer by so much as liberated Jerusalem is more glorious than lost Troy.")

4. Yet there must be few poems in English like *Psyche.* There is some similarity with Edward Benlowes' *Theophila, or Loves Sacrifice: a Divine Poem* (1652), in *Minor Poets of the Caroline Period,* ed. George Saintsbury (Oxford: Clarendon Press, 1905), 1:305–472. As with *Psyche,* here is a "divine poem," a mystical allegory supported by a didactic purpose — though of course *Theophila* is hardly an epic poem.

5. John Cosin, of course, had written *A Collection of Private Devotions* (1627) at the request of Charles I. His *Devotions* may be joined with the many manuals of spiritual exercises, well known in the England of his time, such as Richard Hopkins' popular translation of Luis de Granada, *Of Prayer, and Meditation* (1582). See A. C. Southern's discussion of this work in *Elizabethan Recusant Prose 1559–1582* (London: Sands, 1950), 197–206.

6. Émile Mâle's classic study, *L'Art Religieux après le Concile de Trente* (Paris, 1932), classifies and accounts for the themes in Counter Reformation art in painting, sculpture, and architecture. Mâle demonstrates that Tridentine art defends the dogmas attacked by the protestants and assumes didactic importance by entering into the religious controversies as a graphic defense of catholicism.

7. The quotation occurs in a later passage of the same address noted in the preceding chapter, p. 128 and n. 12. Beaumont has been reviewing Spanish literature; Alonso de Villegas and Garcilasso have written "humana solum suavitate" ("with human sweetness only"). But when Beaumont turns to regard St. Teresa, the divine world opens to him: "Illam siquidem video, cujus calamus divino rore perfusus, nescio quid ipsa dulcedine dulcius stillavit, et totum caelum fudit . . . O quam minime mors esset illius scriptis immori!"

8. One of the most remarkable devotional works by a high churchman was Anthony Stafford's *The Femall Glory* (1635), discussed in chap. 9, on Cosin's *Devotions,* p. 107 and n. 28. Cf. also p. 11.

9. The "minor" poems are all quoted from Eloise Robinson's edition, *The Minor Poems of Joseph Beaumont* (London: Constable, 1914). In his *Transfigured Rites in Seventeenth-Century English Poetry* (Columbia, Mo.: University of Missouri Press, 1992), A. B. Chambers comments on a number of Beaumont's poems, primarily to demonstrate the poet's interest in the liturgy and in the feasts of the church: see esp. pp. 21–32.

10. Cf. Richard Crashaw's "The Weeper," in *The Poems English Latin and Greek of Richard Crashaw,* ed. L. C. Martin, 2nd ed. (Oxford: Clarendon Press, 1957), 79 (and the expanded version, p. 308), with which Beaumont's poem obviously has much in common.

11. *Minor Poems,* 16. Cf. Crashaw's "In the Glorious Assumption of our Blessed Lady," in *Poems,* ed. Martin, 304–306, and also Stafford, who describes the nursing Jesus: "Her Breasts, white as their owne milke, pressed by her delicate fingers, as white as either, He softly pats, and playes with. Sometimes He repaires to them for sport; sometimes for necessity; and He who feeds all things else, draws thence His nourishment" (114).

12. We may distinguish between two general sorts of mysticism, of which Beaumont, through St. Teresa, represents only one. This is *imaged* mysticism, and to it should be opposed the more philosophic and *intellective* mysticism of, for example, St. John of the Cross.

13. Philip I. Herzbrun gives an excellent synopsis of the revised and enlarged edition of 1702 in his "Joseph Beaumont's *Psyche* and Seventeenth Century Poetic Traditions" (Ph.D. diss., Johns Hopkins University, 1955), 246–73.

14. *The Complete Works of Saint Teresa of Jesus,* trans. and ed. E. Allison Peers (London: Burns Oates, 1946), 1:65–66, hereafter cited in the text.

15. *Psyche: or Loves Mysterie. In XX Canto's: Displaying the Intercourse Betwixt Christ, and the Soule* (London, 1648, 1651), 2.97. Quotations from *Psyche* will be made from the first edition unless otherwise noted. The second edition was published postumously in 1702.

16. These lines appear in the second edition of *Psyche,* 16.221, in "The Supply," which is a wholly new canto, being the largest single expansion to the first edition.

17. Beaumont seems to be remembering St. Mary Magdalene. Cf. the stanzas from "S. Mary Magdalen's Ointment," quoted above (p. 140).

18. Inspired by the literature of devotion, Beaumont lets Psyche meditate on God's unity, his truth, his goodness, his immensity, his creative power, his mildness, and his glory. Cf. Benlowes, *Theophila,* canto 7, "The Contemplation"; though not so orderly as Psyche, Theophila does manage to expatiate on all the same attributes.

19. Beaumont's portrayal of spiritual desolation corresponds to St. John of the Cross's Dark Night of the Soul, but this does not mean that he

necessarily had read his works; for St. John of the Cross rendered so eloquently what St. Teresa and other mystics have also experienced and
described. St. John of the Cross, whose *Dark Night of the Soul* now is
celebrated, seems to have been almost unknown in England in the seventeenth century, and, indeed, his works did not appear in Spain until 1618. See
The Complete Works of Saint John of the Cross, ed. E. Allison Peers (London:
Burns Oates, 1943), 1:335–486: "It is well for those who find themselves in
this condition [that is, of the Dark Night of the Sense] to take comfort, to
persevere in patience and to be in no wise afflicted. Let them trust in God,
Who abandons not those that seek Him with a simple and right heart, and
will not fail to give them what is needful for the road, until He bring them
into the clear and pure light of love. This last He will give them by means of
that other dark night, that of the spirit, if they merit that He should bring
them thereto" (379).

12

Henry More's DEMOCRITUS PLATONISSANS
and the Infinity of Worlds

> Let universall Nature witnesse give
> That what I sing's no feigned forgerie.
> A needlesse task new fables to contrive,
> But what I sing is seemly verity
> Well suting with right reason and Philosophie.

HENRY MORE (1614–87), the most interesting member of that group traditionally known as the Cambridge Platonists, lived conscientiously and well. Having early set out on one course, he never thought to change it; he devoted his whole life to the joy of celebrating, again and again, "a firm and unshaken Belief of the Existence of GOD . . . , a God infinitely Good, as well as infinitely Great."[1] Such faith was for More the starting point of his rational understanding: "with the most fervent Prayers" he beseeched God, in his autobiographical "Praefatio Generalissima," "to set me free from the dark Chains, and this so sordid Captivity of my own Will."

More offered to faith all which his reason could know, and so it happened that he "was got into a most Joyous and Lucid State of Mind," something quite ineffable; to preserve these "Sensations and Experiences of my own Soul," he wrote "a pretty full Poem call'd *Psychozoia*" (or *A Christiano-Platonicall display of Life*), an exercise begun about 1640 and designed for no audience but himself. There were times, More continues in his autobiographical remarks, when he thought of destroying *Psychozoia* because its style is rough and its language filled with archaisms. His principal purpose in that poem was to demonstrate in detail the spiritual foundation of all existence; Psyche, his heroine, is the daughter of the Absolute, the general Soul who holds together the metaphysical universe, against whom he sees reflected his own soul's mystical progress. More must, nevertheless, have been pleased with his labor, for he next wrote *Psychathanasia Platonica: or Platonicall Poem of the Immortality of Souls, especially Mans Soul,* in which he attempts to demonstate the immortality of the soul as a corrective to his age. Then, he joined to that *Antipsychopannychia, or A Confutation of the sleep of the Soul after death,* and *Antimonopsychia, or That all Souls are not one;* at the urging of friends, he published the poems in 1642 — his first literary work — as *Psychodia Platonica.*

In his argument for the soul's immortality toward the end of *Psychathanasia* (3.4), More had urged that there was no need to plead for any extension of the infinite ("a contradiction," and also, it would seem, a fruitless inquiry); but he soon changed his mind. The preface to *Democritus Platonissans* reproduces those stanzas of the earlier poem which deny infinity (34 to the end of the canto) with a new (formerly concluding) stanza 39 and three further stanzas "for a more easie and naturall leading to the present Canto," that is, *Democritus Platonissans,* which More clearly intended to be an addition, a fifth canto to *Psychathanasia* (book 3); and although *Democritus Platonissans* first appeared separately, More appended it to *Psychathanasia* in the second edition of his collected poems, this time with English titles, the whole being called *A Platonick Song of the Soul* (1647).

There is little relationship between *Democritus Platonissans* and the rest of More's poetry; even the main work to which it supposedly forms a final and concluding canto provides only the slightest excuse for such a continuation. Certainly, in *Psychathanasia,* More is excited by the new astronomy; he praises the Copernican system throughout book 3, giving an account of it according to the lessons of his study of Galileo's *Dialogo,* which he may have been reading even as he wrote.[2] Indeed, More tries to harmonize the two poems — his habit was always to look for unity. But even though *Democritus Platonissans* explores an astronomical subject, just as the third part of *Psychathanasia* also does, its attitude and theme are quite different; for More had meanwhile been reading Descartes.

More's theory of the infinity of worlds and God's plenitude evidently owed a great deal to Descartes' recent example; More responds exuberantly to him, especially to his *Principes de la Philosophie* (1644); for in him he fancied having found a true ally. Steeped in Platonic and neo-Platonic thought, and determined to reconcile Spirit with the rational mind of man, More thought he had discovered in Cartesian "intuition" what was not necessarily there. Descartes had enjoyed an ecstatic illumination, and so had Plotinus; but this was not enough, as More may have wanted to imagine, to make Descartes a neo-Platonist. But the Platonic element implicit in Descartes, his theory of innate ideas, and his proof of the existence of God from the idea of God, all helped to make More receptive to him. Nevertheless, More did not really need Descartes, nor, as he himself was later to discover, had he even understood him properly, for More had looked at him only to find his own reflection.[3]

But there was nothing really new about the idea of infinite worlds which More described in *Democritus Platonissans;* it surely was not a conception unique to Descartes. The theory was a common one in Greek and Renaissance thought. Democritus and the Epicureans, of course, advocated the theme of infinite worlds in an infinite universe which More accepted; but at the same time, he rejected their view of a mechanistic and fortuitous creation. Although Plato specifically rejects the idea of infinite worlds (in

Timaeus), More imagines, as the title of his poem implies, a Platonic universe, by which he really means neo-Platonic, combined with a Democritean plurality of worlds. More filled space, not with the infinite void of the Atomists, but with the Divine, ever active immanence. More, in fact, in an early philosophic work, *An Antidote against Atheisme* (1652), and again in *Divine Dialogues* (1668), refutes Lucretius by asserting the usefulness of all created things in God's Providence and the essential design in Nature. His reference in *Democritus Platonissans* (st. 20) is typical: "though I detest the sect / Of *Epicurus* for their manners vile, / Yet what is true I may not well reject." In bringing together Democritus's theories and neo-Platonic thought, More obviously has attempted reconciliation of two exclusive world views, but with dubious success.

While More stands firmly in a familiar tradition, his belief in an infinity of worlds evidently has little immediate connection with any predecessors. Even Bruno's work, or Thomas Digges's, which could have occupied an important place, seems to have had little, if any direct influence on More. It was Descartes who stimulated his thought at the most receptive moment; for in 1642 to have denied a theory which in 1646 he proclaimed with such force evidently argues in favor of a most powerful attachment. More responded enthusiastically to what he deemed a congenial metaphysical system; as a champion of Descartes, he was first to make him known in England and first in England to praise the infinity of worlds, yet Descartes' system could give to him little real solace. More embraces God's plenitude and infinity of worlds, he rejoices in the variety and grandeur of the universe, and he worships it as he might God Himself; but Descartes was fundamentally uninterested in such enthusiasms and found them even repellent – as well as unnecessary – to his thought. For More the doctrine of infinity was a proper corollary of Copernican astronomy and neo-Platonism (as well as Cabbalistic mysticism) and therefore a necessity to his whole elaborate and eclectic view of the world.

In introducing Cartesian thought into England, More emphasized particular physical doctrines mainly described in *The Principles of Philosophy;* he shows little interest in the *Discourse on the Method of Rightly Conducting the Reason* (1637), or in the *Meditations* (1641), both of which were also available to him when he wrote *Democritus Platonissans*. In the preface to his poem, he refers to Descartes whom he seems to have read hopefully: surely "infinitude" is the same as the Cartesian "indefinite." *"For what is his* mundus indefinitè extensus, *but* extensus infinitè? *Else it sounds onely* infinitus quoad nos, *but* simpliciter finitus," for there can be no space *"unstuffd with Atoms."* More thinks that Descartes seems "to mince it," that difficulty lies in the interpretation of a word, not in an essential idea. He is referring to part 2.21 of *The Principles,* but he quotes, with tacit approval, from part 3.1 and 2, in the motto to the poem. More undoubtedly knows the specific discussion of "infinity" in part 1.26–27, where he must first have felt uneasy delight on reading "that we must never discuss the infinite, but must simply consider those things in which we notice no limits as indefinite; as, for instance, the extenstion of the world."[4] More asked Descartes to clarify his language in their correspondence of 1648–49, the last year of Descartes' life.

Democritus Platonissans is More's earliest statement about absolute space and time; by introducing these themes into English philosophy, he contributed significantly to the intellectual history of the seventeenth century. Newton, indeed, was able to make use of More's forging efforts; but of relative time or space and their measurement, which so much concerned Newton, More had little to say. He was preoccupied with the development of a theory which would show that immaterial substance, with space and time as attributes, is as real and as absolute as the Cartesian geometrical and spatial account of matter that he felt was true but much in need of amplification.

In his first letter to Descartes, of December 11, 1648, More wrote:

> This indefinite extension is either *simpliciter* infinite, or only in respect to us. If you understand extension to be infinite *simpliciter,* why do you obscure your thought by too low and too modest words? If it is infinite only in respect to us, extension, in reality, will be finite; for our mind is the measure neither of the things nor of truth.

Unsatisfied by his first answer from Descartes (February 5, 1649), he urges his point again (March 5). If extension can describe matter, the same quality must apply to the immaterial and yet be only one of many attributes of Spirit. In his second letter to More (April 15), Descartes answers firmly:

> It is repugnant to my concept to attribute any limit to the world, and I have no other measure than my perception for what I have to assert or to deny. I say, therefore, that the world is indeterminate or indefinite, because I do not recognize in it any limits. But I dare not call it infinite as I perceive that God is greater than the world, not in respect to His extension, because, as I have already said, I do not acknowledge in God any proper [extension], but in respect to His perfection. . . . It is repugnant to my mind . . . it implies a contradiction, that the world be finite or limited, because I cannot but conceive a space outside the boundaries of the world wherever I presuppose them.

More plainly fails to understand the basic dualism inherent in Cartesian philosophy and to sense the irrelevance of his questions. While Descartes is really disposing of the spiritual world in order to get on with his analysis of finite experience, More is keenly attempting to reconcile neo-Platonism with the lively claims of matter. His effort can be read as the brave attempt to harmonize an older mode of thought with the urgency of the "new philosophy" which called the rest in doubt. More saw this conflict and the implications of it with a kind of clarity that other men of his age hardly possessed. But the way of Descartes, which at first seemed to him so promising, certainly did not lead to the kind of harmony which he sought.

More's original enthusiasm for Descartes declined as he understood better that the Cartesian world in practice excluded spirits and souls. Because Descartes could find no necessary place even for God Himself, More styled him, in *Enchridion Metaphysicum* (1671), the "Prince of the Nullibists"; these men "readily acknowledge there are such things as *Incorporeal Beings* or *Spirits,* yet do very peremptorily contend, that they are *no where* in the whole World. . . . Because they so boldly affirm that a Spirit is *Nullibi,* that is to say, *no where,*" they deserve to be called *Nullibists.*[5] In contrast to these false teachers, More describes absolute space by listing twenty epithets which can be applied either to God or to pure extension, such as "Unum, Simplex, Immobile . . . Incomprehensible."[6] There is, however, a great difficulty here; for while Space and Spirit are eternal and uncreated, they yet contain material substance which has been created by God. If the material world possesses infinite extension, as More generally believes, that would preclude any need of its having a creator. In order to avoid this dilemma, which *Democritus Platonissans* ignores, More must at last separate matter and space, seeing the latter as an attribute of God through which He is able to contain a finite world limited in space as well as in time. In writing that "this infinite space because of its infinity is distinct from matter,"[7] More reveals the direction of his conclusion; the dichotomy it embodies is Cartesianism in reverse.

While More always labored to describe the ineffable, his earliest work, the poetry, may have succeeded in this wish most of all. Although he felt that his poetry was aiming toward truths which his *"later and better concocted Prose"*[8] reached, the effort cost him the suggestiveness of figurative speech. In urging himself on toward an ever more consistent statement of belief, he lost much of his beginning exuberance (best expressed in the brief "Philosopher's Devotion") and the joy of intellectual discovery. In the search *"to find out Words which will prove faithful witnesses of the peculiarities of my Thoughts,"* he staggers under the unsupportable burden of too many words. In trying so desperately to clarify his thought, he rejects poetic discourse as "slight"; only a language free of metaphor and symbol could, he supposed, lead toward correctness. Indeed, More soon renounced poetry; he apparently wrote no more after collecting it in *Philosophical Poems* (1647), when he gave up poetry for "more seeming Substantial performances in solid *Prose.*"[9] "Cupids Conflict," which is "annexed" to *Democritus Platonissans,* is an interesting revelation of the failure of poetry, as More felt it; he justifies his "rude rugged uncouth style" by suggesting that sweet verses avoid telling important truths; harshness and obscurity may at least remind one that there is a significance beyond mere words. His lament is characteristic: "How ill alas! with wisdome it accords / To sell my living sense for liveless words."

In spite of these downcast complaints, More was quite capable of lively and meaningful poetic ideas. One is the striking image of the cone which occurs in *Democritus Platonissans* (especially in stanzas 7–8, 66–67, and 88) and becomes the most essential symbol to More's expression of infinitude and extension. The figure first appears in *Antipsychopannychia* (2.9) where his purpose is to reconcile the world Soul with Christian eschatology. In *Democritus Platonissans,* the cone enables More to adapt the familiar Hermetic paradox:

> A Circle whose circumference no where
> Is circumscrib'd, whose Centre's each where set,
> But the low Cusp's a figure circular,
> Whose compasse is ybound, but centre's every where.
>
> (st. 8)

Every point on the circumference, or base of the cone, relates to the single point at the top. The world, More wants to say, has no limits, no center, yet there are bounds in its having none. More recognizes the contradiction when he fancies "some strong arm'd Archer" at the wide world's edge (st. 37). Where shall he send his shafts? Into "mere vacuity"? But More hardly seems aware of the inappropirateness of the cone; he uses a geometrical figure to locate space, time, and numberless worlds within the universal sight of God, but matter is infinite, "distinct / And yet proceeding from the Deitie" (st. 68). Obviously, the archer must forever be sending his arrows through an infinitely expanding surface. Nevertheless, the cone has great value as a metaphor, as a richly suggestive and fascinating conception. More, however, does not want to speak metaphorically; he is attempting to disclose truths, literal and plain, where pretty words and metaphors have no place. Even as he is writing his most effective poetry, we are aware that More is denying his poetic office; for he is pleading a reasoned case where the words crack and strain, where poetic meaning gathers, only to be denied.

But these objections momentarily disappear when More forgets himself enough to let us feel his imagination and does not worry that we might miss the proofs of his philosophy. *Democritus Platonissans* concludes with an apocalyptic vision wherein the poet imagines the reconciliation of infinite worlds and time within God's immensity. He is also attempting to harmonize *Psychathanasia,* where he rejected infinitude, with its sequel, *Democritus Platonissans,* where he has everywhere been declaring it; thus we should think of endless worlds as we should think of Nature and the Phoenix, dying yet ever regenerative, sustained by a "centrall power / Of hid spermatick life" which sucks "sweet heavenly juice" from above (st. 101). More closes his poem on a vision of harmony and ceaseless energy, a most fit ending for one who dared to believe that the new philosophy sustained the old, that all coherence had not gone out of the world, but was always there, only waiting to be discovered afresh in this latter age.

Notes

1. The quotations from More's Latin autobiography occur in the *Opera Omnia* (London, 1675–79), portions of which Richard Ward translated in *The Life of . . . Henry More* (London, 1710). See the modern edition of this work, ed. M. F. Howard (London: Theosophical Publishing Society, 1911), 61, 67–68, the text followed here. There is a reprint of the *Opera Omnia*, 3 vols. (Hildesheim, 1966), with an introduction by Serge Hutin. The "Praefatio Generalissima" begins vol. 2.1. One passage (not appearing in Ward's translation) refers to the genesis of *Democritus Platonissans*. More writes that after finishing *Psychathanasia*, he felt a renewed stirring of heart: "Postea vero mutata sententia furore nescio quo Poetico incitatus supra dictum Poema scripsi, ea potissimum innixus ratione quod liquido constaret extensionem spacii dari infinitatam, nec majores absurditates pluresve contingere posse in Materia infinita, infinitaque Mundi duratione, quam in infinita Extensione spacii" ("In fact, later, having changed my mind, I wrote the aforementioned poem [*Democritus Platonissans*], impelled by some creative inspiration; I relied especially on the idea that it is abundantly clear that the extension of space is given as infinite, and that neither more nor greater absurdities can happen in infinite matter or in the infinite duration of the world than in the infinite extension of space" [ix]).

2. See Lee Haring, "Henry More's *Psychathanasia* and *Democritus Platonissans*: A Critical Edition" (Ph.D. diss., Columbia University, 1961), 33–57. Cf. also John Henry, "A Cambridge Platonist's Materialism: Henry More and the Concept of Soul," *Journal of the Warburg and Courtauld Institute* 49 (1986): 172–95, and Alexander Jacob, "Henry More's *A Platonick Song of the Soul*: A Critical Study" (Ph.D. diss., Pennsylvania State University, 1988).

3. See Rupert Hall, *Henry More: Religion, Magic and Experiment* (Oxford: Blackwell, 1990), who writes of More's curious synthesis of the "triple teaching" of Moses, Plato, and Descartes. Marjorie Hope Nicolson's various articles and books which in part deal with More are important to my discussion, and especially "The Early Stage of Cartesianism in England," *Studies in Philology* 26 (1929): 356–79; *Mountain Gloom and Mountain Glory* (Ithaca: Cornell University Press, 1959), 113–43, and *The Breaking of the Circle* (New York: Columbia University Press, 1960), 158–65. Cf. also Aharon Lichtenstein, *Henry More: The Rational Theology of a Cambridge Platonist* (Cambridge: Harvard University Press, 1962), which includes a very full bibliography, and Earl Miner, *The Metaphysical Mode from Donne to Cowley* (Princeton: Princeton University Press, 1969), 48–117.

4. See René Descartes, *Principles of Philosophy*, trans. Valentine Rodger Miller and Reese P. Miller (Dordrecht, Holland: D. Reidel, 1984), 13. More quotes from Descartes at the end of his preface as if providing an

inscription or epigraph: *"De generali totius hujus mundi aspectabilis constructione ut rectè Philosophemur duo sunt imprimis observanda: Unum ut attendentes ad infinitam Dei potentiam et bonitatem nè vereamur nimis ampla et pulchra et absoluta ejus opera imaginari: sed è contra caveamus, nè si quos fortè limites nobis non certò cognitos, in ipsis supponamus, non satìs magnificè de creatoris potentia sentire videamur.*

"Alterum, ut etiam caveamus, nè nimis superbè de nobis ipsis sentiamus. Quod fieret non modò, si quos limites nobis nullâ cognitos ratione, nec divinâ revelatione, mundo vellemus affingere, tanquam si vis nostra cogitationis, ultra id quod à Deo revera factum est ferri posset; sed etiam maximè, si res omnes propter nos solos, ab illo creatas esse fingeremus" (sig. A4ᵛ). ("In order to reason correctly about the general structure of this whole visible world, we must pay special attention to two things. First, remembering God's infinite power and goodness, we must not be afraid of overestimating the greatness, beauty, and perfection of His works; rather, we must beware of accidentally attributing to them any limits of which we do not have certain knowledge, and of thus seeming to have an inadequate awareness of the Creator's power. Second, we must beware of overestimating ourselves. We would be doing so if we were to attribute to the universe limits of which we had been assured either by reason or by divine revelation; for this would be to assume that our minds can conceive something which is greater than the world which God actually created. We would be overestimating ourselves still more if we were to imagine that God created all things solely for us, or if we were to consider our intellect powerful enough to understand His ends in creating the universe" [84]).

The quotations from the letters that follow occur in Alexandre Koyré's important book, *From the Closed World to the Infinite Universe* (Baltimore, 1957), 114, 122–23, but the complete texts can be consulted in Descartes, *Correspondance avec Arnaud et Morus,* ed. G. Lewis (Paris, 1953).

5. This passage occurs at the beginning of "The Easie, True, and Genuine Notion, And consistent Explication Of the Nature of a Spirit," a free translation of *Enchridion Metaphysicum,* 1.27–28, by John Collins which he included in Joseph Glanvil's *Saducismus Triumphatus* (London, 1681). I quote from the text as given in *Philosophical Writings of Henry More,* ed. F. I. MacKinnon (New York, 1925), 183.

6. See *Enchridion Metaphysicum,* 8.8, trans. Mary Whiton Calkins and included in John Tull Baker, *An Historical and Critical Examination of English Space and Time Theories* (Bronxville, N.Y., 1930), 12. For the original, see *Opera Omnia,* 2.1 (p. 167).

7. *"Infinitum* igitur hoc *Extensum* à Materia distinctum," *Enchridion Metaphysicum,* 8.9, in *Opera Omnia,* and quoted by MacKinnon, 262.

8. This and the following reference appear in *An Explanation of the Grand Mystery of Godliness* (London, 1660), "To the Reader," vi and v.

9. Ibid., 2.11 (p. 52).

IV

VICTORIAN REFLECTIONS

13

Christina Rossetti's
Devotional Prose

ALMOST ALL Christina Rossetti's prose works are "devotional" in one particular sense of that term, for they seek to define and increase religious
knowledge by informing and instructing the Christian worshiper. Rossetti
wrote these books during the last twenty years of her life. The first was *Annus
Domini: A Prayer for Each Day of the Year, Founded on a Text of Holy Scripture* (1874), followed by *Seek and Find: A Double Series of Short Studies of the
Benedicite* (1879), *Called to be Saints: The Minor Festivals Devotionally
Studied* (1881), *Letter and Spirit: Notes on the Commandments* (1883), *Time
Flies: A Reading Diary* (1885), and *The Face of the Deep: A Devotional Commentary on the Apocalypse* (1892). This is a substantial volume of work, but
still of minor significance when set beside the poetry. Poetry was to Rossetti
always the primary and most natural concern of her life; she began to write in
the 1840s, at age eleven or twelve, and continued almost to the end of her life
in 1894. She also continued to write poetry at the same time as the prose,
even interspersing it with appropriately devotional poems. One may feel
tempted to say, indeed, that the best features of some of the prose works are
these poetical interpolations.

But the prose works have an integrity, a solemnity, and a thoughtful-
ness characteristic of much of Rossetti's best writing, although sometimes
they also convey a sense of dutifulness, as if their author felt conscience-
bound to write them. I intend to discuss the imagination that shaped these
books, the historical context within which they were written, and also their
interest to readers of the poetry. Because these books are so little known –
and now very difficult to obtain – I will briefly describe the contents of each
one, and, in doing so, I will begin to explore some of the major issues I have
just identified.

Annus Domini (Oxford: James Parker), the first of Rossetti's devotional prose works, was published in 1874 with a brief commendatory preface
by the Reverend Canon H. W. Burrows, Vicar of Christ Church, Albany
Street, where Rossetti was for many years a parishioner. This little book contains 366 collects, one for each day of the year. Each collect begins with a
scriptural text, opening with Genesis 3.15, and continuing with various texts

from both Old and New Testaments; the last collect is founded on Revelation 23.16. The principle of selection is roughly clear, for Rossetti evidently favored texts of a prophetic nature, such as Isaiah 32.1, "Behold, a King shall reign in Righetousness," or the numerous texts from Revelation; or else she chose New Testament texts that specifically touch the mystery of the Incarnation, such as "The Light shineth in darkness; and the darkness comprehended it not" (John 1.5). It is noteworthy that forty collects are based on texts from Isaiah, and forty-two on the Apocalypse; another thirty-two come from the Gospel of John, and a further sixty-four from the Psalms, many of which can be easily related to Christian sensibility and worship, as, for example, Ps. 43.4: "Then will I go unto the Altar of God, unto God my Exceeding Joy: yea, upon thy harp will I praise Thee, O God my God." Hebrews is another important source (31), as are 1 and 2 Peter (14) and 1 John (10).

A typical collect can be illustrated by no. 198, on John 1.14: "We beheld His Glory, the Glory as of the Only Begotten of the Father":

> O Lord Jesus Christ, the Only Begotten of the Father, lift up our hearts, I entreat Thee, that with Cherubim and Seraphim, with Angels and Archangels, with Saints who labour and Saints who rest, we may love, worship and adore Thee in the Mystery of the Ever Blessed Trinity.

The text becomes the occasion of the beginning of the collect, with an invocation always to Christ − not, as in the Book of Common Prayer, to God the Father. The invocation is followed by an entreaty in the first person "I," a statement of the general intention, and a final gathering up of the prayer in terms of all mankind. Canon Burrows was right to describe these prayers in his preface as "valuable in themselves from their fervour, reverence, and overflowing charity, and [for] . . . the use which should be made of Holy Scripture in our devotions. Each little Prayer may be considered as the result of a meditation, and as an example of the way in which that exercise should issue in worship." He noted also that the book could be used properly only "as supplementary to other devotions," the purpose that their author surely intended.

Rossetti was thinking of a daily prayer that would help people concentrate their thoughts around a meditation on the Incarnate God, the Word made flesh. She also provided for the whole book a calendar-index of the major seasons of the church year from Advent and Christmas through Easter and Trinity, assigning appropriate collects to the different times and including separate sections for Saints' Days, Feasts of the Blessed Virgin, St. Michael and All Angels, Ember Weeks, and Rogation Days. The small format of the book which measures 12.0 cm x 9.0 cm (printed in foolscap 8°), with marginal rules on every page and an ornamental cross at each corner of the rule, and neatly bound in limp, dark red buckram (stamped with double sets of black rules), seems to be declaring itself a suitable accompaniment to the Book of Common Prayer. Rossetti's first devotional book fits nicely into the series that her publisher James Parker was bringing out as the Oxford Editions of Devotional Works. Among the books on his list are Lancelot Andrewes's *Devotions*, Archbishop Laud's *Private Devotions,* Jeremy Taylor's *Holy Living* and *Holy Dying.* Although very different from any of them, *Annus Domini* deserves a place in this worthy company of seventeenth-century manuals, written by some of those who were most representative of the "golden age" of Anglican devotion.

Rossetti's five other works of devotional prose were published with similar elegance: the physical object complements the content itself, reinforces it, helps the reader to move into a specially shaped, aesthetically pleasing religious world. The Society for Promoting Christian Knowledge (SPCK) became her "religious" publisher, beginning with *Seek and Find,* which appeared in 1879, five years after *Annus Domini.* The book is carefully and handsomely produced, though it is not quite so elaborate as the volumes that would follow it. Rossetti's brother Dante Gabriel protested over so much and such committed religious publication, but she objected that "I don't think harm will accrue to me from my SPCK books, even to my standing: if it did, I should still be glad to throw my grain of dust into the religious scale.[1]

The Benedicite, which Rossetti intends to elucidate in *Seek and Find,* is one of the alternative canticles appointed to be said or sung in the office of morning prayer in the Book of Common Prayer. It is known also as the "Song of the Three Children," that is, of Ananiah, Azariah, and Michael, whom Nebuchadnezzar threw into the fiery furnace because they had refused to bow down and worship before his golden statue. This canticle, an apocryphal addition to the Book of Daniel (inserted between 3.23 and 3.24), is a long poem of exaltation and blessing of God's works — the heavens, the waters, the sun and moon, dews and frosts, whales, fowl and beasts, "children of men," and more. In composing her "double series" of studies, Rossetti sets out all the separate objects of praise in a first series that she considers in terms of "creation," drawing together many scriptural passages that could be relevant. Then, in the second series of studies on the "redemption," she gathers other scriptural texts around the same subjects as before. The result is a kind of "harmony" of the Benedicite, with its "Praise-givers" as, on the one hand, the creatures of God, and, on the other, the servants of God, the one side prefiguring the other, but both expressing, with different emphasis or direction, the glory of God.

Little about *Seek and Find* is original, apart from its ingenious structure and the telling arrangement of the biblical texts. Only occasionally does Rossetti allow herself to speak or comment about any of the divisions in the Benedicite and, when she does so, it is usually in rather vague terms. But in one instance, in the "first series," she muses about the stars, and provides us a rare glimpse of her intellectual leanings:

> There is something awe-striking, over-whelming, in contemplation of the stars. Their number, magnitudes, distances, orbits, we know not: any multitude our unaided eyes

discern is but an instalment of that vaster multitude which
the telescope reveals. . . . Knowledge runs apace: and our
globe which once seemed large is now but a small planet
among planets, while not one of our group of planets is
large as compared with its central sun; and the sun itself
may be no more than a sub-centre, it and all its system
coursing but as satellites and sub-satellites around a general
centre; and this again, − what of this? Is even this remote
centre truly central, or is it no more than yet another sub-
centre revolving around some point of overruling attraction,
and swaying with it the harmonious encircling dance of its
attendant worlds?   (35−36)

These comments reveal Rossetti's interest in the new astronomy, which was
undergoing dramatic changes during the last half of the nineteenth century,
especially in its conceptions of stellar structure and evolution.

Rossetti's fascination with the magnitude of the created world (and
sometimes also with its minuteness) is manifested throughout her writings.
Her journey to the continent with her mother and brother William Michael
in 1861 (and again in 1865), and in particular the sight of the Alps, made a
strong impression that deepened with succeeding years. *Time Flies* (1885)
contains numerous references to the Italian and Swiss part of her journey;
the mountains fill her with sadness as well as sober excitement:

Their mass and loftiness dwarf all physical magnitudes
familiar to most eyes, except the low-lying vastness of the
ocean and the boundless overarching sky. They touch and
pass through those clouds which limit our vision. . . .
Well, saddened and probably weary, I ended one delight-
ful day's journey in Switzerland; and passed indoors, losing
sight for a moment of the mountains.
Then from a window I faced them again. And, lo! the evening flush had turned snow to a rose, "and sorrow and sadness fled away."   (entry for June 10)

The observation of mountains in the earlier *Seek and Find* is also evocative:

Mountains bestow, valleys receive: snowy heights form a
water-shed for the low-lying fertility which engarlands their
base. Moreover they bestow necessaries not in mere naked
sufficiency, but in forms which make hill-streams and water-
falls rank among the beauty-spots of this beautiful world:
such streams descend with murmur, tumult and thunder, in
crystal expanses, in ripples, leaps and eddies, in darkness
and light, in clearness and whiteness, and foam and foam-
bow.   (91−92)

In this description, Rossetti reveals something of her imaginative life, whereas in the description of stars she revealed a certain intellectual predisposition. But for the most part *Seek and Find* lacks such moments, for its essential aim is to present a scriptural gloss or interpretation of a well-known canticle.

The next devotional book Rossetti wrote allowed her greater scope for more personal statements. *Called to be Saints,* published in the same year as *"A Pageant" and Other Poems* (1881), was in fact completed five years earlier.[2] In some respects the book is a straightforward, that is, scriptural account of the apostolic saints remembered in the Book of Common Prayer, and of its solemn days set aside for the Holy Innocents, the Presentation or Purification, the Annunciation, St. Michael and All Angels, and All Saints. Starting with St. Andrew (November 30), Rossetti sets out all the scriptural references to the saint, then provides "Biographical Additions" gathered from such traditional stories and legends as would have been available to her in Alban Butler's *Lives of the . . . Saints* (1756–1759, and frequently reprinted) or S. Baring-Gould's *Lives* (1872).[3] There follows a prayer appropriate to the character of the saint − for St. Andrew, this is a prayer for "Large-Heartedness" − evidently of Rossetti's own composition; afterward comes "a memorial" in which scriptural passages about the saint are distributed in one column, with the Psalms appointed for the feast in parallel columns. To each saint, the author assigns a stone and a flower (for St. Andrew, the jasper and the daisy). "The Key to my Book" helps clarify this curious arrangement:

> Those verses in the Book of Revelation [21.19–20] which name the twelve apostolic foundation stones of New Jerusalem, when set against the Calendar naturally assign the jasper to St. Andrew; and thence progressing in a regular order throughout, the amethyst at last to St. Jude: according to which arrangement, in default of any clue to the contrary, I have written concerning them. (xiv)

Rossetti's choice of flowers is even more arbitrary, for there is no catalogue similar to that of the stones:

> But precious things of the earth and of the deep are for those who are gorgeously apparelled and live delicately and are in kings' courts. I think the Gospel records more lessons drawn by our Master from a seed or a plant than from a pearl. So I will, as it were, gather simples and try to spell out their lessons: I will adorn the shrines of Christ's friends with flowers, and plant a garden round their hallowed graves. (xv–xvi)[4]

The most interesting portions of *Called to be Saints* are its "additions": hagiographical, petrographical, botanical. Rossetti is most effective when she writes meditatively about the saints and their festivals, about the stones she assigns to the twelve apostles, and about the single-flower gardens she plants for each one of them, but much else seems mechanically ordered, as if with the help of a large memory or a good concordance.

The section on St. Michael and All Angels is especially full, and includes much scripture but also much of Rossetti's distinctive prose.[5] One interesting passage describes the desolate life, with the antidote offered by the seraphic vision (Isa. 6.1–8):

> When it seems (as sometimes through revulsion of feeling and urgency of Satan it may seem) that our yoke is uneasy and our burden unbearable, because our life is pared down and subdued and repressed to an intolerable level: and so in one moment every instinct of our whole self revolts against our lot, and we loathe this day of quietness and of sitting still, and writhe under a sudden sense of all we have irrecoverably foregone, of the right hand, or foot, or eye cast from us, of the haltingness and maimedness of our entrance (if enter we do at last) into life, – then the Seraphim of Isaiah's vision making music in our memory revive hope in our heart.
>
> For at the sound of their mighty cry of full-flooding adoration, the very posts of the door moved and the house was filled with smoke. No lack there, nothing subdued there; no bridle, no curb, no self-sacrifice: outburst of sympathy, fulness of joy, plesures for evermore, likeness that satisfieth; beauty for ashes, oil of joy for mourning, the garment of praise for the spirit of heaviness; things new out of God's treasure-house, – things old also, please God.[6]

The contrast of the dull spirit with the vision of joy in its fullness provides a happy example of Rossetti's prose style. The circumstances of deprivation, described abstractly yet in plaintive detail, are nicely presented within the controlling view of praise and worship. A similar kind of genius touches the curious description of the flower assigned to St. Michael and All Angels – flowerless flowers, the ferns, especially bracken and maidenhair. Through close observation, we may realize tender meanings: fronds have much to teach us, "for if instead of merely plucking a well-developed frond we sever its thick stalk in a smooth slant, the surface thus disclosed exhibits markings which (more or less) resemble the figure of the imperial spread eagle, the outline shifting according to the angle of the cut. Which leads us to a thought of wings out of sight, and angels unawares" (449).

Called to be Saints is one of the most attractively printed of Rossetti's books. Every page is set out by rules (an ornamental device in each corner), with running headlines and section titles in gothic type. There are ornamental, engraved initial letters at the beginning of each sub-section, accompanied by engraved illustrations of each flower (or plant). The paper is an antique white, and the whole book is bound in dark blue, fine-ribbed buckram; the title is stamped in gold on the spine. Such care for the physical appearance of the book is, of course, typical of much Tractarian publishing, and all Rossetti's books, beginning, as we have seen, with *Annus Domini,* received devoted attention.

Letter and Spirit appeared only two years after its predecessor, using the same rules and devices on each page and the same type. It is clear upon opening this book that one is, as it were, entering a devotional work, as if George Herbert's admonition in *The Temple* (1633) had been given a literal translation:

> Avoid, Profanenesse; come not here:
> Nothing but holy, pure, and cleare,
> Or that which groneth to be so,
> May at his perill further go.[7]

This little book on the commandments, like all the companion volumes Rossetti wrote, communicates a certain spare chastity, a purity of intention, a sense of duty and calling. Like the other devotional books, this one also depends upon another book or writing, which it intends to elucidate, support, and sustain. Possibly more than the others, *Letter and Spirit* strikes a chord for charity, which is part of one's continuing duty. The two great commandments — and in them lies the spirit of the Old Testament letter of Mosaic code — lead to this knowledge: "Thou shalt love the Lord thy God with all thy heart, and with all thy soul, and with all thy mind, and with all thy strength. . . . Thou shalt love thy neighbour as thyself."

If we approach the book "in charity," we may better recognize both its strengths and its failings. The latter lie in the easily formulated and superficially considered theological statements, the former in Rossetti's kind and affectionate wish "to throw [her] grain of dust" into sustaining the devotional life of the ordinary faithful Christian. We can learn little from Rossetti's discussion of the Trinity: "A self-surrendering awe-struck reverence is all that beseems us in contemplating this Mystery of Mysteries, the Trinity in Unity" (12), for this statement describes a devotional, not an intellectual understanding of doctrine. Rossetti similarly says we must be faithful to the Church and to "the Catholic religion" (Rossetti's inverted quotation marks), which teaches the unity and trinity of the Godhead:

> It seems that to grasp, hold fast, adore the Catholic Mystery
> leads up to man's obligation to grasp, hold fast, adore the
> Christian Mystery; rather than this to the other. What is
> Catholic underlies what is Christian: on the Catholic basis
> alone can the Christian structure be raised; even while to

> raise the superstructure on that foundation is the bounden
> duty of every soul within reach of the full Divine Revela-
> tion.   (8–9)

The appeal to charity is more helpful:

> Party feeling, whether called religious zeal or national
> antagonism or political creed, becomes simple malice and is
> simply devilish when it leads us not only to condemn
> opponents . . . but to wish that they may really be as
> unworthy as history or rumour makes them, to court and
> hug and blaze abroad every tittle of evidence which tells
> against them, to turn a dull ear and lukewarm heart to
> everything which tells in their favour. "Charity . . . rejoiceth
> not in iniquity, but rejoiceth in the truth." It is a solemn
> thing to write history.   (157–58)

William Michael Rossetti recalls in the *Memoir* of his sister that she
lived above all by the precept, "Judge not, that ye be not judged." Her life
was one of charity, long-suffering, and ready affection for everyone. William
Michael's judgment that her faith was pure and absolute is clearly reflected in
such a work as *Letter and Spirit:* "To learn that something in the Christian
faith was credible *because it was reasonable,* or because it rested upon some
historic evidence of fact, went against her. . . . 'My faith is faith; it is not
evolved out of argumentation, nor does it seek the aid of that.'"[8] This last
remark might well be the epigraph or motto for all Rossetti's devotional
prose.

   Letter and Spirit is somewhat awkwardly organized, for it attempts
both to show how the Ten Commandments of the old law are reflected in the
two commandments of the new covenant and to display the different commandments in relation to one another. The text contains numerous
reminders of these divisions and branches; nonetheless, it leaves the impression of a peculiar and unnecessary confusion of parts without headings or
obvious breaks — an unusual feature, not characteristic of the other devotional works. Another quality unique to *Letter and Spirit* is its use of
"characters," such as (and notably) The Idler and The Money-grubber, both
egregious trangressors of the fourth commandment, "that thou keep holy the
Sabbath-day." The Idler is "the last man to draw an unswerving line of sacred
demarcation around the seventh day. His mind is lax; his habits are unstable
as water, dribbling out in this direction, overflowing in that, running short
somewhere." The Money-grubber is also grossly indolent, but he repudiates
Sunday for different reasons:

> If importunate decency transports our Money-grubber into
> his pew on Sunday morning, then before his mental eyes
> ledgers and their kind flaunt themselves, where neighbours

only discern Bibles, Prayer-books, Hymn-books, on the desk. His bales of goods, cattle, hay-ricks, would be no more out of place in Church than is he himself; his money-bag would occupy a seat as worthily; they would put full as much heart into their attendance, and full as much spirituality. (180)

In these portraits, Rossetti follows the tradition going back to the Greek writer Theophrastus and continuing in such English authors as Sir Thomas Overbury, John Earle, and Thomas Fuller, especially in his *Holy and Profane State* (1642), which Rossetti may have read (we know she was reading Fuller's *Worthies* because she alludes to it in *Called to be Saints*).[9] But the English writer Rossetti's characters first bring to mind is William Law. In *A Serious Call to a Devout and Holy Life* (1728, and frequently reprinted), Law not only draws notable "characters," such as the tradesman Calidus who is too busy to keep the Sabbath, but he also writes with an uncompromising and austere view of religion, filled nevertheless with charity and honest devotion. Of "imaginary conversations," I can fancy few more amiable than one between William Law and Christina Rossetti.

Rossetti's next prose work followed soon after her "notes" on the commandments. In 1885 she published *Time Flies,* descriptively subtitled "A Reading Diary." For this volume, SPCK provided an especially handsome format using heavy, laid hand-made paper with uneven deckle edges. The book has much in common with *Called to be Saints,* physically resembling it in size and binding. As for content, the earlier book concentrates on the prayer book saints, whereas the later one describes not only these saints but many others, especially martyrs of the church and such British saints as Alban, David, and Chad. Thus every day of the year has an entry, and all the prayer book feasts are mentioned, as are many minor saints' days. Rossetti provides no commemoration for some days, however; rather she includes a poem or writes a meditation, occasionally related to the season of the year. *Time Flies,* like *Called to be Saints,* contains numerous personal observations, but it comes closer to being a book of commonplaces, thus reminding us of its diary-like composition.

Reading *Time Flies,* we seem to overhear Rossetti's speech, and since this book brings us so close to her attitudes and views, it enables us to fill out her portrait. The portrait is of a somber, sensible person, moved by the infinite and unremitting sadness of life, who is alternately touched by grief and quiet joy. The full entry for November 7, written about her sister Maria, who had died in November 1876, shows these bittersweet qualities well:

One of the dearest and most saintly persons I ever knew, in foresight of her own approaching funeral, saw nothing attractive in the "hood and hatband" style toward which I evinced some old-fashioned leaning. "Why make everything as hopeless looking as possible?" she argued.

And at a moment which was sad only for us who lost her,
all turned out in harmony with her holy hope and joy.

Flowers covered her, loving mourners followed her,
hymns were sung at her grave, the November day
brightened, and the sun (I vividly remember) made a minia-
ture rainbow in my eyelashes.

I have often thought of that rainbow since.

May all who love enjoy cheerful little rainbows at the fun-
erals of their beloved ones.[10]

In another entry (September 4), Rossetti writes again of human affection: we
love others without wanting them to be different, and we readily overlook
blemishes. Yet when one whom we have loved dies, the faults become
memorable, even growing in beauty and helping "our 'vale of misery' [turn]
to a perennial well of very sweet and refreshing water."

We are not likely to forget such sensitively felt passages as these, no
more than we can ignore the particular kind of religious devotion that shaped
Rossetti's life. Rossetti was an Anglican in the high church tradition, and
much of her writing reflects the depth of her belief. One need hardly know
more about her biography than that she was above all else an inheritor of
Tractarianism in the supreme flowering of the Oxford Movement. Consequently, she saw the Church of England as a true and historical part (some
would say "branch") of Catholic Christendom. She can speak naturally,
without really being smug or arrogant, of "our venerable Anglican Mother
Church" (entry for June 28), and write:

Great is our privilege as members of the English Church,
in that we are not commanded, or invited, or in any way
encouraged to assert what contradicts history, or to override
facts by pious beliefs, or in any form to hold "the thing that
is not."

When we reflect on points susceptible of improvement in
our beloved Mother Church, it is well to betake ourselves to
prayer; well also to give thanks for her grace of sin-
cerity.   (March 18)

This comment comes in her commemoration of St. Edward, King of the West
Saxons, who might have been martyred (the Anglican calendar is quite
proper in its silence on this point).

Rossetti's interest in the natural environment is especially apparent in
her devotional prose, but nowhere so clearly as in *Time Flies*. Rossetti saw
the natural world as emblematic of God's incarnational presence: "To him
'that hath ears to hear,' any good creature of God may convey a message"
(March 31). Thus she observes the significance of a millipede, jackdaws and
starlings, a four-leaf clover, frogs, a tame robin, a spider in its web. Her

observation of a water rat, or possibly "a water-haunting bird," illustrates how she sees nature and interprets it:

> One day long ago I sat in a certain garden by a certain ornamental water . . . so long and so quietly that a wild garden creature or two made its appearance. . . . I was absorbed that afternoon in anxious thought, yet the slight incident pleased me. If by chance people noticed me they may have thought how dull and blank I must be feeling: and partly they would have been right but partly wrong.
>
> Many . . . whom we pity as even wretched, may in reality, as I was at that moment, be conscious of some small secret fount of pleasure: a bubble, perhaps, yet lit by a dancing rainbow.
>
> I hope so and I think so: for we and all creatures alike are in God's hand, and God loves us. (April 10)

Everything in nature can teach the love of God and his presence. Rossetti recalls her first experience of death when, in early childhood, she found a dead mouse in the grounds of a cottage. In sympathy, she buried the mouse in a mossy spot. Remembering the place, she went back a day or two later and, moving the moss away, discovered a black insect: "I fled in horror, and for long years ensuing I never mentioned this ghastly adventure to anyone." The initial sympathy, and the horror of decay, were both childish reactions, she now understands: "Contemplating death from a wider and wiser viewpoint, I would fain reverse the order of those feelings: dwelling less and less on the mere physical disgust, while more and more on the rest and safety; on the perfect peace of death, please God" (March 4).

In order to read Rossetti's many accounts of martyrdom and saintly deaths appropriately, one must appreciate in them the spirit of an intense incarnationalism, in which the Word made flesh discourses with those who can speak and hear. St. Richard (April 3) edifies us in his death: having collapsed when hearing Mass, he later spoke gently from his deathbed, "I was glad when they said unto me, We will go into the house of the Lord." St. Boniface (or Winfrid), another English martyr, had "from early childhood . . . set his heart on piety and the service of God"; when he was about to be executed, he placed under his head a volume of the Gospels, on which he stretched forth his neck for the blow of the executioner. Although Rossetti borrows from various sources, particularly in writing her martyrologies — *Time Flies* is after all "a reading diary" — she shapes these materials to accord with her own design. This design emphasizes her incarnational orientation, her high church devotion to sacramental worship with its encouragement of a lively sense of God at work in all creation.[11]

The last of Rossetti's devotional prose works is also the longest. *The Face of the Deep* (1892) contains more than 500 pages of close commentary on the Apocalypse. But it is not so much a commentary as a loosely connected and free-ranging discussion of many topics and ideas that concerned Rossetti. The entire Book of Revelation is set out a verse at a time; for each verse, Rossetti provides some discussion, often extended, at other times rather abbreviated, depending on her inclination. But if one is hoping to discover a theological or analytical exegesis of Revelation, this is not the work in which to find it. Rossetti more than once apologizes for what she is doing, because she hopes no one will misundertand her purpose: "What I write professes to be a *surface* study [Rossetti's italics] of an unfathomable depth: if it incites any to dive deeper than I attain to, it will so far have accomplished a worthy work. My suggestions do not necessarily amount to beliefs; they may be no more than tentative thoughts compatible with acknowledged ignorance" (365). The book is difficult to read consecutively from beginning to end, for it seems to make no progress, and it develops by a loose association of ideas.

In the discussion of Revelation 8.2, "And I saw the seven angels which stood before God; and to them were given seven trumpets," Rossetti sees first Jericho and its destruction, then the ark of the Lord placed before Jericho; she then remembers that Christ is "our true and sole Ark of Safety" and that he has promised to be with his church even to the end of the world. Christ's promise of salvation to his church and to his people reminds us that we are to worship him regularly; thus the sabbath day should be kept holy and undefiled, for it "ranks amongst venerable and immutable Divine institutions, dating back to unfallen man in the Garden of Eden" (243). This observation gives Rossetti the chance to comment on contemporary worship, which is desultory and mean:

> Already in England . . . the signs of the times are ominous:
> Sunday is being diverted by some to business, by others to
> pleasure; Church congregations are often meagre, and so
> services are chilled. Our solemn feasts languish, and our
> fasts where are they? . . . So Joshua and his host when sum-
> moned to storm Jericho day after day for seven days, must
> amongst those days have kept one unexampled Sabbath, if
> not in the letter yet in the spirit.   (243–44)

Thus we return to Jericho, but not before a string of more or less related ideas are laid before us.[12]

The Face of the Deep is a patchwork of scriptural citations, meditations, admonitions, studies of spiritual climate, and self-criticism − of almost everything except the proposed subject, the Apocalypse itself. In *The Face of the Deep,* Rossetti is engaged in a self-study similar to that of "holy George Herbert," to whom she makes one notable reference: the concluding line of "Miserie." In this poem Herbert has been complaining of man's foolishness, his imperfection, and consequently his loss of Paradise; but whom he has really meant to criticize is, as he says in the final line, "My God, I mean my self." Rossetti's self-study, though less subtle than Herbert's, is more explicit; she prays that "God grant us . . . self-knowledge and humility" (226).

Self-knowledge, charity, avoidance of judgment of others, and energetic and ceaseless instruction characterize Rossetti's devotional prose, and evidently her own personality. Her attraction to these qualities is at work in the "commentary" on the Apocalypse, as in the studies of the Benedicite and of the commandments. But there is another, complementary, aspect of the prose works, illustrated most obviously in the book of collects, the consideration of the festivals and diary of daily reflections. And that aspect is the impossible desire to prepare oneself to know something of the incomprehensible mystery of God. The attitude is familiar in the Anglo-Catholicism that Rossetti practiced: God cannot really be known except as he wishes to reveal himself; and to find him, one must exercise patience and prayer, and everywhere in the created world look thoughtfully. Patience, indeed! In her prefatory note to *The Face of the Deep,* Rossetti tells us that patience is the lesson in the Book of Revelation: "I seek and hope to find Patience in this Book of awful import. Patience, at the least: and along with that grace whatever treasures beside God may vouchsafe me."

Perhaps this last work in fact combines dutiful, regulated study and its waiting on patience with the happiness of fulfillment, or at least the joy of expectation, which may, after all, be the greatest gift of sacramental understanding and faith in the Incarnation. As the commentary in *The Face of the Deep* demonstrates, Revelation 8.4, "And the smoke of the incense, which came with the prayers of the saints, ascended up before God out of the angel's hand," offers an especially rich text for someone such as Christina Rossetti, whose affections always desired stirring, but only as she so determined. Rossetti observes that

> the incense and smoke of the incense should kindle us to utmost adoration and love, by thus setting before us Christ Who for our sakes made Himself once for all a whole Burnt Offering, an Offering and a sweet-smelling Savour to the Glory of God the Father; and Who in the Blessed Sacrament of His Body and Blood having left to His Church a perpetual Memorial of His sole sufficient Sacrifice, receives us and our petitions into the "secret place" of that Presence and sets us in heavenly places with his own Self. (245)

Notes

1. Quoted by Lona Mosk Packer, *Christina Rossetti* (Berkeley: University of California Press, 1963), 329. Packer also quotes (329–32) a number of interesting passages from Rossetti's unpublished notes on Genesis and Exodus, which she may have been writing at the same time as *Seek and Find*.

2. Rossetti offered the book to Alexander Macmillan in a letter of November 4, 1876: "I have by me a completed work, a sort of devotional reading-book for the red-letter Saints' Days, which of course is longing to see the light & which I shall be glad if you will consent to look at." The letter is quoted by Packer, *Christina Rossetti*, 328.

3. Rossetti acknowledges Baring-Gould as the source of her "black letter Feasts" in *Time Flies* (entry for March 1). His *Lives of the Saints* (London: John Hodges, 1872–1889), which finally filled seventeen volumes, was being published even as Christina wrote. My references to *Time Flies* are by entry, rather than by page, and thus they apply to any of the several editions of the book.

4. Immediately following this explanation, Rossetti refers to Thomas Fuller, *The Worthies of England* (1662) who writes of flowers in his description of Norwich (under "Natural Commodities"): "In the morning when it groweth up, [the flower] is a lecture of Divine Providence. In the evening, when it is cut down withered, it is a lecture of human mortality." (Rossetti misquotes "withered" as "and withereth.") Fuller is writing of the reputation of flowers in the city, which was advanced by the Dutch who brought many "pleasurable curiosities" with them (*Worthies of England*, ed. John Freeman [New York: Barnes & Noble, 1952], 419). Rossetti probably consulted one of the nineteenth-century editions (1811, 1840). Fuller's *Church History of Britain* (1655) also went through several nineteenth-century editions, including J. S. Brewer's edition of 1845. Victorian interest in Fuller is further manifested in J. E. Bailey's *Life* (1874) and his edition of the *Sermons* in two volumes (1891).

5. The epigraph of the book, which appears on a third separate leaf, following the title page and the dedication, is from Richard Hooker, *Of the Lawes of Ecclesiastical Polity* (1597), 5.71.11, the chapter of "Exceptions against our keeping of other festival days besides the Sabbath." Hooker is defending the keeping of saints' days against the objections of the protestant reformers; he concludes by saying that "to celebrate these religious and sacred days is to spend the flower of our time happily." What follows is quoted in *Called to be Saints*: "They are the splendour and outward dignity of our religion, forcible witnesses of ancient truth, provocations to the exercise of all piety, shadows of our endless felicity in heaven, on earth everlasting records and memorials, wherein they that [Hooker writes "which"] cannot be

drawn to hearken unto that we teach, may only by looking upon that we do, in a manner read whatsoever we believe." Rossetti is quoting from John Keble's edition (1836, 1841, etc.). Packer (*Christina Rossetti,* 328) thinks that "the sonority and stately rhythms of the rhetorical prose of the great Anglican divines resound in her sentence-paragraphs," implying Hooker's particular importance in shaping Rossetti's prose style. This is a loose judgment that is difficult, perhaps impossible, to prove.

6. Georgina Battiscombe quotes most of this passage in her biographical study, *Christina Rossetti: A Divided Life* (New York: Holt, Rinehart and Winston, 1981), 169, but for the purpose of demonstrating her point that Rossetti "knew moments of inward rebellion against the limitations and sameness of her life in a dull London house with only three old ladies for company." Such a reading takes a limited vision of Rossetti's artistic ability; surely this passage shows above all Rossetti's creative and imaginative power as a writer.

7. *The Works of George Herbert,* ed. F. E. Hutchinson (1941; repr. Oxford: Clarendon Press, 1959), "Superliminare," ll. 5–8.

8. See *The Poetical Works of Christina Georgina Rossetti,* ed. William Michael Rossetti (London: Macmillan, 1904), liv, lxxvii.

9. See n. 4, above.

10. See Battiscombe, *Christina Rossetti,* 169. The copy of the first edition of *Time Flies* at the University of Texas-Austin contains the author's marginal notes identifying persons and places mentioned in the text.

11. G. B. Tennyson cogently describes Rossetti as "the true inheritor of the Tractarian devotional mode in poetry" in *Victorian Devotional Poetry: The Tractarian Mode* (Cambridge: Harvard University Press, 1981), 198, thus reinforcing Raymond Chapman's view of Rossetti as a full product of the Oxford Movement: see Chapman's *Faith and Revolt: Studies in the Literary Influence of the Oxford Movement* (London: Weidenfeld and Nicolson, 1970), especially the chapter "Uphill All the Way." Rossetti collected her devotional poetry, nearly all of which had appeared in the prose works, in *Verses* (1893). William Michael Rossetti included all this verse in his edition of the poetry in 1904, but he distributed it among a rather confusing set of headings; even so, it is obvious that much of the poetry is either narrowly "devotional" or generally religious. What has been said about the Tractarian temper of Rossetti's poetry applies almost equally well to her prose.

12. Packer writes that Rossetti first knew the Bible, and particularly the Book of Revelation, from childhood, when her mother read it to her (*Christina Rossetti,* 5). Another favorite of Frances Rossetti was Jeremy Taylor whose *Holy Living* and *Holy Dying* must have touched a sympathetic listener in Christina Rossetti. Taylor's manuals possess that kind of systematic austerity and orderly, sometimes elevated devotion that underlies so much of Rossetti's own work. She alludes approvingly to Taylor, though in passing, in *Time Flies* (entry for August 19).

14

"Thou Art Indeed Just, Lord":
Hopkins, Donne, and Herbert
and the Sonnet of Affliction

GERARD MANLEY HOPKINS'S POETRY has frequently been compared to the devotional writing of earlier English poets, and especially to the "metaphysicals," John Donne and George Herbert. But the significance of these seventeenth-century poets to Hopkins is best understood not so much in the general terms of their influence, but first in the particular theological outlook common to them all, and second, in their poetic imagery and technique. My wish is to demonstrate these points by discussing one of Hopkins's well known sonnets, "Thou art indeed just, Lord" in connection with Donne's Holy Sonnet 3, "O might those sighes and teares returne againe," and Herbert's "The Sinner," "Lord, how I am all ague."[1]

"Justus quidem tu es, Domine" is the Vulgate translation of Jeremiah 12.1, which Hopkins turns into the opening lines of his poem, one of the last he was to write, probably early in 1889:

> Thou art indeed just, Lord, if I contend
> With thee; but, sir, so what I plead is just.
> Why do sinners' ways prosper? and why must
> Disappointment all I endeavour end?
>
> Wert thou my enemy, O thou my friend,
> How wouldst thou worse, I wonder, than thou dost
> Defeat, thwart me? Oh, the sots and thralls of lust
> Do in spare hours more thrive than I that spend,
>
> Sir, life upon thy cause. See, banks and brakes
> Now, leavèd how thick! lacèd they are again
> With fretty chervil, look, and fresh wind shakes
>
> Them; birds build — but not I build; no, but strain,
> Time's eunuch, and not breed one work that wakes.

Mine, O thou lord of life, send my roots rain.

Hopkins had already written the six "sonnets of desolation," probably about 1885–86, and certainly a somber, brooding, and final mood touches them and this sonnet, too, linking them all as one.

Donne's nineteen Holy Sonnets, written perhaps around the years 1609–10, reflect a variety of moods; but Sonnet 3 appeared in a group of four, first printed in 1635, thus forming a kind of sequence. Helen Gardner prints them together in her edition of *The Divine Poems* in order to emphasize their common subject, namely, penitence, with a mutual "emphasis on sin and tears for sin" – a traditional subject for meditation:

> O might those sighes and teares returne againe
> Into my breast and eyes, which I have spent,
> That I might in this holy discontent
> Mourne with some fruit, as I have mourn'd in vaine;
> In my Idolatry what showres of raine
> Mine eyes did waste? what griefs my heart did rent?
> That sufferance was my sinne, now I repent;
> Because I did suffer'I must suffer paine.
> Th'hydroptique drunkard, and night-scouting thiefe,
> The itchy Lecher, and selfe tickling proud
> Have the remembrance of past joyes, for reliefe
> Of comming ills. To (poore) me is allow'd
> No ease; for, long, yet vehement griefe hath beene
> Th'effect and cause, the punishment and sinne.

Although the poet repents his past – the good work of his present experience – he still suffers, ever grieving, ever thirsting.

Herbert expresses similar sorrow in many of the poems of *The Temple* (1633), and similar disappointment. He uses most lyric forms of the earlier seventeenth-century, devising also some of his own; yet especially frequent of metrical kinds in his book is the sonnet, with at least ten scattered through the 154 poems of *The Temple*. One of these, and one which describes the problems of penitence, is "The Sinner":

> Lord, how I am all ague, when I seek
>   What I have treasur'd in my memorie!
>   Since, if my soul make even with the week,
> Each seventh note by right is due to thee.
> I finde there quarries of pil'd vanities,
>   But shreds of holinesse, that dare not venture
>   To shew their face, since crosse to thy decrees:
> There the circumference earth is, heav'n the centre.
> In so much dregs the quintessence is small:
>   The spirit and good extract of my heart

Comes to about the many hundred part.
Yet Lord restore thine image, heare my call:
And though my hard heart scarce to thee can grone,
Remember that thou once didst write in stone.

Hopkins's "sots and thralls of lust" recall Herbert's "pil'd vanities" and his "shreds of holiness"; and both sonnets point to Donne's "holy discontent," his "hydroptique drunkard, and night-scouting thiefe." This trinity of sonnets locates an attitude of suffering, disappointment, wretchedness, and it asks the question of why one's best hopes end in disorder. Bewildered and uncertain, Hopkins, like his predecessors, discovers dryness in himself where he should find freshness.

Grief, pain, idle pleasure, and vanity form the necessary foundation of life, while at the same time forming the basis of our own prayer that Christ may raise up those who fall down. This is the fundamental idea, contained in the economical sonnet form, of these poems. The questions raised in each of them is inspired by sorrow, but each asks for joyful resolution: "send my roots rain"; "mourne with some fruit"; "heare my call."

Let us consider Hopkins's sonnet more carefully. The key word at first is "contend," for Hopkins is imagining himself in a cause that he must plead, and is pleading, as if he were in litigation. The term of address is properly "sir," suggesting deference but also some irritation; for "sinners' ways prosper," and his somewhat distant friend, who must know what is best for him, seems to reward those who are least deserving, while he struggles both to promote and believe in this curiously ungrateful Lord. In the second part of the sonnet, beginning with "See, banks and brakes / Now, leavèd how thick!," Hopkins turns from the questions of God's justice applied to himself and to others; here he looks at the world of nature, the freshness of new growth, the wind that blows in the leaves, and the birds that build their nests. But he can see no growth in himself, nor begetting, only "dull privation and leane emptiness" (cf. Donne, "A Nocturnall upon S. *Lucies* day"). Instead of "sir," the poet begins now to call his master "thou lord of life," for he has moved from pleading a narrow case of law to analogizing himself with all of organic nature, where there is growth: why should not he who has roots that require water, also be touched by the nourishing rain?

Hopkins describes in his Retreat Notes of January 1, 1889 (St. Stanislaus' College, Tullabeg) the distress he was feeling. Being unable to do more than repeat *Justus es, Domine, et rectum judicium tuum,* he fell asleep, then awoke with a start:

What is my wretched life? . . . I am ashamed of the little I have done, of my waste of time. . . . What is life without aim, without spur, without help? All my undertakings miscarry: I am like a straining eunuch. . . . O my God, look down on me.[2]

Hopkins was of course ill when he wrote these notes, and evidently when he wrote this sonnet. But while the poem clearly has some biographical significance, its interest extends far beyond a description of the poet's personal feelings. Hopkins is describing, in terms given greater poignancy by his own circumstances, a universal difficulty; for affliction regularly strains us. He is particularly brilliant in crying from the depths of his own sorrow, in a fashion that is both personal and universal: he sees himself in dialogue with God, on the one hand, and then he identifies himself with all of God's creation, on the other. The isolation he feels must be due to misperception, he implicitly says, for all around there is growth – can his roots be long without water?

The first part of the poem is fraught with dryness as he pleads, but the last, and answering part of the poem is filled with the contrasting growth, not his own, but that which should be his. In his "Metaphysical Poets and Their Readers," Patrick Cruttwell contrasted this sonnet with Herbert's much longer "Affliction (I)," in which Herbert gives the history of his spiritual progress and suffering: "When I got health, thou tookst away my life," he says. But at the end, he writes, "Let me not love thee, if I love thee not." Here is, says Cruttwell, "a serenity in the midst of anguish," whereas Hopkins "seems disturbed and muddy."[3] But such a distinction does not see the growth that is implied even in pain, nor understand the comfort of "world-sorrow," the knowledge that "all / Life death does end and each day dies with sleep."

The comfort of woe and pain is the joy of the penitent. In Donne's Holy Sonnet, the "sighes and teares" that return once more into the griever's eyes, rending him with deep sorrow and discontent, rain uselessly. Mourning is vain; and the poet's questions receive no ready answer. "Sufferance" was a sin, for which now one feels repentance; that is, the past discontent is unholy, but the present discontent is not, though one still suffers in the good work of repentance. Why? Even the "dropsical" drunken man, whose thirst increases the more he drinks, or the thief that prowls by night, or the lecher's unsatisfied hankerings, or the self-absorption of the proud man all have the pleasure of recalling their past joyful indulgences "for reliefe / Of comming ills." Yet for the poet there is no easeful remembrance of the past, for in it lies the source of his present sorrow. His weariness is both personal and typical of all who labor in the generality of suffering; infirmity is endless, and endlessly oppressive, with melancholy and woe always looking on. Even so, Donne hints at completeness in the conjunction of redemption and sin, an implicit source of true pleasure.

In his description of "The Sinner," George Herbert also writhes in agony: "how I am all ague," he complains, when he seeks out the whispering vices stored in his memory. Vanities are piled there, and the shreds and tatters of good intentions; but they dare not appear for having once fallen "crosse to thy decrees." *Cross* means "perverse" or "contrary"; it also doubles in another sense by anticipating the transformation of sins (or crosses) in the cross of Christ's Passion. Herbert, in an unexpected turn or paradox, sees heaven as the center of earth, but the Cross is indeed at the center of his earth, of his sins which make possible and encircle the Cross. The very dregs, the distillation of "the cream of all his heart" comes to little; yet he calls on God to restore His divine image in him, which has never really disappeared, for it was always there. Finally, Herbert resolves the troubles of his hard and shriveled, but contrite heart through groans of beseeching: "Remember that thou once didst write in stone," he pleads. While Moses received the Law on Tables of Stone (Exod. 31.18), Herbert, writing as a Christian of the New Covenant, instead asks to receive "fleshy tables of the heart" (2 Cor. 3.3).

The personal situation of despondency, of soulful disease and trembling "ague," becomes in Herbert, as in Donne and Hopkins, too, a universal malady. The figure is of the struggling penitent, deeply mired in sin that may yet yield to salvation. The situation is like that of Bunyan's Christian, who, having fallen into the Slough of Despond early in his pilgrimage to the Celestial City, is saved by Faithful; or having been detained in Doubting Castle where Giant Despair and his wife Diffidence want to kill him, goes free when he finds the Key of Promise which he keeps in his own bosom. Herbert recognizes such circumstances as these in "The Sinner," or when he writes in "Easter Wings" that "Affliction shall advance the flight in me."

The witty use of musical imagery in "The Sinner" may send us also to another sonnet of Hopkins, his early "Let me be to Thee as the circling bird," where he finds "the dominant of my range and state." Hopkins is referring to the dominant seventh of the common chord, suggesting that in his resolved faith he finds God; so also does Herbert invoke the seventh note "by right due to thee" in order to register an essential, Godlike rest. In affliction one hopes for an answer to one's call for help, only to discover that the Redeemer Himself is both calling and responding, that in affliction there is joy and paradise at the last.

Notes

1. Hopkins's poem is quoted from *Gerard Manley Hopkins,* ed. Catherine Phillips, The Oxford Authors (Oxford: Oxford University Press, 1986), 183; Donne's sonnet is in *The Divine Poems,* ed. Helen Gardner, 2nd ed. (Oxford: Clarendon Press, 1978), 13–14; Herbert's "The Sinner" is quoted from *The Works of George Herbert,* ed. F. E. Hutchinson (Oxford: Clarendon Press, 1941), 38.

2. See *Hopkins,* ed. Phillips, 303.

3. See "The Metaphysical Poets and Their Readers," *Humanities Association Bulletin* (Canada), 28 (1977): 39.

Volumes in the Peter Lang series **Seventeenth-Century Texts and Studies** are under the general editorship of Anthony Low, Professor of English at New York University. This series is primarily concerned with English non-dramatic writings, prose and poetry, from the time of Donne and Jonson to the death of Milton. It includes monographs on individual writers, wider studies employing a variety of critical and historical methods, collections of original essays on special topics, and editions of texts from the period.